W9-BKX-758

180 DAYS TO SUCCESSFUL WRITERS

This book is dedicated to our supportive families,
the talented teachers we worked with in Marion County,
Florida, and our students, whom we hope will continue to enjoy writing.

180 DAYS TO SUCCESSFUL WRITERS

Lessons to Prepare Your Students for Standardized Assessments and for Life

LIBRARY
FRANKLIN PIERCE COLLEGE
RINDGE, NH 03461

KAREN DONOHUE AND NANDA N. REDDY

CORWIN PRESS
A SAGE Publications Company
Thousand Oaks, California

Copyright © 2006 by Karen Donohue and Nanda N. Reddy

All rights reserved. When forms and sample documents are included, their use is authorized only by educators, local school sites, and/or noncommercial or nonprofit entities who have purchased the book. Except for that usage, no part of this book may be reproduced or utilized in any form or by any means, electronic or mechanical, including photocopying, recording, or by any information storage and retrieval system, without permission in writing from the publisher.

For information:

Corwin Press
A Sage Publications Company
2455 Teller Road
Thousand Oaks, California 91320
www.corwinpress.com

Sage Publications Ltd.
1 Oliver's Yard
55 City Road
London EC1Y 1SP
United Kingdom

Sage Publications India Pvt. Ltd.
B-42, Panchsheel Enclave
Post Box 4109
New Delhi 110 017 India

Printed in the United States of America

Library of Congress Cataloging-in-Publication Data

Donohue, Karen.
180 days to successful writers: Lessons to prepare your students for standardized assessments and for life/Karen Donohue, Nanda N. Reddy.
        p. cm.
Includes index.
ISBN 1–4129–2448–0 (cloth) — ISBN 1–4129–2449–9 (pbk.)
    1. English language—Composition and exercises—Study and teaching (Elementary) 2. English language—Composition and exercises—Ability testing. 3. Education, Elementary—Curricula. I. Title: One hundred eighty days to successful writers. II. Reddy, Nanda N. III. Title.
LB1576.D655 2006
372.62′3—dc22   2005019385

This book is printed on acid-free paper.

06   07   08   09   10   9   8   7   6   5   4   3   2   1

Acquisitions Editor:	Kylee Liegl
Editorial Assistant:	Jaime Cuvier
Production Editor:	Beth A. Bernstein
Copy Editor:	Colleen B. Brennan
Typesetter:	C&M Digitals (P) Ltd.
Proofreader:	Dennis W. Webb
Indexer:	Rick Hurd
Cover Designer:	Terry Taylor
Graphic Designer:	Rose Storey

Contents

Preface

Eighty-six percent of our students qualified for free or reduced lunch. Fifty-five percent were transient. Thirty-eight percent came from families working at or below the poverty level. Yet none of them failed.

Instead, one hundred percent of our students passed the state writing test. One hundred percent of them wrote quality poetry, chapter stories, plays, and autobiographies. And all of them were motivated to write. This is because we provided structured writing instruction and tools that worked.

Our students learned to organize their thoughts with graphic organizers such as the "pickle sandwich" and the "tier cake." They crafted interesting essays and stories using "Dress Me Up" devices such as Vivacious Verbs, Awe-Inspiring Adjectives, and Mind-Bending Metaphors. They employed our TCUPSS editing tool and rubrics to revise and polish their work, and they completed the writing process by publishing.

These tools are part of this book's curriculum. The method emphasizes careful modeling and guided practice to foster independence. We found that struggling writers became more confident when they used the scaffolds, while more able writers stretched the tools to their limits. This program can help your third- through sixth-grade students write well also.

Detailed lesson plans, clear objectives, and a multitude of reproducible figures and resources will allow you to easily duplicate our success. Your students will begin with simple essays and stories and build on their knowledge weekly. By the end of the year, they will craft notable chapter stories and newspaper articles. Furthermore, specific chapters help to diagnose and fix common writing problems and to prepare students for state writing tests.

Teaching writing is a process, not a formulaic task, and there are many ways to achieve success. We are confident that this method makes writing instruction easier, and, as a result, we believe all of your students will write as successfully as ours wrote.

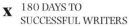
ACKNOWLEDGMENTS

Corwin Press gratefully acknowledges the contributions of the following reviewers:

Liz Mullins, NBCT
Lead Teacher
Oakland Heights Elementary School
Russellville, AR

Bethany Orr, NBCT
Grade 4 Teacher
Lake Norman Elementary School
Mooresville, NC

Melanie Conaway, NBCT
Grade 4 Teacher
Tyler Run Elementary School
Powell, OH

Stephanie Hall, NBCT
Grade 3 Teacher
Wake County Public School System
Wake County, NC

Stephanie Manuel
K–5 Classroom Teacher
East Greenbush Central Schools
East Greenbush, NY

Laura A. Flynn
Author and Teacher
Chelwood Elementary School
Albuquerque, NM

Deborah Hersh Carter, NBCT
Academically Gifted Teacher
Moore County Schools
Carthage, NC

Renee Peoples, NBCT
Classroom Teacher
Swain Elementary School
Bryson City, NC

Ellen M. Flynn
Author and Teacher
Chelwood Elementary School
Albuquerque, NM

About the Authors

Since earning her MEd from the University of Florida in 2000, **Karen Donohue** has worked to develop and implement a writing curriculum for elementary students. She has experience with Early Intervention programs with students in first-, third-, and fourth-grade classrooms in both Reddick Collier Elementary in Reddick, Florida, and Pine Forest Elementary in Marietta, Georgia. With student writing becoming a benchmark for students as young as first grade, Karen has researched, developed, and taught Staff Development courses for K–5 teachers. Her workshops titled "Writing to a Prompt (Grades K–5)," "Write Way to Success (Grades 3–5)," and "Writer's Workshop—Getting Started" have been implemented schoolwide at Pine Forest Elementary where she was a Grade 1 Team Leader. She is currently a Grade 1 Team Leader at Lockheed Elementary in Marietta, Georgia, where she is a member of the International Reading Association.

Nanda N. Reddy earned her MEd from the University of Florida in 1999 and subsequently worked as a fourth-grade teacher in Marion County, Florida. At her school, she served as a team leader and worked to develop a writing curriculum to accommodate the pressures of standardized tests and student writing needs. Nanda taught the curriculum at the school, and for that, she was honored as Rookie Teacher of the Year. She has workshopped this material under the titles "Teaching Reluctant Writers" and "Teaching Kids to Write" in both Floridaz and Reno, Nevada, where she now resides. Nanda, a member of the National Council of Teachers of English (NCTE), currently works full time raising her family and writing fiction. She hopes to continue conducting writing workshops for teachers.

1 No-Brainers and Bosses: Laying the Foundation

I t is the beginning of a new school year. The interior decorator in you emerges as you hang posters and arrange desks. You practice your mean face for the first day as you obsess over discipline, books, curriculum, and county mandates. And, if you're like most teachers, you worry about your kids achieving state and national benchmarks.

You're probably confident your kids will reach their reading and math goals—at least you have a curriculum. But what about writing? Chances are your teaching arsenal for writing is full of grammar lessons, spelling words, journal activities, and prompts. However, your students need more than ingenious prompts and well-executed grammar lessons to learn to write and to become lifelong writers.

Your students need structured lessons that build on what they already know and continuously add to their knowledge. They need easy-to-use writing tools that take them through the writing process. They need to watch you write and listen to you think as you write. And they need to write with support before tackling the task on their own. What your students need is explicit writing instruction.

CURRICULUM OVERVIEW

This book's writing curriculum allows you to control what your students learn and the order in which they learn it. Carefully crafted, unscripted lessons cover a scope and follow a sequence that aims for success.

The lessons begin with the assumption that your students have rudimentary grammar knowledge and can construct sentences and paragraphs. Students first study prompts and two basic types of writing—expository and narrative. Next they learn to use graphic organizers to organize their thoughts. Through modeling, you will teach them how to draft essays and stories, then how to edit and revise their work. Finally you will guide your students' work to foster independence.

The curriculum focuses strongly on growth and accountability. You will continually assess your instruction, diagnose student problems, conference with students, and reteach. As such, we discuss writing assessments, including standardized writing tests, in detail. You may amend lessons or deviate from the curriculum to accommodate your teaching philosophy, students' needs, and state's guidelines.

Goals

All instruction plans must be based on clearly defined goals. The scope and sequence of this curriculum were designed to help you achieve the following five goals with your third- through sixth-grade students.

1. Become a confident writing teacher.

2. Prepare your students for all practical applications of writing.

3. Prepare your students to succeed on standardized writing tests.

4. Accommodate your students' strengths and weaknesses.

5. Create confident writers of your most reluctant students.

Instruction Framework

Throughout the school year, you will follow five steps to achieve your instruction goals.

1. Plan. Review lessons before instructing to streamline them for your students' needs. We recommend collaborating with a team of teachers if possible.

2. Teach. Model every new skill and guide students closely. Promote independence slowly.

3. Test. Assess students after they have worked independently.

4. Analyze results. Grade and analyze student work with a rubric. Document students' strengths and weaknesses and establish areas to reteach.

5. Teach again. Reteach according to weaknesses.

PREPARING TO TEACH

1. Schedule a specific writing instruction time.
   - Ideally, this is a daily forty-five minute block. But you can accomplish the same goals with two twenty to twenty-five minute blocks each day.

2. Research language arts benchmarks and your students' writing strengths and needs.

- Review your county and state benchmarks.
- Review your state's writing rubric (guidelines for grading writing) and compare it to the generic rubric and rubric posters provided as Resources B and C. Do the rubrics assess required benchmarks?
- Meet with teachers in grades above and below yours to discuss their views of students' strengths, weaknesses, and writing needs. Ask for writing samples.

3. Familiarize yourself with the types of writing, the lessons, and this book's general plan.
   - Review the two main types of writing taught. For the first terms, lessons focus on expository essays (a subset of informational) and narrative stories (both fantastical and realistic). After that time, students learn poetry and the practical aspects of exposition and narration (e.g., autobiographies, plays, and newspaper writing).
     a. *Informational:* Usually in the form of expository, persuasive, or descriptive essays. Expository essays, the type taught in this book, offer detailed fictional or factual explanations regarding a topic. Expository essays often include aspects of persuasive and descriptive writing. An expository essay prompt: How would you spend a million dollars? Persuasive essays offer opinions with supporting reasons; they also discredit opposing opinions. A persuasive essay prompt: Convince me to buy a dog. Descriptive essays impart sensory experiences. Writers are expected to evoke an emotional response from readers, using smell, sound, sight, touch, and taste, as applicable. A descriptive essay prompt: Describe your dream house. None of these essay types require strict time sequences in the prose.
     b. *Narrative:* A story, factual or fictional, told with a definite time sequence and containing a conflict. Examples: Tell about your most embarrassing moment (realistic); you awake to find you're an inch tall (imaginary).
   - Note that this writing curriculum discusses spelling, grammar, and vocabulary but does not offer regular lessons. We recommend teaching vocabulary as part of your reading program. Provide daily grammar practice and mini lessons to address the following important grammar skills: capitalization; periods; commas; contractions and apostrophes; homonyms; conjunctions, run-ons, and fragments; and subject-verb agreement. Spelling and handwriting may be assigned for homework and tested weekly outside the curriculum.

4. Address writing assessments and make necessary amendments to the general structure.
   - If your state does not test writing, skip Chapters 7 and 8 and reduce the amount of time spent alternating between the two types of prompts in Chapter 6. Plan to administer a posttest after Chapter 6. Determine your student goals and how you will measure student gains, and decide how and when you will use time limits. Finally,

determine how you will use or extend projects in Chapters 9 and 10 and incorporate advanced strategies from Chapter 11.

- If your state tests writing, review its demands and address test preparation. Note that Chapters 7 and 8 assume that state tests are timed, are given approximately two-thirds of the way through the traditional school year, and ask students to write to either an expository or narrative prompt. Adapt the structure to fit your guidelines and consider administering your own posttest after Chapter 8, before teaching applications.

- If you would like to focus on persuasive or descriptive writing, adapt the expository prompts (using Resource A), the sample writings, and the expository lessons. Adaptation notes are provided during Weeks 1 and 2, in Chapters 1 and 2.

- If you would like to focus only on one type of narrative writing, realistic or imaginary (sometimes called fantastical), rewrite narrative prompts using Resource A.

- If your state tests only one type of writing, teach that type of writing first and focus on its applications. Then teach the other modes of writing. Note that all modes of writing have important applications.

- If you want to create themes, reorganize or rewrite the prompts and sample writings. Choose prompts to coincide with reading, science, or social studies.

5. Learn special terms and aspects associated with this book.
   - Notes for daily plans indicate ways to prepare for lessons before class.
   - If a day is designated as a "Copy Day," it is important for your students to copy your writing model.
   - If a day is designated as a "No Help Day," your students are expected to write without your help. Offer close assistance any other day.
   - If a day is designated as a "Pair Day," prepare for student collaboration, paired or grouped.
   - Figures are numbered as they appear in chapters.
   - Each week has a focus. Use this to help plan when you need to reteach skills.
   - Certain lessons call for previously modeled papers. Be sure to save all models you write.
   - Certain lessons call for previously written student papers. Students should store all written papers and handouts in their binders (see materials list in Step 8).
   - All weeks consist of five daily plans, except for Week 14. Week 14 is a three-day week with two timed writings and a lesson on friendly letters.

6. Review in detail the lesson plans for Week 1.
   - Consider the pretest prompts. If you need to change or reformat them, do so.
   - Determine the time limit you would like to set if you aren't in a state that tests writing.
   - Review the notes for Days 4 and 5. Follow recommendations.

7. Determine regular and special methods of student publication.
   - Ideally, students should publish all of their writing. However, you might not be able to afford instructional time for this task, especially if preparing students for standardized tests. We recommend providing class time at least once a month for publication. Otherwise, routinely allow students to rewrite final drafts and publish their work as homework. Display works in the room.
   - An easy publication idea is to provide each student with report folders that contain title-page inserts on the cover. Allow students to illustrate blank paper to accompany their writings and place in the cover. Students will secure completed final drafts inside. To publish new works, students simply replace the cover sheet and change out the essay or story inside. Provide a method to display the "reports"—students should be able to read each other's work and change their own work easily.
   - Offer different ways to publish occasionally. Students may transfer final drafts to construction paper and decorate; students may write and illustrate paragraphs on separate pages to create small books; students may enter contests or publish with trusted online sites; you may put together "classroom books" by binding illustrated final drafts.

8. Gather general materials. These should be on hand for every lesson.
   - Overhead projector, blank transparencies, and overhead markers for daily use. If these aren't available, determine a reliable method to model and display writing.
   - Chart paper, basic markers, various sized construction paper, poster boards, notebook paper and pencils for students, and materials for student publication.
   - Student binders. To save instructional time, consider putting these together now. Otherwise request students to purchase materials and set aside class time during the first week for students to put their binders together. Students will need one 3-ring binder and five dividers each. Dividers should be labeled as follows: expository; narrative; reference; conferences; other writing. Students will place written work and handouts in appropriate sections.

9. Make posters. We suggest making posters of figures and other resources to supplement the lessons. Consider making these posters now, while you have the time. Some require 22- by 28-inch poster board, while others require several pieces of 12- by 18-inch construction paper or 24- by 32-inch chart paper. A list of posters, their locations, and their recommended materials follow in the order they are used.
   - Figure 1.1. Page 9. Prompt Differentiation. Chart paper.
   - Figure 1.2. Page 11. Prompt Dissection. Chart paper.
   - Figure 2.1. Page 18. Pickle Sandwich With Hints. Poster board.
   - Figure 2.2. Page 19. Expository Transition Words. Chart paper.

- Figures 2.3 and 2.4. Pages 20–23. TCUPSS. Poster board and colored construction paper.
- Resources B and C. Pages 261–263. Rubric and Rubric Posters. Use these or your state's rubric. Construction Paper. Use your own or Resources B and C.
- Figure 3.2. Page 33. Rainbow Words. Eight pieces of colored construction paper.
- Figure 3.3. Page 36. Awe-Inspiring Adjectives. Ten pieces of construction paper.
- Figure 4.1. Page 47. Tier Cake With Hints. Poster board.
- Figure 4.2. Page 50. Narrative Transition Words. Chart paper.
- Figure 5.2. Page 64. Vivacious Verbs. Ten pieces of construction paper.
- Figure 5.3. Page 67. ASk fOR LIKEly Similes. Chart paper.
- Figure 6.1. Page 73. Mind-Bending Metaphors. Chart paper.
- Figure 6.4. Page 84. Sensory Details. Chart paper.
- Figure 6.5. Page 88. Street Talk. Chart paper.
- Figures 7.13 and 7.14. Page 123. Dress Me Up Doll. Poster board and four pieces of construction paper.

10. If you're working with a team, agree on regular meeting times.
    - Informal meetings should occur weekly for fifteen to twenty minutes. During this time you will review lessons, make amendments, and discuss progress and problems.
    - Formal meetings should occur monthly or every term when you will grade each other's student work and analyze graded work for growth and weaknesses. You may also address systematic classroom problems and ways to reteach skills.

WEEK 1 LESSON PLANS

Focus: Pretests and Prompt Differentiation

It is important to begin with an assessment of your students' skills and knowledge. This week's testing will help you determine your students' strengths and weaknesses. Students will also learn to tell the difference between expository and narrative writing.

Day 1

Objectives: Students will write and illustrate poems to decorate the room.

Materials: Varies according to your chosen project.

Note: Before class, prepare to implement your behavior management program and get your students used to your scheduled writing time.

1. At your scheduled writing time, tell students they will write every day at this time.

2. Describe the assignment. If you have a favorite "first day" writing assignment, do it. Otherwise, choose one of the two examples that follow: name poems under self-portraits or "I am" poems with illustrations.
   - *Name poems:* Students write their names vertically and come up with descriptions of themselves for each letter in their name. Start with scrap paper to generate ideas, then transpose to construction paper. Students could write single words, phrases, or complete sentences— you set the rules. Students should illustrate the final product with portraits or according to what they've written.
   - *"I am" poems:* Students will write poems with three stanzas, each containing five sentences. The first two words of the sentences in the stanzas follow:
     a. Stanza 1: I am, I live, I love, I hope, I believe.
     b. Stanza 2: I am, I can, I want, I won't, I wonder.
     c. Stanza 3: I am, I say, I wish, I cherish, I dream.
     d. Discuss the following "I am" lines to prompt creativity: I am not ever going to win the lottery; I am the luckiest kid in the world; I am (name); I am forgetful (or other adjective); I am the middle child in my family; I am a basketball player (any hobby or sport); I am a daydreamer; I am going to be a star, etc.
     e. Students should write final drafts of their poems on large construction paper, then illustrate.

3. Allow students to share their final, illustrated work with each other.

Day 2 (No Help Day)

Objective: Students will complete an expository writing pretest.

Materials: Expository prompt.

Note: Before class, choose an expository (or other informational) prompt that will be applicable for an end-of-year posttest. If your state assesses, mimic the format of your state's test when writing the prompt and consider printing the prompt along with planning and answer sheets as presented by your state. Examples of all three informational prompts follow.
   - Expository: Everyone does different things on weekends. Think about how you normally spend your weekends. Now write to explain how you spend your weekends.
   - Persuasive: Your school wants to get a class pet. What would your choice be? Write an essay convincing your teacher to get the pet of your choice.
   - Descriptive: Everyone has a strong memory. Think of your strongest memory. Describe that memory to your readers.

   1. Begin by telling students you will be testing them to see how well they write.
   2. Discuss the genre of the prompt students will write to. Describe the length of time students will have to write, and, if appropriate, begin discussing how this test relates to your state's standardized test. Tell

students they will have to answer the prompt by writing an essay without your help.

3. Set a timer for your designated time limit. Pass out the test and begin timing students.

4. Students will probably get done early, but stick firmly to the time limit. Do not reward fast workers by allowing them to read or draw in the time that remains. Students need to get used to using all of their time.

Day 3 (No Help Day)

Objective: Students will complete a narrative writing pretest.

Materials: Narrative prompt.

Note: Before class, choose either a realistic or an imaginary narrative prompt that will be applicable for the end-of-year posttest. Format and present the prompt similar to the expository pretest. Examples follow.

- Realistic: Everyone has had a bad day. Think about the worst day of your life. Now write a story about a day you would hate to relive.
- Imaginary: Imagine finding yourself locked in a supermarket. Think about how this could happen and what you would do. Now write a story about being locked in a supermarket.
  1. Briefly discuss that there are two main kinds of prompts, expository and narrative, and that students are getting the second kind today, the narrative. If your state tests only one mode of writing, discuss briefly which of those modes will be tested. However, tell students they will learn both types of writing.
  2. Administer the test as described above for the expository pretest.
  3. After administering both tests, assess them according to your state's rubric or use Resource B. Use student scores to indicate beginning writing levels and to assess growth over the year.

Day 4

Objective: Students will differentiate expository and narrative prompts, and they will organize writing resource binders.

Materials: Figure 1.1.

Note: Before class, prepare a display of the pretest prompts and prompts listed following Step 4. If your state formats its prompts differently, make the necessary changes. Also, use chart paper to make a poster of Figure 1.1. If you are focusing on persuasive or descriptive writing, create new prompts and new key words using Resource A as a guide. For persuasive essays, key words might be "convince," "persuade," and "prove". For descriptive essays, key words might be "sensory details," "describe" and illustrate. Finally, plan to pass out or prepare student binders.

Figure 1.1 Prompt Differentiation

Expository	Narrative
Tells you to **explain**.	Asks you to tell a **story**.
Usually asks you to discuss **real life**.	Often asks you to **make-believe**.
Sometimes asks you to **tell what you would do**.	Sometimes asks you to **remember a time**.
Needs you to **list information or reasons in any order; you choose the order.**	Needs you to **tell something in the order it happened.**

Copyright © 2006 by Karen Donohue and Nanda N. Reddy. All rights reserved. Reprinted from *180 Days to Successful Writers: Lessons to Prepare Your Students for Standardized Assessments and for Life* by Karen Donohue and Nanda N. Reddy. Thousand Oaks, CA: Corwin Press, www.corwinpress.com. Reproduction authorized only for the local school site or nonprofit organization that has purchased this book.

1. Display and read the pretest prompts. Label the prompts expository or narrative.

2. Draw a simple t-chart labeled expository and narrative. Ask students to study the two prompts for differences and list these on the chart. Guide students to include the following key phrases for expository: about real life, asks for a list of different things, wants you to give reasons or explain something; and the following for narrative: can be made up; imaginary things can happen, asks about one main event, wants to hear about something in the order it happened.

3. After the most important differences have been highlighted, review them. Then tell students to take out scrap pieces of paper and number from one to five.

4. Display and read the following five prompts. Ask students to write E for expository or N for narrative next to their numbers after you read each prompt, based on the key phrases listed on the t-chart. Key words in the following prompts are italicized.
   - *Imagine* that you've won a million dollars. Think of *all the things you can do* with a million dollars. Now *explain* what you would do with your million dollars.
   - You wake up from a nap and find that you are three inches tall. *Imagine* what life would be like if you had to stay three inches tall for a whole day. Write a *story about a time* you were three inches tall *for a whole day.*
   - Everyone has a favorite day of the week. Think about your favorite day and the *reasons* you like it. Now *write to explain* what your favorite day is and why.
   - Everyone has had embarrassing moments. Think about your most embarrassing moment. Now *tell about a time* you were embarrassed.

- Think about your first day back to school. *What did you like* about returning to school after summer vacation. Now *explain what you like* about going back to school.

5. After allowing students to differentiate, review each prompt and provide the following correct answers. Discuss each prompt's key words and why certain prompts might have been difficult to differentiate. Key words and phrases are italicized.
   - Expository. This is difficult. It uses the word "imagine" and asks you to make believe something. But you have to *explain and make a list.*
   - Narrative. This is easy. It uses the word "story" and asks you to imagine and *tell something in the order* that it happened.
   - Expository. This is easy. This asks you to *explain and make a list* of reasons.
   - Narrative. This is difficult. This asks for a real life event and does not use the words "story" and "imagine." However, you have to *tell events in order.*
   - Expository. This is difficult. The first sentence may make kids think of a sequence of events on the first day of school. The key is students need to *list and explain the reasons* they like going back to school.

6. Discuss why clues like "real life" and "make believe" aren't always good indicators of prompt type. Cross out these items on your t-chart. Discuss that students may make up or imagine answers for expository prompts. For example, if they had trouble thinking up interesting things they like to do during the weekend, they could have made them up during the pretest. Also some people have had very strange things happen to them, for example being stuck in a supermarket, so they may be telling the truth when writing "imaginary" stories. Furthermore, all good essays and stories will have truthful and made-up elements. Cross out other items on the t-chart that led your students astray as they differentiated prompts.

7. Help students see that the main key words for narrative prompts are "story" and "tell about a time," while key words for expository prompts are "explain," "list," and "reasons."

8. Display and read Figure 1.1, the prompt differentiation poster. Discuss that the best way to differentiate prompts is to determine if the prompt wants students to tell events in order (narrative) or list things in any order (expository).

9. Following directions in the preplanning section, address writing binders.

Day 5

Objective: Students will dissect expository and narrative prompts.

Materials: Five prompts; Figures 1.2 and 1.3.

Note: Before class, choose or create five prompts (three expository, two narrative) using Resource A as your guide. Use chart paper to make a poster of Figure 1.2. Make a teacher display and student copies of Figure 1.3, and use this figure as a template if you decide to make a quiz. Make necessary amendments to accommodate your state's format.

Figure 1.2   Prompt Dissection

Type of Prompt:	
Everyone has a favorite holiday.	**No-Brainer.** The topic is holidays.
Think about your favorite holiday.	**Brain.** I have to think about holidays and choose one favorite.
Now write to explain what your favorite holiday is and why.	**Boss.** I have to name my favorite holiday and tell all the reasons I like it.
Most people have gotten lost at least once.	**No-Brainer.** The topic is being lost.
Think about a time you were lost or imagine being lost.	**Brain.** I have to remember being lost or make it up, imagine being lost somewhere.
Now tell a story about a time you got lost.	**Boss.** I need to write a story about getting lost and what happened to me.

Copyright © 2006 by Karen Donohue and Nanda N. Reddy. All rights reserved. Reprinted from *180 Days to Successful Writers: Lessons to Prepare Your Students for Standardized Assessments and for Life* by Karen Donohue and Nanda N. Reddy. Thousand Oaks, CA: Corwin Press, www.corwinpress.com. Reproduction authorized only for the local school site or nonprofit organization that has purchased this book.

1. Review Figure 1.1, the prompt differentiation poster.

2. Display the five prompts you've written or collected. Allow students to differentiate. Put aside for Steps 5 and 6.

3. Display Figure 1.2, the prompt dissection poster. Discuss that prompts usually have three parts. The first part tells the topic: the No-Brainer. The second part asks you to think: the Brain. The last part tells you exactly what to do: the Boss.

4. Review the example prompts and ask students to differentiate the prompts before you begin dissecting. Write in the prompt types and discuss.

5. Pass out student copies of Figure 1.3, the prompt dissection worksheet, and redisplay the five prompts from Step 2. Model the dissection process with two prompts, one expository and one narrative. Discuss what each sentence of the prompt directs you to think or do as you dissect. Students should copy your work.

Figure 1.3   Prompt Dissection Worksheet

1. Teacher will dissect one expository prompt.

	No-Brainer. The topic is
	Brain. I have to . . .
	Boss. I need to . . .

2. Teacher will dissect one narrative prompt.

	No-Brainer. The topic is
	Brain. I have to . . .
	Boss. I need to . . .

3. Class will dissect one expository prompt.

	No-Brainer. The topic is
	Brain. I have to . . .
	Boss. I need to . . .

4. Class will dissect one narrative prompt.

	No-Brainer. The topic is
	Brain. I have to . . .
	Boss. I need to . . .

5. Students will dissect one narrative or expository prompt alone.

	No-Brainer. The topic is
	Brain. I have to . . .
	Boss. I need to . . .

6. Class will make up an expository prompt.

	No-Brainer. The topic is
	Brain. I have to . . .
	Boss. I need to . . .

7. Class will make up a narrative prompt.

	No-Brainer. The topic is
	Brain. I have to . . .
	Boss. I need to . . .

Copyright © 2006 by Karen Donohue and Nanda N. Reddy. All rights reserved. Reprinted from *180 Days to Successful Writers: Lessons to Prepare Your Students for Standardized Assessments and for Life* by Karen Donohue and Nanda N. Reddy. Thousand Oaks, CA: Corwin Press, www.corwinpress.com. Reproduction authorized only for the local school site or nonprofit organization that has purchased this book.

6. Allow students to lead the dissection of another expository and narrative prompt, identifying the No-Brainer topic sentence, the Brain sentence, and the Boss sentence. Have students describe exactly what each sentence of the prompt forces them to do or think.

7. Ask students to dissect the fifth prompt on their own, then share their answers.

8. Help students create their own expository and narrative prompts using the last two blank charts. Allow students to volunteer ideas to create the No-Brainer, Brain, and Boss sentences. Dissect both prompts as you write them.

9. If desired, end this lesson with a short quiz. Provide prompts for differentiation and give students blank charts to dissect those prompts. Students may create prompts for extra credit.

2 Pickle Sandwiches and TCUPSS: Beginning Expository Writing

Alas, your first week is over—that glorious period of no timeouts, awestruck students, and fun getting-to-know-you activities. Even though the charm of back to school is wearing off, you should experience smooth sailing because you've laid the foundation for a strong discipline plan and are dedicated to preparing your lessons well.

As far as writing is concerned, you have waded through initial housekeeping procedures by administering pretests, ironing out the schedule, and introducing your students to two general kinds of writing. You should also begin to get an idea of your students' writing abilities, including strengths and deficiencies. This should prepare you for the real work, which begins now.

WEEK 2 LESSON PLANS

Focus: The Expository Writing Process

You will begin modeling writing, focusing on expository essays, unless you've chosen a different informational genre. As you teach the basics of planning, writing, and editing an essay, it is important to model the thinking process related to writing.

As such, you should "think out loud like a writer" as you model. Students need to learn the natural self-editing process that writers practice, and this is the only way to demonstrate it. Teach your students to not settle for the first sentences they write and to not write the first things that come to mind. Encourage constant self-editing and revision, revising items in both the plan and first drafts, as needed.

Day 1 (Copy Day)

Objectives: Students will review expository and narrative genres and learn to plan an expository essay.

Materials: Four prompts; Figure 2.1; Figure 8.1 (optional).

Notes: Before class, make a poster of Figure 2.1. Choose or create four prompts using Resource A as your guide. You do not have to follow the provided example exactly. However, save the paper you create this week for use on Day 3 of Week 18. The following information will help you amend lessons for persuasive or descriptive writing.

- If you are preparing your students for persuasive writing, amend as follows. The topic sentence should directly state your opinion, and the three main details should support them. However, each main details paragraph should list at least two supporting details in favor of your opinion and one supporting detail in opposition to your opinion.

- To prepare for descriptive writing, focus on describing "personality" and one or two of the following senses: sight, sound, smell, taste, and touch. In your topic sentence, briefly discuss the subject you'll be describing and why you've chosen the item. Your three main details should discuss the sense or senses you will focus on, along with personality. If an object, person, or place is worth describing, it has to have some aspect of "personality." You may also combine senses such as sight and touch to give paragraphs more richness.

1. Begin with a quick review of Figures 1.1 and 1.2. Highlight the parts of a prompt and the main difference between expository and narrative writing: events in order versus list and explain.

2. Display the four prompts. Ask students to quickly differentiate.

3. Tell the students that they are going to learn how to make an organized plan to answer an expository prompt. Display the following prompt.

   - Everyone does different things during their summer vacations. Think about the things you did. Now explain how you spent your summer vacation.

4. Display and read Figure 2.1, the expository plan sheet with hints; refer to this as "the pickle sandwich." Explain that this is the correct graphic organizer to use every time students plan an expository paper.

5. Model drawing the pickle sandwich, then ask students to draw their own. Observe students. Guide them to use all of the space on their

papers and discuss that the ovals need not look perfect. Pickle sandwiches are supposed to be messy.

6. Each oval in the graphic organizer represents a paragraph. Count the ovals—there are five, two buns and three pickles. Explain that students will write five paragraph essays to answer expository prompts.

7. Tell students you will explain each paragraph's name and content by labeling your planning sheet. As you work, ask students to label their hand-drawn plans. Using the figure as your guide, label the graphic organizer to include the following: introductory paragraph; introductory sentence; three main details; three supporting paragraphs; three supporting details for each main detail; and conclusion. Discuss each term and review the hints when you are done.

8. On a piece of chart paper, draw another planning sheet, and have students do the same on blank pieces of paper.

9. Explain that the introductory sentence is the first sentence you write when answering a prompt. This sentence is pulled, or stolen, from the No-Brainer section of the prompt. Students enjoy knowing this is one time stealing is okay. Using the prompt as a crutch helps students start out in the right direction. Later, students will learn more creative ways to hook readers.

10. Reread the prompt and demonstrate the stealing process. Emphasize that you will not use complete sentences in the pickle sandwich, as it's just a sheet for planning. The words you write are meant to jog your memory for the first draft, where you will use complete sentences. Examples follow.
    a. No-Brainer sentence. Everyone does different things during their summer vacations.
    b. Stolen introductory sentence: Everyone does different things during their summer vacation, and I spent mine having fun.
    c. As written in top bun: Different things, summer vacation, fun.

11. Model the process of coming up with three main details to support your introductory sentence. Stress that these details need to be general and interesting, allowing you to write more specific details about them later. Provide examples of things that are too specific or dull before choosing yours: rode my bike to the store once; read a book; slept a lot; told a joke. Your examples may include the following; note they are numbered to mimic the figure's format.
    • Main details: (1) Swam a lot. (2) Hung out with friends. (3) Family vacation.

12. Show students where to copy the three main reasons at the top of the pickles. Use Figure 8.1, a prewritten expository plan, for extra guidance if necessary. Explain that is it important to keep the three main reasons in the same order as they appear in the introductory bun to maintain an organized essay.

13. Demonstrate how to come up with the three supporting details for your main points. As you do this, "think out loud" to demonstrate the natural process of writing. Also observe students' copies regularly. Examples follow, numbered and lettered as in the hints sheet.

    (1) Support for "Swam a lot": a. YMCA pool. b. Friends' pool parties. c. Beach trip.

    (2) Support for "Hung with friends": a. Shopped at the mall. b. Sleepover parties. c. Rode bikes to library.

    (3) Support for "Family vacation": a. Fishing. b. Camping. c. Comfy RV.

14. As you complete the final bun, the summary, point out that it is merely a reiteration of your introductory paragraph. Repeat the three main reasons in the same order they appear in the first bun, but tell students you will state them differently when you write the full sentences.

15. Announce that you will use the plan to begin a first draft tomorrow. Students should keep the hints sheet and their plan in their binders.

16. Post the complete plan on the classroom wall.

Day 2 (Copy Day)

Objectives: Students will learn to use transition words and create first drafts from written plans.

Materials: Two prompts; Figure 2.2; yesterday's plan.

Note: Before class, make a poster and student copies of Figure 2.2. Also, choose or create two prompts using Resource A as your guide.

1. Show the two prompts. Have students differentiate the expository from the narrative.

2. Ask students to retrieve their plans from yesterday and point out the one you posted on the wall. Review the prompt you are writing to and this plan. Ask students if you are staying on topic so far and answering the Boss.

3. Display Figure 2.2, the expository transition words poster, and pass out student copies. Discuss that transition words help to keep writing organized and give essays "flow." Discuss that "flow" refers to how easy an essay is to read and understand. Flow helps readers to figure out what the writer was thinking and "get into" the writer's mind.

4. Read some of the words out loud. Discuss that there are different ways to use the transition words. For example, first, second, and third are okay to use together, and some writers choose to maintain uniformity by using transitions like "my first reason," "my second reason," etc. However, a writer who wants variety might use "first of

Figure 2.1   Pickle Sandwich With Hints

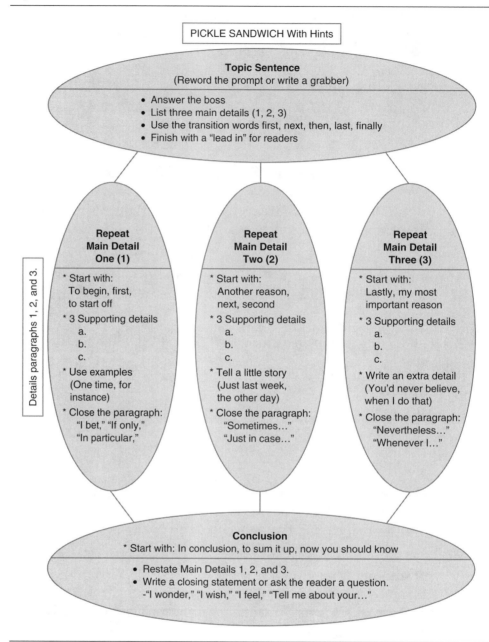

Copyright © 2006 by Karen Donohue and Nanda N. Reddy. All rights reserved. Reprinted from *180 Days to Successful Writers: Lessons to Prepare Your Students for Standardized Assessments and for Life* by Karen Donohue and Nanda N. Reddy. Thousand Oaks, CA: Corwin Press, www.corwinpress.com. Reproduction authorized only for the local school site or nonprofit organization that has purchased this book.

all," "second," and "another reason" in one paragraph. Discuss that the choice is partly a matter of individual writers' styles and voices.

5. Begin the writing process by referring to your plan. Take the words from the first bun to create your topic sentence. According to the example plan, your topic sentence is as follows:
   - Everyone does different things during their summer vacation, and I spent mine having fun.

Figure 2.2   Expository Transition Words

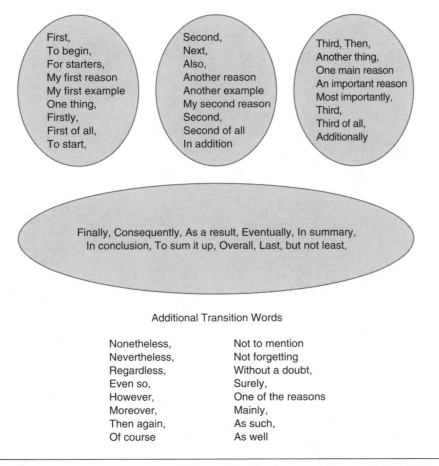

Copyright © 2006 by Karen Donohue and Nanda N. Reddy. All rights reserved. Reprinted from *180 Days to Successful Writers: Lessons to Prepare Your Students for Standardized Assessments and for Life* by Karen Donohue and Nanda N. Reddy. Thousand Oaks, CA: Corwin Press, www.corwinpress.com. Reproduction authorized only for the local school site or nonprofit organization that has purchased this book.

6. Continuing with the introductory paragraph, write each of the three main reasons in complete sentences. Engage students as you choose transition words from the poster. Continue to think out loud and self-edit as you construct the sentences, being aware that you are modeling the most difficult aspect of writing. Finally, finish the introductory paragraph with a "lead in" for the reader. Example sentences follow.

   • To begin, I swam nearly every day this past summer. Also, I got to be lazy and hang out with friends a lot. Finally, my family took a great RV vacation this summer. Read on to hear all the wonders of my summer.

7. Point out that the paragraph has five sentences. Tell students paragraphs need to have four to seven sentences, but never less than four. This is a rule that can be broken after students develop as writers.

8. On completion, reread the paragraph. Discuss how the transition words maintained flow and how the last sentence also accomplishes that.

Figure 2.3 TCUPPS

Copyright © 2006 by Karen Donohue and Nanda N. Reddy. All rights reserved. Reprinted from *180 Days to
Successful Writers: Lessons to Prepare Your Students for Standardized Assessments and for Life* by Karen Donohue
and Nanda N. Reddy. Thousand Oaks, CA: Corwin Press, www.corwinpress.com. Reproduction authorized
only for the local school site or nonprofit organization that has purchased this book.

9. With your students, choose a transition word or phrase to begin the
   second paragraph. Model the second paragraph just as you did the
   introductory paragraph. This paragraph can also be called the first
   details paragraph. An example follows.
   - One thing I did a lot this past summer was swimming. For starters,
     I participated in the YMCA program and got to swim in the big indoor
     pool at the Y most days. Also, my best friends Ali and Sue threw excel-
     lent pool parties this summer where we played water games. I was
     best at pool volleyball. Finally, my family took a trip to Andrew's
     Beach one weekend. Basically, I swam non-stop this past summer.

10. Begin making basic grammar errors related to capitalization, punctuation, and spelling for TCUPSS editing later this week. Do not make errors with the fundamentals such as with indentation and transition words.

11. Be sure students are copying your model correctly.

Day 3 (Copy Day)

Objective: Students will create a first draft.

Materials: Previously written plan and paragraphs.

Note: If you choose to give a mid-week quiz, make up ten prompts using Resource A or another source as your guide.

1. Begin with a mini mid-week quiz if desired. Show a list of up to ten prompts, narrative and expository. Have students differentiate them.

2. Review the plan and paragraphs you wrote yesterday. Point out transition words, proper indentation, and how well you're following and/or revising the plan.

3. Choose transition words or phrases and begin modeling Paragraphs 3 and 4. Keep referring back to the plan, and ask students to make sure you've written at least four sentences per paragraph. Examples for both paragraphs follow.
    a. Another thing I did this summer was act lazy and hang out with my friends. Sometimes when I was good, my mom dropped me off at the mall with my friends to shop all day. She even gave me money. I also went to three sleepover parties, and one was on a Tuesday night. Finally, my best friend Sue and I rode our bikes to the library once a month. We usually checked out at least twenty books each. I loved the freedom of being lazy with my friends this past summer.
    b. However, the most wonderful thing I did this summer was to take an RV trip with my family. We started at Lake Michigan, where we spent a weekend fishing and swimming. Then we spent two weeks driving around, camping and hiking all over the Appalachian Mountains. Camping was fun in the RV because we got to do things others campers couldn't, like watch TV. I had a blast driving around in that RV.

4. Check student copies.

Day 4 (Copy Day)

Objective: Students will complete a first draft and edit their work.

Materials: Figure 2.4; previously written plan and paragraphs.

Note: Before class, make a poster and student copies of Figure 2.4 using the following illustration (Figure 2.3) as a guide.

1. Review the plan and Paragraphs 1 through 4 of your first draft.

2. Referring to Figure 2.2, choose an appropriate transition for the conclusion paragraph. "In conclusion," "So let's review," and "As you can see" are reliable choices. Remind students that the conclusion mirrors the introduction, but it is worded differently. Furthermore, it can end with a closing statement to the reader. Model how to reword the introduction. An example follows.

   • As you can see, I did many fun things this summer. First, I swam in pools, a lake, and at the beach. Of course since I didn't have school, I got to be lazy and bum around with my friends. Furthermore, my family took the best RV vacation this summer. What fun things did you do this past summer?

3. Discuss other applicable closing statements: How was your summer vacation? Did you also have a fun summer? This summer was, hands down, the best one ever.

4. Display your poster of Figure 2.4, the TCUPSS Checklist, and pass out student copies. Introduce the TCUPSS process and explain that students will use it to edit their first drafts. Explain what each letter represents.

5. Model the TCUPSS process on your paper. Students should follow and "TCUPSS" their copies. Make sure your students track by moving their fingers across each word on their papers. In the beginning, complete each part of the TCUPSS process separately. As students become more practiced, they may begin to combine parts. Note, Umph and Support will give students trouble until they learn various elaboration techniques. Tell your students you are looking for the way you worded things this first time around. As for support, tell them you are looking for the correct number of sentences per paragraph right now.

6. Use editing symbols to mark and correct mistakes. It is important that students become familiar with editing symbols as they will be TCUPSSing each other's papers and receiving TCUPSSed papers from you later.

7. Students should rewrite final drafts for homework. You should also display a final draft on chart paper in your classroom for a few days. Save all materials for Week 18, Day 3. Also, note that during Week 13, Day 1, the hook will be changed to "Splash! I heard a lot of that this summer at the pool."

Day 5

Objective: Students will use a prewritten expository paper to review planning.

Materials: Figure 2.5.

Note: Before class, make a display copy of Figure 2.5.

Figure 2.4   TCUPSS Checklist

☐ **T- Track with your fingers**

To find . . .

☐ **C- Capital letters**

    ☐ Beginning of all sentences

    ☐ For names and proper places

    ☐ At the beginning of quotes

☐ **U- Umph!**

    ☐ Exciting, unique ideas

    ☐ Awe-inspiring adjectives and vivacious verbs

    ☐ LIKEly similes and Mind-Bending Metaphors

    ☐ Sensory details: see, smell, taste, feel, and hear

☐ **P- Punctuation**

    ☐ Periods or question marks at the end of sentences

    ☐ Commas and apostrophes

    ☐ Quotation marks

☐ **S- Spelling and Sound**

    ☐ Commonly misspelled words and homonyms

    ☐ No slang or street talk; use "school" grammar

    ☐ Author's voice and excitement

    ☐ Transition words for a good "flow"

☐ **S- Support**

    ☐ Anecdotes and examples

    ☐ Many interesting details

    ☐ Different kinds of complete sentences

    ☐ Have you answered the prompt?

Copyright © 2006 by Karen Donohue and Nanda N. Reddy. All rights reserved. Reprinted from *180 Days to Successful Writers: Lessons to Prepare Your Students for Standardized Assessments and for Life* by Karen Donohue and Nanda N. Reddy. Thousand Oaks, CA: Corwin Press, www.corwinpress.com. Reproduction authorized only for the local school site or nonprofit organization that has purchased this book.

Figure 2.5   Aunt Rhea Relates the Best

I have a large family with many relatives, and of all of them, I like Aunt Rhea best. To begin, Aunt Rhea always makes me laugh. Also, she buys the best presents. But most important, Aunt Rhea is easy to talk to. Read on to find out how great my Aunt Rhea is to have around.

One reason Aunt Rhea is so cool is because of her sense of humor. Aunt Rhea tells jokes non-stop and does cartoon voices like a pro. She also pulls priceless practical jokes. Once, before our family's reunion picture, she hid my grandparents' false teeth and made them smile toothless for the picture. One of my favorite things to watch Aunt Rhea do is make up the words for muted TV shows. She makes me laugh till my sides hurt.

Another reason Aunt Rhea is my favorite has to do with the gifts she gives. On my birthdays, I can count on getting a fashionable, new outfit, from shoes to accessories. Aunt Rhea has great taste. She also usually brings me a cool new book to read whenever she pops over to visit my mom. Furthermore, Aunt Rhea always slips me extra money to buy ice cream and candy without mom knowing. She is the most generous person I know.

Finally, Aunt Rhea makes high marks with me because she's easy to talk to. She always gives useful advice. Her advice once helped me and my best friend stop fighting. Also, she treats my problems like they're important. Finally, she can discuss serious things like drugs, without lecturing. When it counts, Aunt Rhea can get serious and become a great listener.

It should be clear why my Aunt Rhea is one of my favorite relatives. Not only is she funny, but she can get serious and give great advice. Plus, she gives the best gifts ever. I feel lucky to have Aunt Rhea in my life.

Copyright © 2006 by Karen Donohue and Nanda N. Reddy. All rights reserved. Reprinted from *180 Days to Successful Writers: Lessons to Prepare Your Students for Standardized Assessments and for Life* by Karen Donohue and Nanda N. Reddy. Thousand Oaks, CA: Corwin Press, www.corwinpress.com. Reproduction authorized only for the local school site or nonprofit organization that has purchased this book.

1. Announce that today is Backward Day. Tell students they will read a complete essay, then help you work backward to plan the essay. They will also determine the prompt that the paper might be trying to answer.

2. Display and read Aunt Rhea Relates the Best, Figure 2.5. After reading, bring attention to organizational details such as indentation, number of paragraphs, number of sentences per paragraph, and transition words chosen. Underline all of the transition words, and discuss how the words help the essay's flow. Discuss other transition words that might or might not work in the essay.

3. Discuss the paper's content, word choice, and voice. Ask students if they can get an idea of the author's personality and Aunt Rhea's personality. Ask students what they might have written differently to enhance the paper.

4. Ask students to volunteer what the prompt might have been for the paper. Write the prompt according to the No-Brainer, Brain, and Boss model unless you follow a different format. You may even allow student volunteers to write these sentences.

   - Everyone has a favorite family member. Think about your favorite relative and what makes that person special. Now write to tell who your favorite relative is and why.

5. Draw a pickle sandwich on chart paper or the chalkboard. Starting with the introductory paragraph, proceed paragraph by paragraph to "plan" the paper. Engage students' help to determine the three main details and the supporting details for each of these. As you fill in the blank plan, remember to write only words and phrases, not complete sentences.

   a. Three main details: funny, generous, easy to talk to
   b. Supporting details for "funny": jokes or voices; pranks; soundtrack to shows
   c. Supporting details for "generous": birthday outfits; books; secret cash
   d. Supporting details for "easy to talk to": good advice; treats my problems seriously; talks without lecturing

6. After completing the plan, discuss how well the plan and paper mirror each other. Ask students to explain what they know about the pickle sandwich.

3 Rainbow Words and Awe-Inspiring Adjectives: Enhancing Expository

It's a rare thing for teachers to feel their students are in the palms of their hands, but we hope that is akin to what you're feeling. Until now your students have been on very tight leashes, learning discrete skills. Now that they know the basics, it's time to loosen the leash and teach students how to make their writing unique and personal. However you cannot do this too fast; your students need to move toward independence slowly.

As you proceed with modeling, focus strongly on the "je ne sais quoi" of writing. It is especially important to constantly self-edit as you choose words and sentences, showing students how to think like writers and imbue their writing with strong voices. Maintain a steady, thoughtful pace and your students will be prepared to succeed when you finally release the leash.

WEEK 3 LESSON PLANS

Focus: Author's Voice

A story with a strong voice is one where the narrator's personality, humor, and honesty shine through. Students often struggle with this concept, and the only way to teach this skill is to continuously demonstrate it. You will introduce voice this week by instilling your essay with a strong character and pointing out the elements that strengthen the essay's personality.

Day 1 (Copy Day)

Objectives: Students will differentiate prompts and practice expository planning.

Materials: Four prompts; Week 2's plan and essay.

Note: Before class, choose or write four prompts using Resource A as a guide. Also, display this plan and essay on chart paper.

1. Display the four prompts. Ask students to differentiate.

2. Direct students' attention to last week's plan and essay. If your students need very basic instruction, show how each oval in the plan sheet corresponds to a written paragraph in the finished essay. Discuss organization, indentation, number of sentences per paragraph, transition words, and TCUPSS.

3. Tell students you will plan another essay today. Ask students to list the basic rules of planning: writing only key phrases and words; generating three main details and three supporting details for each main detail; answering the Boss.

4. Display the following prompt.
   - Everyone has a favorite food. Think about the food you love best. Now write to explain what your favorite food is and why.

5. On chart paper, draw an oversized pickle sandwich (see Figure 2.1). Students should draw their own plans.

6. Remind the students how to steal from the prompt. Using the No-Brainer part of the prompt as a guide, brainstorm an introductory sentence out loud. Ask students if it answers the Boss of the prompt. Then write key words in the plan.
   - Example No-Brainer sentence: Everyone has a favorite food.
   - Stolen introductory sentence: Everyone has a favorite food and mine is pizza.
   - As written in the top bun: fave. food, pizza

7. Come up with the three reasons that support your introductory sentence.
   - Examples: (1) Great ingredients. (2) Anytime food. (3) Easy to make.

8. Thinking out loud and engaging students, come up with supporting details for each main reason.
   - Examples for "great ingredients": Cheese + sauce + bread = yum; many toppings for any mood; unlimited tastes (pepperoni, BBQ, veggie)
   - Examples for "anytime food": Delivery when tired or lazy, no utensils; leftovers for breakfast, lunch, or snack; good for friends, parties, etc.
   - Examples for "easy to make": Dough easy to buy, or use bread; always have a topping around; becomes calzone or dessert quickly

9. When completing the conclusion, repeat the reasons in the same order. Remind students that this paragraph reviews the main reasons, but is reworded to sound different from the introduction paragraph.

10. Review the plan and check student copies.

Day 2 (Copy Day)

Objective: Using an expository plan, students will help write two paragraphs.

Materials: Plan from Day 1.

1. Review the Day 1 plan. Tell students you will write Paragraphs 1 and 2 today with their help.

2. Discuss that you will focus on letting your personality shine through your writing.

3. Begin the writing process. Using the written key words, remind students of the topic sentence you came up with: Everybody has a favorite food, and mine is pizza.

4. Tell students that this simple sentence is okay, but it doesn't "sound like you." Think of three other sentences that have more of a "voice"; you may use the examples that follow. Allow students to help you choose the one that fits your personality best. If your students are not ready for this process, stick with the simplest sentence.
   - There is one food on this planet I am sure I'll never get sick of, the glorious pizza.
   - Like water and air, pizza is one thing I cannot live without.
   - I have a confession to make—I'm a pizza fanatic.

5. Students should begin to get an idea of what "personality" means in writing; discuss that personality fulfills both Umph and Sound in TCUPSS (see Figures 2.3 and 2.4). Continue to demonstrate this as you write the three main details in complete sentences. Examples follow.
   - I have a confession to make—I'm a pizza fanatic. To begin, pizzas are made up of the most delicious ingredients on the planet. Also, anytime is a good time to eat pizza. Finally, pizza is a simple, fun food to make. If you want to hear all the virtues of pizza, read on.

6. Refer to the transition words poster when you use transitions. Students need this repetition now so that it will become habitual for them to use the posters.

7. On completion, count the number of sentences in Paragraph 1. Discuss the need for at least four sentences. Then discuss flow and voice. Do the transition words provide flow and is there a voice? Did you end with a lead in?

8. Allow students to suggest transitions to begin the second paragraph, details Paragraph 1. Write Paragraph 2 with a distinct voice. Remember

to make some minor errors in spelling, punctuation, and grammar that can be edited later. An example follows.

- The first reason pizzas rock is that they're made up of purely delicious foods. The combination of cheese, sauce, and bread has to be one of the best inventions ever. As if that weren't enough, I get to put things like pepperoni, barbeque chicken, and even pineapple on top. With so many combinations of ingredients, I can have a different tasting pizza every day to suit my mood.

9. Check student copies.

Day 3 (Copy Day)

Objectives: Students will differentiate prompts and continue helping to write a first draft.

Materials: Four prompts; previously written plan and paragraphs.

Note: Before class, choose or write four prompts using Resource A as your guide.

1. Display the prompts. Ask students to differentiate.

2. Review the plan and paragraphs you wrote. Discuss words or phrases that allow a distinct author's voice to come through the writing, providing Umph. Discuss how they add punch to the work, making it interesting and fun to read.

3. Tell students you will be adding more Umph today by writing an extra detail sentence in each paragraph. This sentence will provide extra support and add more interest, but it is important that the sentence is on topic and continues to answer the Boss.

4. When you add the extra supporting details to the paragraphs, verbally model examples of sentences that are on topic and sentences that are off topic.
   - On-topic example of extra detail after "good for friends, parties": My friends and I once ate a whole pizza each at a sleepover party.
   - Off-topic example: My friends and I like going to parties a lot.

5. Begin Paragraphs 3 and 4 with appropriate transitions, and demonstrate how to add appropriate extra details. Examples are provided with extra details italicized.
   - Paragraph 3: Another reason I love pizza is that I can eat it anytime. If I'm hungry, and there's no time to cook, all mom has to do is call for delivery. Also, leftover pizza makes a delicious breakfast and a lunch my friends drool over. Third, if I have friends at my house for a party, pizza is what I serve. *Not only do my friends love it, there is hardly anything to clean up.*
   - Paragraph 4: Another excellent thing about pizza is that it is easy to make. Grocery stores sell dough, but in a pinch, I use plain bread.

Also, you only have to glance in the fridge to find a topping. Finally, it's fun to experiment with pizza recipes to make calzones or dessert pizzas. *If you know how to turn on an oven, you can definitely make a pizza.*

6. Check student copies.

Day 4 (Copy and Pair Day)

Objectives: Students will help to complete a first draft and TCUPSS it.

Materials: Previously written plan and paragraphs.

Note: Before class, plan to create five student groups to write final drafts.

1. Review the plan. Be sure you've stayed on topic and answered the Boss.

2. Ask students to choose an appropriate transition for the conclusion paragraph. "In conclusion" and "To sum it up" are easy choices.

3. Remind students of this paragraph's objectives before writing. An example follows.
   - So, let's review the reasons why pizza is my favorite food. First, pizzas combine the world's best ingredients into one food. Also, it's a food I can eat anytime. Finally, I have a lot of fun making my own pizzas at home. Aren't those the reasons you love pizza too?

4. Refer to the TCUPSS poster (see Figures 2.3 and 2.4) and briefly review.

5. Begin editing. Change at least one word or phrase to improve the Sound, or author's voice, and add one more Umph detail. If necessary, edit transition words for flow.

6. Group students. Assign each group to transfer one final paragraph onto chart paper for display.

7. Save this model for use during Week 15, Day 4.

Day 5

Objective: Students will practice adding extra details to a basic essay.

Materials: Four prompts; Figure 3.1.

Note: Before class, make a display and student copies of Figure 3.1. Also choose or write four prompts using Resource A as your guide. You may use more prompts for a quiz.

1. Display the prompts. Allow students to differentiate. Provide as a quiz if desired.

2. Briefly review the expository planning hints and discuss Umph and Sound.

Figure 3.1   I'm Special

Everyone in this world has special traits, and I am special, too. To begin, I am a very good son and brother. Also, I am a good friend. Last, I'm fun to be around. Read on to hear why I'm special.

First, I'm special because I am a good son and brother. I make good grades, so my parents are always proud of me. *Last year,* _____. Also, I never cause trouble and always do my chores. Finally, I am really nice to my baby sister. *One time I even* _____.

Another thing that makes me special is that I am a good friend. I listen to my friends' problems and give them great advice. *My friend* _____

_____. Furthermore, I never pick fights with my friends, and I always stand up for them. Last, I often invite my friends over to hang out at my house. *We usually* _____.

The final reason I'm a special person is that I'm really fun to be around. I like to tell and make up jokes, and they always crack my friends up. Also, I love to do daring things, like stunt riding and tricks on my skateboard. *I can even* _____. To top it off, I love to play sports, and people like to play with me because I just have fun with it.

To conclude, I consider myself special for many reasons. For starters, I know I'm an excellent brother and son. Also, I am really good to my friends and I am fun to hang out with. Wouldn't you say those things make me pretty special?

Copyright © 2006 by Karen Donohue and Nanda N. Reddy. All rights reserved. Reprinted from *180 Days to Successful Writers: Lessons to Prepare Your Students for Standardized Assessments and for Life* by Karen Donohue and Nanda N. Reddy. Thousand Oaks, CA: Corwin Press, www.corwinpress.com. Reproduction authorized only for the local school site or nonprofit organization that has purchased this book.

3. Tell students that to provide enough support in response to a prompt, they will often need to write more than four sentences per paragraph. Generally, they need to add at least one extra sentence to explain their reasoning, and sometimes they may have to add up to three extra sentences. While this is Umph, it is not optional.

4. Tell students that you will practice adding extra details to an essay.

5. Pass out and display your copy of Figure 3.1, I'm Special. Read it or have student volunteers read it aloud, omitting the italics and blanks.

6. Discuss the Boss this essay possibly answers: "Now tell what makes you a special person." Ask students if the essay answers the prompt. It does, but it cannot be considered a good response because it does not provide sufficient information.

7. With student input, add extra details in the blanks provided to spice up the essay with a specific voice. Examples follow in order.
   - Last year, I made the principal's honor roll three times.
   - One time I even let her use my Hot Wheels cars for a school project.
   - My friend Tony got in fights last year until we talked about how pointless fights are.
   - We usually play video games and ride our skateboards.
   - I can even do a one-footed 90-degree spin.

8. Read the improved essay and discuss the details that add a more distinct author's voice. Discuss how the voice could be changed to reflect a kid who struggles in school; a kid who is interested in art or music; or even a child who is a genius.

9. Ask students if they believe the essay is the best it could be. They should detect that the essay is still somewhat "flat," lacking personality. Tell them you will work on that later, but that it is important for them to see how a perfectly fine essay can still fall short of being excellent.

10. Students should secure these improved copies for use later during Week 18, Day 1.

WEEK 4 LESSON PLANS

Focus: Word Choice

A good essay can become a great essay simply by changing a few choice words. This week you will begin demonstrating how words can make images pop off the page and bring stories to life.

Day 1

Objectives: Students will review prompts and help to plan an expository paper.

Materials: Figure 3.2.

Figure 3.2 Rainbow Words

Red	Orange	Yellow	Green
Crimson	Pumpkin	Lemon	Lime
Blood red/Bloody	Tangerine	Fair	Olive
Brick red	Melon	Golden	Emerald
Candy apple red	Mango	Blond	Mint/Spearmint
Flame/Flaming	Coral	Flaxen/Straw colored	Sea green
Scarlet	Salmon	Pale	Chartreuse
Ruby	Fiery	Sunshiny	Aquamarine
Raspberry	Carroty	Goldenrod	Jade
Cherry	Ginger	Sunflower yellow	Kiwi
Watermelon	Peach	Jaundiced	Avocado
Strawberry	Apricot	Banana	Pea green
Tomato	Gold/Golden	Daffodil	Grassy/Leafy
Fire engine red	Sun-colored	Almond	Springlike
Lipstick red	Basketball orange	Cream	Bottle green
Beet red	Light cinnamon	Sandy	Algae/Ivy green
Vermilion	Tanned	Corn/Cornmeal	Verdant

Blue	Purple	Black	White
Navy	Violet	Midnight	Milky
Baby blue	Plum	Jet black	Pearly/Creamy
Sky	Orchid	Sooty/Smudged	Bleached
Cornflower	Fuchsia	Tar black	Floury/Powdery
Sapphire	Magenta	Inky	Papery
Cobalt	Mauve	Ebony	Snowy
Azure	Lilac	Charcoal/Coal black	Clear/Watery
Midnight blue	Lavender	Shadowy	Sparkling white
Slate blue	Wine	Leaden	Albino
Blueberry	Amethyst	Gloomy/Dusky	Coconut white
Indigo	Bruised	Unlit/Unclear	Faded/Faint
Cerulean/Cyan	Mulberry	Raven	Washed out
Peppermint blue	Raisin colored	Opaque	Colorless/Light
Turquoise	Maroon	Depressing	Ashen/Pale
Peacock blue	Burgundy	Dirty/Muddy	Rice white

Brown		Pink	Gray
Burnt/Scorched	Khaki/Beige	Rose/Rosy	Silver
Chocolaty/Cocoa	Bronze/Copper	Blushing/Blush	Ashy
Rust/Rusty	Hazel	Flushed	Iron/Steely
Cinnamon	Auburn/Chestnut	Glowing	Oatmeal gray
Nutmeg	Fawn	Fleshy	Dove gray
Toast/toasty	Mousy	Coralline	Grizzly
Nutty/Walnut	Brunette	Lobster-pink	Smoky
Coffee	Sepia/Sienna	Ruddy	Wolf gray
Leathery	Mahogany	Baby pink	Leaden

Copyright © 2006 by Karen Donohue and Nanda N. Reddy. All rights reserved. Reprinted from *180 Days to Successful Writers: Lessons to Prepare Your Students for Standardized Assessments and for Life* by Karen Donohue and Nanda N. Reddy. Thousand Oaks, CA: Corwin Press, www.corwinpress.com. Reproduction authorized only for the local school site or nonprofit organization that has purchased this book.

Note: Make posters for the first eight colors listed on Figure 3.2, and make student copies of the resource. It's helpful to write the words on aptly colored construction paper. You may also enhance this lesson by acquiring paint chips from a hardware store. Often, the chips' unique, thought-provoking names foster discussion.

1. Start with a quick drill on the parts of a prompt and the expository writing process.

2. Point out Figure 3.2, the Rainbow Words poster, and pass out student copies. Explain that Rainbow Words are another aspect of Umph.

3. Review the words. Clarify meaning and pronunciation if necessary. Discuss that students should not use words if they are unsure of the meanings, and that they should continue to use the simpler color words in their writing when they fit. Ask students to volunteer favorite Rainbow Words. Introduce paint chips if you have them.

4. Spend up to five minutes allowing students to describe items in the classroom using these alternative color adjectives.

5. Display the following expository prompt.
   - Everybody knows interesting people. Think about the most interesting person you know. Now write to explain who that person is and why you find the person interesting.

6. Ask students to clarify what the Boss requires.

7. Announce that this week will be Students in Control Week. This means the students control the writing and that you will merely guide them.

8. Ask a volunteer to draw the pickle sandwich on chart paper.

9. Lead students to brainstorm a list of interesting people who work at the school. However, do not use people unless all students know them. If there isn't anyone specific, ask students to make up a fictional person with interesting traits. After students brainstorm, help them narrow down their choices to one most interesting person. Help them generate three traits this person has that lend themselves to vivid descriptions. Students may vote from a brainstormed list of traits. Write these in the introductory bun.

10. Continue planning to develop details for each main trait. Guide students to stick to the topic, but allow them to dictate where you should write information on the plan. If you limit your input, this exercise should serve as an informal assessment of students' planning skills.

11. Review the collaborative plan and ask students to determine if they answered the Boss. Post the plan for use this week.

Day 2

Objective: Students will write two paragraphs from yesterday's expository plan.

Materials: Yesterday's plan; Rainbow Words sentences.

Note: Prior to class, write the five example sentences below for display. Leave room below each sentence to rewrite them with Rainbow Words.

1. Point out the following sentences.
   - The police car chased a sports car.
   - Susan always wears mismatched socks and a ribbon in her hair.

- Mrs. Levy keeps twelve cats in her house and feeds them birds.
- Jill sneered at the meatloaf and cake her mother made for dinner.
- Tom raced down the dusty racetrack, waving our school's flag.

2. Tell students these sentences need Umph from Rainbow Words. Ask students to find words from their color adjectives list and class posters to improve the sentences. Discuss that some choices are better than others and that less can be more. Share the following examples of appropriate and inappropriate choices.
   - The jet-black police car chased a flaming red sports car. Not: The sooty police car chased a bloody sports car (sooty implies dirty, and bloody implies covered in blood).
   - Susan always wears mismatched socks and an emerald ribbon in her blond hair. Not: Susan always wears mismatched purple and white socks and a blue or green ribbon in her dirty blond hair (too many colors distract).
   - Mrs. Levy keeps twelve albino cats in her brick house and feeds them raven-black birds. Not: Mrs. Levy keeps twelve calico, orange, gray, and black cats in her pink house and feeds them purple birds (too outrageous).
   - Jill sneered at the pale meatloaf and olive cake her mother made for dinner. Not: Jill sneered at the bronzed meatloaf and cinnamon cake her mother made for dinner (*sneer* implies "not appetizing").
   - Tom raced down the dusty orange racetrack, waving our school's crimson and white flag. Not: Tom raced down the dusty sepia racetrack, waving our school's fuchsia and snow-white flag (too many colors distract).

3. Review yesterday's plan and encourage students to start thinking about ways to incorporate two good color words in today's paragraphs.

4. Remind students that it is Students in Control Week so your input is limited.

5. Referring to the plan, begin writing the introductory paragraph. If the students do not remind you to indent the first sentence, don't. Structure sentences according to students' suggestions.

6. Guide students to choose an appropriate transition from the resource poster, and begin writing Paragraph 2 with their suggestions.

7. On completion of Paragraph 2, read the paragraphs and refer back to the plan. Ask students if they stayed on topic and are imbuing their writing with a strong voice.

8. Post these two paragraphs for student reference this week.

Day 3 (Pair Day)

Objectives: Students will learn alternative adjectives and write one paragraph of an essay semi-independently.

Materials: Previously written plan and paragraphs; Figure 3.3.

Figure 3.3   Awe-Inspiring Adjectives

Fun		Boring		Big	
Amusing	Agreeable	Dull	Flat	Abysmal	Bulky
Exciting	Pleasurable	Dry	A snoozer	Brawny	Colossal
Enjoyable	Pleasant	Tedious	Lackluster	Enormous	Gigantic
Entertaining	Eventful	Tiresome	Tiring	Hulky	Immense
Inspiring	Interesting	Unexciting	Depressing	Inflated	Massive
Merry	Joyful	Uninspiring	Uninteresting	Monstrous	Monumental
Adventuresome	Stimulating	Monotonous	Dreary	Obese	Sizable
Delightful	Satisfying	Lifeless	Uneventful	Substantial	Titanic
Gratifying	Lovely	Mind-numbing	Passionless	Tremendous	Vast

Little		Happy		Sad	
Atomy	Bite-sized	Carefree	Cheerful	Cheerless	Dejected
Cramped	Dinky	Chipper	Delighted	Depressed	Despondent
Dwarfed	Inadequate	Elated	Excited	Dismal	Down
Infinitesimal	Insignificant	Exhilarated	Exuberant	Dull	Gloomy
Meager	Microscopic	Frivolous	Gleeful	Glum	Heartbroken
Miniature	Particle	Irrepressible	Jovial	Low	Melancholy
Runt	Scant	Joyous	Lighthearted	Miserable	Morose
Scrawny	Speck	Merry	Mirthful	Somber	Upset
Stunted	Trifle	Optimistic	Radiant	Unhappy	Wretched

Pretty		Ugly		Good	
Appealing	Attractive	Disfigured	Displeasing	Appropriate	Benevolent
Beautiful	Charming	Dreadful	Foul	Considerate	Comfortable
Dazzling	Divine	Grotesque	Hideous	Delicious	Excellent
Eye-catching	Fresh-faced	Horrid	Marred	Fulfilling	Genuine
Gorgeous	Graceful	Nasty	Nauseating	Gratifying	Honest
Handsome	Lovely	Offensive	Pockmarked	Impressive	Magnificent
Made-up	Natural	Repulsive	Revolting	Pleasant	Remarkable
Ornamented	Pleasant	Unattractive	Unpleasant	Skillful	Splendid
Pleasing	Spectacular	Unsightly	Vile	Superb	Terrific
Striking	Stunning			Talented	Wonderful

Bad		Easy		Hard	
Appalling	Abominable	Accommodating	Breezy	Austere	Bitter
Corrupt	Decayed	Child's play	Cinch	Burdensome	Difficult
Deplorable	Disgraceful	Comfortable	Convenient	Firm	Harsh
Disgusting	Embarrassing	Effortless	Facile	Inflexible	Laborious
Frail/Ill	Impish	Foolproof	Gentle	Painful	Pitiless
Malodorous	Mischievous	Lax	Lazy	Rigid	Rigorous
Naughty	Prankish	Lenient	Mild	Severe	Solid
Roguish	Rowdy	Painless	Permissive	Steely	Strict
Terrible	Wicked	Pliable	Simplistic	Tough	Unyielding

Copyright © 2006 by Karen Donohue and Nanda N. Reddy. All rights reserved. Reprinted from *180 Days to Successful Writers: Lessons to Prepare Your Students for Standardized Assessments and for Life* by Karen Donohue and Nanda N. Reddy. Thousand Oaks, CA: Corwin Press, www.corwinpress.com. Reproduction authorized only for the local school site or nonprofit organization that has purchased this book.

Note: Before class, write your modeled version of the paragraph and display the sentences from Step 3. Also, make and post the adjectives posters for "fun" and "boring" from Figure 3.3. Do not hand out student copies yet as they contain all twelve words.

1. Point out the two adjectives posters you've displayed. Discuss that the new posters are of Awe-Inspiring Adjectives and that you will display two new posters daily for the next five days. Ask if students know that *awe-inspiring* means "impressive."

2. Read the adjectives on the posters and allow time for questions. Give volunteers a chance to use the alternative words in sentences.

3. Point out the following sentences:
   - Fun 1: Everybody had fun in our school's cornfield maze.
   - Fun 2: Mr. Jones is a fun PE teacher.
   - Bored 1: I felt bored at the class picnic.
   - Bored 2: Mrs. Deter assigned a boring worksheet for homework.

4. Discuss the following appropriate and inappropriate replacements for fun and boring in these sentences. Discuss the role of helping verbs and the need to modify synonyms and the articles "a" and "an" for grammatical correctness.
   - Fun 1: Everybody (had a blast, had an adventure, enjoyed themselves) in our school's cornfield maze. Not: Everybody (felt merry; was amused; felt inspired; felt satisfied) in our school's cornfield maze.
   - Fun 2: Mr. Jones is an (amusing; exciting; inspiring; entertaining) PE teacher. Not: Mr. Jones is a (delightful; satisfying; merry) PE teacher.
   - Bored 1: I felt (uninterested; unenthusiastic; aloof) at the class picnic. Not: I felt (dull; casual; calm; irritable) at the class picnic.
   - Bored 2: Mrs. Deter assigned a (dull; uninteresting; irritating) worksheet for homework. Not: Mrs. Deter assigned a (casual; aloof; calming) worksheet for homework.

5. Tell students they will work in pairs today to write Paragraph 3. They should use an Awe-Inspiring Adjective and a Rainbow Word in their writing today. However, students should write on their own papers.

6. Read over Paragraphs 1 and 2 and review the plan carefully for Paragraph 3. Discuss details you might add, adjectives you might use, and how you might phrase certain things if you wrote the paragraph. Explain that you have written your own version of the paragraph and that you will compare paragraphs after they have written theirs since it is still Students in Control Week. Remind students to choose appropriate transitions and provide a time limit.

7. Pair up students and set a timer if desired. Monitor students.

8. When time is up, display your model. Point out indentation, extra details, adjectives, and transition words. Discuss your flow and the aspects of your writing that give it personality. Allow student pairs to compare their details, transition words, and adjective choices. If possible, ask students to discuss the voice and flow of their pieces. Ask students what they had problems with and try to solve those problems right away.

Day 4 (Pair Day)

Objectives: Students will learn alternative adjectives and write the final two paragraphs of an essay semi-independently.

Materials: Previously written plan and paragraphs; Figure 3.3.

Note: Before class, make and post the "big" and "little" adjectives posters and sentences. Complete your model of Paragraphs 4 and 5.

1. Point out the two new posters and introduce the words. Allow students to practice them orally in sentences and use the following sentences for written practice.
   - After I fell, I felt a big bump form on my head.
   - Sheila's little puppy does big tricks and is always fun to be around.

2. Have students retrieve their paragraphs and get together with their partners.

3. Reread the paragraphs written as a class as well as the one you modeled yesterday. Then carefully review the plan for paragraphs four and five. Discuss student options while writing the paragraphs, and tell students you will show them your version after they have written theirs. Encourage students to use words from the adjectives posters today as well as one color word.

4. Provide a time limit. Remind students to begin with appropriate transition words and allow them to begin working with their partners to write the final two paragraphs.

5. Observe students closely and offer feedback when needed.

6. After time is up, read your paragraphs and allow students to compare theirs. Allow students to discuss their successes and mistakes and let them read sentences aloud to demonstrate how they imbued their paragraphs with personality. Praise exemplary use of Awe-Inspiring Adjectives and Rainbow Words.

Day 5 (Pair Day)

Objectives: Students will review expository transition words and edit a first draft.

Materials: Completed essays; Figures 3.3 and 3.4.

Note: Before class, plan to pair students up with different partners, cover the expository transition words poster, and make copies of Figure 3.4. Make and display the "happy" and "sad" adjectives posters and sentences.

1. Start this lesson by asking students to write down all the expository transition words they can think of in two minutes. Uncover the transition words poster and discuss how many students remembered each of the words. Draw particular attention to words the students forgot.

2. Point out the two new posters and introduce the words. Allow students to practice them orally in sentences. Use the following sentences for written practice.
   • I was never as happy as I was the day I won the tennis championship.
   • After his goldfish died, John was sad for weeks.

3. Tell students they will TCUPSS the three paragraphs they wrote this week with different partners. Pair students up.

4. Review the TCUPSS poster and editing procedures. Have students tell you what each letter of the acronym stands for.

5. Pass out a copy of Figure 3.4, the Checklist for Peer Editing, to each student. Review this sheet. Tell students they will be using it to edit their partners' papers as their partners look on. Students will look for each TCUPSS item as they track; they will note a good example and tally the mistakes their partners made in each category. As they track and edit, they could whisper read. If possible, they should look for ways their partners can add Umph to their papers with interesting words. Afterwards, partners will write what they learned about themselves as writers and will give themselves what they consider a fair grade at the bottom of the checklist.

6. Place a time limit so that both partners can complete the assignment.

7. Observe students as they track and edit the papers. Encourage them to keep pace and remind students when to switch and begin TCUPSSing the second paper.

8. After editing, students should copy Paragraphs 1 and 2, which you posted, and begin writing final, polished drafts of their paragraphs. They may finish these for homework and display them in the classroom.

WEEK 5 LESSON PLANS

Focus: Pace and Independence

This week, you will begin to foster independence. This is a delicate process, and your students will require a great deal of support. By the end of the week, you should expect students to plan and write an easy essay with confidence.

Day 1

Objectives: Students will review prompt differences, learn new adjectives, and plan an expository paper.

Materials: Four prompts; Figure 3.3; A Prized Photograph.

Note: Before class, choose or write four prompts using Resource A as your guide. Also, post the prompt from Step 3 and the "pretty" and "ugly" adjective posters and sentences. Finally, review the plan in Step 7 and A Prized

Figure 3.4 ✓ Checklist for Peer Editing ✓

Checker's name: _____ Writer's name _____

T = Track with your finger; Touch EVERY word as you read.

What to find	Yea! A good example found	Uh-Oh! # of mistakes found
C = Capitals (Sentence; quotes)		
U = Umph! (Ideas; vocabulary; voice/style)		
P = Periods & Punctuation		
S = Support (Details; organization; on topic)		
S = Spelling & Sound (Slang; transitions; easy to read; flow)		

Hint from the peer checker:

_____

_____

Writer: The thing I learned is . . . _____

_____

_____

The grade I give myself is _____.

_____

_____

Copyright © 2006 by Karen Donohue and Nanda N. Reddy. All rights reserved. Reprinted from *180 Days to Successful Writers: Lessons to Prepare Your Students for Standardized Assessments and for Life* by Karen Donohue and Nanda N. Reddy. Thousand Oaks, CA: Corwin Press, www.corwinpress.com. Reproduction authorized only for the local school site or nonprofit organization that has purchased this book.

Photograph, the finished essay, to make desired changes. You may also plan and write your own essay before class instead.

A Prized Photograph

Everyone has a prized possession, and mine is a framed photograph of my family. To begin, the picture was taken on an unforgettable, special day in my life. In addition, I received it as a gift. Finally, the photo is meaningful because it reminds me of my family, who lives far away.

The first reason I love the photograph is because it was taken on my sister's wedding day. Whenever I look at everyone's beautiful, smiling faces, I remember how thrilled my family was that day. I was especially excited since I was the maid of honor. I also remember why we were all smiling so hard. A blue-green peacock had insisted on riding on my sister's train during the photo shoot in the park. The photo always reminds me of how much fun I had that day.

The photo is also special to me because it was a thank you present from my sister and brother-in-law. They framed it professionally with the wedding colors, sapphire and silver. The photo is a large 8-by-10, so it's the centerpiece on my mantle where everyone can see it. I love having such a lovely memento to show off my family to friends.

The most important reason I love the photo is that it allows me to see my family every day. My parents, sisters, and brother all live in different states, and we rarely get together. Our next family reunion isn't until Christmas. Because I miss them often and am very close to them, I enjoy seeing their faces daily.

As you can see, I cherish the photo of my family. It reminds me of my sister's magical wedding day, and I appreciate that it was a thank you present. Plus, since I don't see my family often, the photo means a lot to me.

---

1. Display the four prompts. Ask students to differentiate.

2. Point out the two new posters and introduce the words. Allow students to practice them orally in sentences. Use the following sentences for written practice.
   - The girls all chose pretty dresses for the prom.
   - My aunt redecorated her house and now it's ugly.

3. Tell students they will finally begin their own papers today, using their own ideas. Reveal the following prompt.
   - Everyone has a favorite possession. Think about the things you own that are special to you. Discuss what your favorite possession is and why you cherish it.

4. Discuss the topic of the prompt and possibly the meaning of "possession." Describe what the Boss is asking. Be sure to emphasize that the Boss wants to hear about only one possession.

5. Brainstorm possible possessions. Discuss that certain possessions are difficult to write about, such as a favorite pen or a chair. However, a favorite bicycle will let you discuss how you got it, what it allows you to do, and how it makes you feel. To write an interesting essay, students may tell the truth, make up the information, or do both. Examples of items to consider include the following: tree house; doll; sports equipment; library card; video game, CD, or DVD player; computer; bedroom; go-cart; skates; telephone; television.

6. Draw a pickle sandwich and allow students to draw theirs. Ask students to note the possession they want to focus on somewhere on their papers so they won't forget.

7. Tell students you will model your plan first and that you chose to write about a picture of your family. Think out loud as you plan, considering interesting ways of wording eventual sentences and editing uninteresting thoughts.
   - Introduction. Favorite thing, framed picture of family: very special day; was a present; live far away
   - Second paragraph. First, picture of special day, sister's wedding: everyone dressed up, happy; mishaps with peacock during the shoot; reminds me of fun I had
   - Third paragraph. Next, a "thank you" gift; framed with wedding colors; large 8-by-10 on mantle; like to show it off
   - Fourth paragraph. Most important, lets me see my family every day; live far away; won't see until Christmas; miss them often and am close to them
   - Conclusion. So let's review: wedding; thank you; see family

8. After you have modeled your plan, review it quickly.

9. Provide time for students to complete their plans. Observe and offer feedback.

Day 2

Objectives: Students will use a previously created plan to start a first draft and include adjectives they've learned.

Materials: Yesterday's plans; Figure 3.3; A Prized Photograph.

Note: Before class, make and post the "good" and "bad" adjectives posters and sentences.

1. Point out the two new posters and introduce the words. Allow students to practice them orally in sentences. Use the following sentences for written practice.
   - I had a good day at school.
   - Ron was being bad, so his mother punished him.

2. Review your plan. Then, thinking out loud, model Paragraph 1 according to A Prized Photograph. Self-edit, use adjectives you've introduced, and complete quickly. You may choose to impose a time limit on yourself.

3. Instruct students to review their plans and to write their introductory paragraphs. Set a time limit if desired. Observe student work and offer help as needed.

4. After time is up, model Paragraph 2.

5. Allow students to review their plans and write Paragraph 2.

6. Model Paragraph 3.

7. Allow students to write Paragraph 3.

Day 3

Objective: Students will complete their first drafts.

Materials: Previously written plans and paragraphs; Figure 3.3; A Prized Photograph.

Note: Before class, make student copies of Figure 3.3. Also make and post the "easy" and "hard" posters and sentences.

1. Hand out student copies of Figure 3.3, the Awe-Inspiring Adjectives list. Encourage students to use this list, along with the Rainbow Words from their binder's resource section, to add Umph to their writing today. Point out the final two posters and new words. Allow students to practice the words orally in sentences. Use the following sentences for written practice.
   • Math has always been an easy subject for me.
   • The hard thing about telling the truth is that it can get you in trouble.

2. Have students take out their plans and incomplete essays.

3. Review your plan, then model Paragraph 4 according to A Prized Photograph.

4. Set a time limit if desired and allow students to complete Paragraph 4. Observe.

5. Model your conclusion.

6. Allow students to write their conclusions. Observe.

7. TCUPSS your paragraphs, adding adjectives where applicable.

8. Allow students to TCUPSS their paragraphs. Monitor closely and provide feedback.

9. Students should hand in completed essays for assessment.

Day 4

Objective: Students will learn to use a grading rubric.

Materials: Select student papers; rubric; rubric posters; A Prized Photograph.

Note: Before class, prepare a student version of your state writing rubric unless you plan to use the generic rubric provided in Resource B. Make an overhead display and student copies of the rubric, and amend the lesson to reflect your rubric's qualities. If you are following your own rubric, make rubric posters and student copies following Resource C as a guide. Otherwise, make posters using this resource. Finally, review student papers to choose four examples: one that would receive a score of four or five; two that might score a three; and one that is a two.

1. Tell the students they will learn how teachers grade students' writing. As such, they will know what is expected of them and can work to get the highest score possible.

2. Explain that when grading most other class work, answers are either right or wrong. But with writing, there are no right or wrong answers. This is why teachers use a rubric to grade writing.

3. Display the rubric.

4. Explain that a rubric lists all of the things an essay must have to get a perfect score. If the essay is missing items, the score is reduced. Review each section of the rubric thoroughly. Make sure students understand the wording and elements of a "perfect" paper.

5. Discuss that a perfect score of six (according to the generic rubric) is very difficult to achieve. Three, four, and five are good, more attainable scores. Poor scores are one and zero. A two needs improvement.

6. Read A Prized Photograph. Have students guess its score by holding up fingers.

7. Use your overhead copy of the rubric to grade the paper according to the six categories (if using the generic rubric). Award a maximum of two points per subcategory. Then add up the subcategory points. A paper can achieve up to six points per section. This paper should achieve four to six points in every category for a total of twenty-four to thirty points and a mean of four to five.

8. After scoring each category, find the mean score by adding each category's points and dividing by six. Ask students if they were accurate when they guessed the score.

9. Tell students you will anonymously grade a few of the papers they wrote this week by reading them out loud and analyzing them with the rubric.

10. Read a chosen student paper. Ask students to guess its grade (with fingers) before analyzing it according to the rubric.

11. Grade the paper in the manner described above and discuss students' guesses.

12. Repeat the process with the three other papers you've preselected.

13. After scoring the papers, ask students to help you write examples of papers that would score a zero or one. Discuss that even a well-written off-topic paper can score a zero. Examples follow.

   • One: My favrite poseshun is a book. Frist, I read it. Evry night. I likes it. Also, Its a good storie for me. It help my learn morals. It got good Bible stories in it. And my sister read it too.

- Zero: I really like to help my Aunt Sophia with her sewing. She lets me pick out the material and patterns. I love the store where we shop for these things. Then we cut the pattern out. Finally I help keep things in place as she sews. I love seeing the final product. (Even if this were five paragraphs long, its score would not improve.)
- Zero: A dog. It's fun to play with.

14. Point out or post your rubric posters and pass out student copies. Discuss that each poster represents a writing grade from six to zero, listing the requirements for each grade. Discuss the posters and ask students what they learned.

Day 5 (No Help Day)

Objectives: Student will write an expository essay independently.

Materials: Expository prompt; grading tools.

Note: Format and present the following prompt as you did the pretests. You may use Resource E or a similar tool to assess this essay and diagnose problems.

- Everyone has a favorite teacher. Think about a teacher you really appreciate. Now write to explain who your favorite teacher is and why.

    1. Tell students that you are testing them today and so will not provide writing help. They may use posted references and those in their binders, including expository essays you've written together. Discuss that they should feel free to embellish or make up information if they get stuck in the writing process or can't come up with ideas.

    2. Set the timer and pass out the test. Allow students to plan and write their essays. Remind them to leave enough time for editing.

    3. When time is up, pick up student papers. If possible, ask two other teachers on your team to blindly grade the papers according to the rubric, circling student scores in each area. Average the students' final scores and analyze them using Resource E or a similar tool. Use the tool to determine the areas of writing your class struggles with as a whole.

    4. You may allow students to polish these pieces and present them as gifts to the teachers they wrote about.

4 It All Started With a Tier Cake: Directing Narrative Structure

Narratives, or stories, are just plain fun, and most students feel comfortable with narrative writing because it's familiar. They grew up surrounded by stories. However, that does not mean narrative writing is easy. It is actually the more difficult of the two genres you are teaching. Whereas expository writing fits easily to a form, narrative writing seems to defy form. There are general rules to narratives, however. If you teach these rules and provide a graphic organizer to guide your students' thoughts, you can show them how to master the art of stories.

WEEK 6 LESSON PLANS

Focus: Narrative Story Structure

Stories contain different elements from essays, including characters, setting, a conflict, and a resolution. Although there is no perfect story formula, you will teach your students a generic structure they may apply to any six-paragraph short story.

Day 1 (Copy Day)

Objectives: Students will differentiate prompts and learn to plan a narrative.

Materials: Figures 4.1 and 4.2; Figure 8.2 (optional).

Note: Before class, display the posters and make student copies of Figures 4.1 and 4.2. Also, post the prompt in Step 3. If you need a completed sample narrative plan for guidance, use Figure 8.2.

Figure 4.1   Tier Cake With Hints

Hook your reader: quote, funny example, a LOUD sound, a feeling or reaction, invitation

Setting	Characters	Problem
Describe—what do you see? Hear? Feel? Smell? Talk about colors and the scene. Tell the time of day, month, season, holiday, or special event that might be happening	Introduce one or two. If it fits into the story, briefly describe them. Tell a detail about the character (what is he/she doing, saying, wearing, eating, acting like?)	Tell the problem or hint at it. You'll never believe what happened next! One thing ruined the day; The downfall was; The most amazing thing happened; Read on to hear the exciting adventure

Action Paragraph 1

- Start with: To begin with, One day, On January 1st (any specific day), It all began, First of all, Three days ago, Let me take you back, It was 8 a.m.

- Tell the first 4 or 5 things that happened in a row that are important to know before you get to the problem.

- Describe what you see, hear, taste, smell, feel, wondered, and thought.

Action Paragraph 2

- Start with: Later on, Just hours later, A split second later, I woke up the next day and, All I did was, or Then.

- Tell the next 4 or 5 things that happen in a row leading up to the problem or involving the problem.

- Get to the problem: Use senses (eyes, nose, tongue, skin) and juicy color words to tell what is going on.

Action Paragraph 3

- Start with: Hours later, Some time later, When, After, or some other line that continues the story.

- Tell the next 4 or 5 events in a row that will lead up to the solution. Introduce a new event or "savior" character.

- Change paragraphs when something BIG happens, TIME changes, or the speaker changes (if using quotes).

Action Paragraph 4

- Start with: Out of the blue, In the middle of nowhere, A savior arrived, I knew that everything would be OK when, The adventure couldn't have ended better, I can't think of a happier ending than, To close this story up.

- Be sure to solve or eliminate the problem.

- Don't write "The End"

Take away: The thing I learned; I promise never, ever; I wish; I hope; I wonder; I believe; Have you ever had an adventure like this? I would love to hear more; Nothing can beat . . .

Copyright © 2006 by Karen Donohue and Nanda N. Reddy. All rights reserved. Reprinted from *180 Days to Successful Writers: Lessons to Prepare Your Students for Standardized Assessments and for Life* by Karen Donohue and Nanda N. Reddy. Thousand Oaks, CA: Corwin Press, www.corwinpress.com. Reproduction authorized only for the local school site or nonprofit organization that has purchased this book.

Generic Story Structure

a. Paragraph 1: Comes from the four boxes on top (the top tiers), including the hook, setting, characters, and conflict. Its main goal is to introduce the story to readers without giving it away. So students should not transfer everything from the plan into the written paragraph, as is done in expository writing. They should only get the reader's attention.

b. Paragraph 2: The "it all began" paragraph, which tells how everything was right before the problem occurs. It's the first action paragraph because it shows the action leading up to the problem. It only includes information important to the problem and story.

c. Paragraph 3: The "problem" paragraph is where the problem or conflict arises. The problem may occur at the beginning or end of this second action paragraph.

d. Paragraph 4: The "what next" paragraph aims to intensify the story and make the problem worse. A resolution may begin to form at the end of this third action paragraph.

e. Paragraph 5: The "resolution" paragraph, or fourth action paragraph, shows how the character deals with the problem. The problem should be resolved at the middle or end of this paragraph.

f. Paragraph 6: The "take away" paragraph aims to show what the characters learned or how they grew in the story. Part of this paragraph may also be used for resolution if needed.

1. Tell students they will begin narrative writing today.

2. Remind students that narratives are stories, either true or made up. The made-up stories may also be realistic or fantastical. Remind students that all narratives show the passing of time: something happens, and then something happens later, and so on. Narratives also feature problems or conflicts; otherwise the stories are boring to readers. Give an example of a bland story, a fun day at the beach, for example, where nothing out of the ordinary happens. Finally, discuss that your narratives will include six paragraphs, not five.

3. Direct the students' attention to the following narrative prompt.
   • Everyone has lost a belonging at least once. Think about a time you lost something. Now write a story about a time you lost something.

4. Clarify word meanings in the prompt and what the Boss wants. Tell the students that you know this is a narrative prompt because the Boss directs you to write a story. Remind them of how carefully they worked with you to learn expository. Discuss that they will learn narratives the same way. As such, they will need to follow and copy your model this week.

5. Point out Figure 4.1, the narrative graphic organizer with hints, and hand out student copies. Refer to this plan as the "tier cake" to contrast it from the pickle sandwich. Explain that students will use this graphic organizer each time they plan a narrative.

6. Draw a tier cake on chart paper as the students copy it. Observe students. Make sure they use their entire sheets of paper to draw the plans.

7. Now use the hints on Figure 4.1 and the generic story structure to introduce the elements in a story. Also, refer to the blank tier cake you drew to reinforce which part of the plan corresponds with each paragraph of the story.

8. Point out Figure 4.2, the narrative transitions poster, and hand out student copies. Allow students to read some of the transition words and phrases. Discuss how they show the passage of time.

9. If you need to further illustrate the differences between narrative and expository, verbally remind students of your last expository. Discuss the order of items you wrote and ask if the order mattered. Students should realize that order matters little in expository writing. The order in which things occur matters heavily in narratives.

10. Tell students you will now show them how to plan a narrative. Reread your prompt before brainstorming. Think of several ideas to answer the prompt before settling on one, even if you're using the example. Remind them that good writers rarely settle for their first ideas.

11. Point out that the first tier of your cake is for the hook or grabber, meant to "hook" or "grab" the reader's attention. Brainstorm some simple hooks that answer the prompt and grab attention. Write one in the plan as a complete sentence since the wording matters. It should be the only complete sentence in the plan. Students should copy your work. An example follows.
    • "I will never forget the day I lost my most favorite thing in the world."

12. Refer again to the tier cake poster. Remind students that the next tier at the top of your plan includes your setting, characters, and problem.

13. Explain that sometimes the character and setting can be found in the prompt; however, the problem will usually come from the Boss. Ask students if they see the characters, setting, or conflict in the prompt. They should see "you," a character, and "lost something," the conflict. The setting is up to the writer.

14. Fill in the boxes, thinking out loud. Indicate to students that if they can "see" a story clearly as they plan, it should be easier to write. A completed paragraph is provided to help you guide your students through the story as you plan.

- Characters: my mom and I
- Setting: the mall
- Problem: I lost my purse.

15. Monitor the students as they copy your words. Tell students they do not need complete sentences in these boxes.
    - Complete paragraph: I will never forget the day I lost my most favorite thing in the world. My mom had taken me to the mall to buy a gift. I got caught up looking around, and somehow, I misplaced my beautiful pink purse. Read on to find out the details.

Figure 4.2 Narrative Transition Words

It all started	After a while,
It all began when	Later that morning (night, etc.)
To begin with	Soon after,
The day began normally	Minutes (seconds, hours) later,
Let me take you back to the start	Not long after,
Unusually,	Fortunately,
That day (morning, night, etc.)	Back at school (home, etc.)
Nothing was going right	Not surprisingly,
Nothing was unusual until	It was no surprise
It was 10:30 (or other time)	The shocker was
A couple of days ago	In the meantime (meanwhile)
On March 23rd (or other day)	Just then
Last week (month, year, etc.)	All I did was
	I went on with my business and . . .
Out of the blue,	Eventually,
Out of nowhere,	After a little while,
Shockingly,	The next thing I know
To my surprise,	Moments later,
That evening,	As I rounded the corner,
The next day (morning, etc.)	There before me
After a long night,	A split second later
When (event) happened	Just when I thought
When (name) did that,	A savior arrived
At exactly the same moment,	I saw the light at the end of the tunnel
Simultaneously,	I rejoiced when
After (event),	We were ecstatic to see (person)
Needless to say,	It turned out that
When all hope was gone,	The whole time

Finally,	I learned	I wish
As a result	I came to realize	I hope
Consequently,	It became clear to me that	I believe
As such,	I now know	I know
With much relief,	The lesson I learned	I wonder
To our relief and surprise,	It is important to	I imagine
Thankfully,	The truth is	I promise

Copyright © 2006 by Karen Donohue and Nanda N. Reddy. All rights reserved. Reprinted from *180 Days to Successful Writers: Lessons to Prepare Your Students for Standardized Assessments and for Life* by Karen Donohue and Nanda N. Reddy. Thousand Oaks, CA: Corwin Press, www.corwinpress.com. Reproduction authorized only for the local school site or nonprofit organization that has purchased this book.

Day 2 (Copy Day)

Objectives: Students will differentiate prompts and continue to help plan a narrative.

Materials: Previously written plan.

Note: Although you are only planning the narrative today, completed example paragraphs are provided to help you make the story clear to your students as you plan. Use the completed paragraphs during Days 3, 4, and 5 if you are using the example provided.

1. Review the tier cake, story structure, transition words, and what you've planned so far. Tell students you will complete the plan today.

2. Remind students that the next box to fill in is Paragraph 2, the first action paragraph. Here you will tell the first four or five things that happen before the problem. Direct students' attention again to the narrative transition words poster. Choose a transition word appropriate for the beginning of your story (e.g., It all started, The day began, It all began when, etc.). Then write the first four or five things that happened using only phrases, attending carefully to sensory details (what you see, hear, taste, smell, feel, wonder, etc.). Make it clear that you are only writing notes to trigger your memory for the actual story writing.

   - It all started—I wanted to buy a present; had to use my allowance; got purse, went to mall; mall was loud and crowded

   - Complete paragraph: It all started when I begged my mom to take me to the mall. It was my friend Eliza's birthday, and I wanted to get her a present. My mom said I'd have to use my allowance to buy it. So, I got my purse, and my mom drove me to the mall in her brand new truck. The mall was loud and crowded, and I was excited to look around.

3. Move on to the second action paragraph (Paragraph 3). Direct students' attention back to the narrative transition words poster and have them help you select an appropriate transition. Point out that you have to get to the problem by the end of this paragraph. Think aloud about the next four or five things that will happen and write them on your plan. If you are using the example, here is where you actually lose your purse.

   - After four or five stores, hungry; got tacos; mom paid, we ate; getting up, realize I don't have my purse

   - Complete paragraph: After we hit four or five stores, I was exhausted and hungry. Mom suggested getting tacos, and I waited for her at a booth while she ordered. I was so tired, I rested my head on the table even though it was smeared with ketchup. I got energy after I gobbled up the taco, but that's when I realized something was missing. "My purse!" I screamed.

4. Continue with the third action paragraph (Paragraph 4). Elicit student help to choose an appropriate transition. Then refer to the tier cake and remind them that in this paragraph you need to show what happened as

a result of the problem. Also, you may begin to resolve the problem. However, the problem will be resolved completely in your next paragraph. Complete this section of the plan and monitor the students' progress in duplicating it into their binders.

- Hours later, searched stores; cried; lost Christmas present from dad; checked lost and found; told security guard
- Complete paragraph: Hours later, after we had searched every store, I sat down and cried. I couldn't believe I lost twenty-five dollars and my favorite pink purse that my dad had given me for Christmas. I didn't even get Eliza something. I was so careless. As I cried, mom went to lost and found. They didn't have it, so she reported it lost to a security guard.

5. With the students' help, choose your last transition phrase for the fourth action paragraph (Paragraph 5) and write it on your plan. Remind your students that this is where you need to resolve the problem for sure. You might choose one of the following: Out of the blue, In the middle of nowhere, I knew everything would be okay when, etc. Plan for the last four or five events that will occur in your story. If you're using the example prompt, you may find the item or react to the realization that you will never get it back.

- Example: Out of blue, spotted purse; kid dragging it in store; ran after it; little girl had it; her mom returned it
- Complete paragraph: Out of the blue, as we were walking past a toy store, I spotted a familiar pink purse. Someone was dragging it around the store. "My purse," I shouted, "You have my purse!" I ran toward the purse and realized the thief was just a little kid. She smiled at me and held up the purse. Her mom handed the purse to me and said the little girl must have just picked it up somewhere. I was so thankful. I wanted to kiss that little girl.

6. Your final paragraph tells what happens after the problem is resolved and gives a "take home message." This message is a lesson learned or something gained from the experience. Think several options aloud and come up with the best for your plan. Check students' copies one last time for mistakes.

- Example: In the end, buy gift for little girl and Eliza; lucky; learned to be careful; don't lose belongings anymore
- Completed paragraph: In the end, I decided to buy a small gift for the little girl who found my purse and for Eliza. I realized I was lucky. I could have lost my beloved purse and my hard-earned allowance, all because I got careless. Now, I'm very careful with my belongings. I haven't lost a thing since that day.

7. Point out that "lose" and "belonging" are key words from the Boss, and using them helps to show you were on topic. If time permits, you might want to give a verbal example of an "off-topic" story plot: you visit an amusement park, ride roller coasters, lose something, find it soon after, then continue the day.

8. Review your first complete tier cake. Post it on chart paper for use this week.

Day 3 (Copy Day)

Objectives: Students will differentiate prompts and begin a narrative draft.

Materials: Previously written plan.

1. Review the narrative transition words poster. Ask why it is important to use these types of transition words instead of those for expository. Students should respond that transitions for narratives help show the passing of time.

2. Today you will use the plan you created yesterday to begin a first draft of your story. You will write Paragraphs 1 and 2. Be sure to review the plan carefully before you begin writing. Refer to the tier cake poster to make sure your plan follows the proper story form.

3. Post a new piece of chart paper on the board and ask students to get ready to copy the story on clean sheets of paper. They should also have their plans available for reference.

4. Referring to the tier cake poster, point out that the hook, character, setting, and problem boxes all go into the first paragraph. Pull your hook from your plan word-for-word. Be sure to indent, and write it on the first line of your paper. Just as you did for expository, remember to make a few deliberate spelling and grammar errors to be corrected during TCUPSS.

5. As shown in yesterday's example, you might want to end with a lead in: "Read on to find out what happened when . . ." or, "Keep reading and I'll tell you everything."

6. A different example for the introduction follows.
   - "Oh no! It's gone!" I screamed. I was shopping with my mom at the grocery store one ordinary Saturday afternoon. When I woke up that morning I had no idea, this would be the day I would lose my precious pink purse. Read on to find out what happened on that fateful day.

7. Check students' papers for accuracy and begin reviewing the plan for your next paragraph. Using the tier cake poster, remind the students that your second paragraph is your first action paragraph. Copy your transition onto your paper and begin writing, referring to yesterday's example if desired.

8. Think of two or three ways to word certain sentences before choosing the best one. Discuss voice, wording, and that real writers constantly edit during their first drafts. Refer to the Rainbow Words and Awe-Inspiring Adjectives posters to add Umph.

9. End the lesson by asking the students to share something they have learned about narrative writing.

Day 4 (Copy Day)

Objectives: Students will take a narrative transitions quiz and continue working on a narrative first draft.

Materials: Previously written plan and paragraphs.

Note: Before class, cover the narrative transitions poster.

1. Announce that students will be taking a quick quiz to see how many narrative transitions they can come up with. Provide five minutes. Instruct students to keep going until the time runs out. When time is up, ask the students to share their answers. Review and define forgotten transitions.

2. Read the paragraphs you wrote and review your plan. Focus on the two paragraphs you are adding today.

3. Remind students that the second action paragraph (Paragraph 3) is where you must introduce the problem. Indent and write your transition phrase to start. Transfer the next four or five events onto your plan into complete sentences, thinking out loud and self-editing as you go. Use the examples given on Day 2 to aid your writing.

4. Indent and pull your transition phrase from your plan into your fourth paragraph. This is action paragraph three. Using the narrative hints poster, point out that this paragraph shows what happens as a result of the problem. Also, you can start to resolve the problem here or see the "light at the end of the tunnel." Or you may resolve it during Paragraph 5 (fourth action paragraph).

5. Check student copies.

Day 5 (Copy Day)

Objectives: Students will take a quiz on the narrative plan, then complete and edit the paper.

Materials: Previously written plan and paper.

Note: Before class, cover the tier cake poster.

1. Begin the lesson with a quiz of the tier cake. Give students five minutes to draw it and write hints and transition words in each box. Collect the quiz, and review the answers.

2. Let students know they will finish the paper they started yesterday with the fourth action paragraph and conclusion. Review the plan and the four paragraphs you have written so far.

3. Indent and begin the fourth action paragraph (Paragraph 5) with the transition word you chose earlier. The problem needs to be resolved in this paragraph.

4. Review the rules for the final paragraph. Inform students that this paragraph tells exactly what happened after the problem was resolved and

contains the take home message. You may remind students of morals found in fairy tales and fables. Discuss that the main characters usually learn a lesson or "grow" in the process of the story. Discuss your take home message.

5. Indent, write your last transition, and complete this paragraph according to your plan. Sum up how the problem was resolved (if necessary), what happened after the resolution, and write the take away.

6. Model how to review the prompt to check that you are answering the Boss. Reread the final sentence of the prompt and ask your students if you wrote about what the Boss asked and if you stayed on topic.

7. TCUPSS the paper. Model the process on your paper as the students follow along with their copies. Post the completed paper in the classroom for a few days.

5 Ask for Likely Similes and Vivacious Verbs: Enhancing Narratives

As you probably discovered last week, students love to hear a good story. These next weeks, you'll find out that they love telling stories, too. All kids delight in thinking up bizarre plots with great twists and turns. They simply need a little stimulation.

WEEK 7 LESSON PLANS

Focus: Syntax

Syntax refers to word order and sentence relationships. Students often experience difficulty recognizing poor syntax or may not see the value of improving it. The subtle skill of word arrangement is best taught through continuous modeling and describing your thought process as you write.

Day 1

Objective: Students will review narrative planning with a prewritten narrative.

Materials: Figure 5.1.

Note: Before class, make a display and student copies of Figure 5.1.
  1. Announce that it's Backward Day. Remind students they will work backward from a prewritten story to fill in a plan sheet.

Figure 5.1   My Least Proud Moment

It's tough to admit, but I committed one of the worst crimes ever. I used to blame my ex best friends, Arlene and Diane, for what happened that fateful Friday afternoon. But I now know I'm a big part of the reason Leona broke her leg in the woods behind my house. Let me tell you about that shameful day when I mistreated a trusting friend.

It all started when Leona moved to our school and tried to befriend Arlene, Diane, and me. She hung around like a puppy dog. Diane and I liked her, but Arlene didn't, and what Arlene said went. So we made fun of her. Still, Leona kept being nice to us and would even bring us gifts.

One day, Arlene, Diane, and I were walking to my house after school. Leona wanted to join us. I was about to make an excuse, but Arlene quickly said, "Sure." As Leona tagged along behind us, Arlene whispered her plan. She thought it'd be funny to play a practical joke on Leona and leave her stranded in the woods behind my house. "She'll never bother us again," Arlene said.

At the time, I thought it was a funny prank, but deep down, I knew that I was doing something mean. We told Leona that we played a game called blind scavenger hunt, where we put objects in the woods and then blindfolded ourselves to find them. I put a ruby ball behind a tree. Leona chose a Frisbee, Diane hid a book, and Arlene stuck a polished rock on an old trunk.

As soon as we were sure Leona was blindfolded, Arlene, Diane, and I took our blindfolds off. We moved the objects around, snuck off, and left Leona searching in the darkening woods. Back in my room, we played with makeup, but I felt guilty. An hour later, we hadn't heard from her. I went to check on Leona and found her crying, stuck in a pothole with a broken leg.

Leona never forgave me and I don't blame her. I made her feel like she didn't deserve me as a friend, when the truth was I didn't deserve her. My parents punished me, but I learned my lesson the moment I saw Leona in that pothole. I will never treat anyone with disrespect again.

Copyright © 2006 by Karen Donohue and Nanda N. Reddy. All rights reserved. Reprinted from *180 Days to Successful Writers: Lessons to Prepare Your Students for Standardized Assessments and for Life* by Karen Donohue and Nanda N. Reddy. Thousand Oaks, CA: Corwin Press, www.corwinpress.com. Reproduction authorized only for the local school site or nonprofit organization that has purchased this book.

2. Pass out copies of Figure 5.1, My Least Proud Moment. Read or allow volunteers to read it aloud.

3. Instruct students to draw tier cakes as you draw one on chart paper.

4. Brainstorm to figure out the prompt and Boss that this narrative answers.
   - Prompt: Everyone does things they're not proud of. Think about a time you did something you regret. Now write a story about a time you did something regretful.

5. Think out loud and brainstorm with students to find out the topic sentence, characters, setting, and conflict. Ask students if all of the information was found in the introductory paragraph. A main character (Leona) and conflict (deciding to play a mean prank and strand a friend) are not in that first paragraph.

6. Complete the tier cake for the first two paragraphs of the story with student help. Remember to emphasize transition words and write only

the most vital information related to the story's plot in as few words as possible.

7. Allow students to plan the next two paragraphs of the story as you monitor them and provide hints.

8. Finally, allow students to plan the final paragraph without your input. Review the plan when they are done and instruct students to keep it for reference.

Day 2

Objectives: Students will review story structure and help plan a narrative.

Materials: Prompt.

Note: Plan details are provided in this lesson, and the complete essay is given this week. However, you may choose to change details or allow students to help you write the narrative.

1. Post the following narrative prompt.
   - Imagine getting lost and finding something bizarre. Where could you get lost and what could you find? Write a story about getting lost and finding a strange thing.

2. Ask students to draw individual tier cakes as you draw one on chart paper.

3. Point out the poster displaying transition words for narratives. Tell students you will choose the ones you prefer in advance and change them later if they don't work. Choose words to prompt each paragraph. Emphasize that these are "time" words, the hallmark of stories.
   - For example: You'll never believe (introduction); It all began (second); Later (third); An hour later (fourth); Suddenly (fifth); In the end (final)

4. Discuss that the prompt calls for an imaginary story, not a realistic one. Then review the general goals for each paragraph. You introduced this differently last week.

Alternative Generic Story Structure

a. Paragraph one: The introduction; it grabs readers' attention and begins answering the Boss. This paragraph sets the scene (setting), introduces main characters, and hints at the conflict or states it outright.

b. Paragraph two: The "it all began" paragraph tells how everything is before the conflict (problem) arises.

c. Paragraph three: Introduces the tension and conflict. You may introduce the conflict in the beginning or at the end of this paragraph.

d. Paragraphs four and five: Show results of the conflict and how the character gets in trouble. The trouble intensifies and a solution emerges.

e. Paragraph six: Resolution. Shows how the conflict is resolved. It also refers back to the Boss to be sure you stayed on topic.

---

5. Model answering the Boss and grabbing readers' attention with an introductory sentence. For example: You'll never believe what happened to me when I got lost in the woods.

6. Brainstorm, then write down a setting, characters, and the conflict.
   - Characters: Me; my dog, Muriel
   - Setting: Sunny, wet Saturday morning
   - Conflict: Got lost, found footprints, and met miniature people.

7. Tell the students to note that the Boss only told them part of their problem. They have to come up with the details.

8. Fill in the plan with phrases as you create a plot.
   - It all began . . . when Muriel woke me; took her out; she pulled me into woods
   - Seconds later . . . leash got cut; she ran off; I got lost; no trail
   - After an hour . . . heard noises; saw tiny footprints, door; saw a tiny person
   - Suddenly . . . it bit me; all went black; I fell; heard Muriel; heard little voices
   - In the end, miniature people got under me; moved me like ants move things; felt twigs, leaves, and mud; heard Muriel; woke up outside the woods; no one believes me

9. When you are through, review the plan and then post it for reference this week.

Day 3

Objective: Students will help write Paragraphs 1 and 2 from yesterday's plan.

Materials: Previously written plan.

1. Review yesterday's prompt and plan, paying careful attention to the part you'll use today.

2. Referring to the posters, remind students of the basics: indentation; sticking to the plan; using transition words to show time change; writing with a clear voice; using Rainbow Words and Awe-Inspiring Adjectives.

3. As you write, try to use weak verbs to aid next week's lesson: move, walk, said, and see. Also, remember to make minor spelling and grammar errors.

4. Thinking out loud and pointing out strong use of voice, write the introduction.
   - You'll never believe what happened to me when I got lost in the woods. It occurred when I was walking my dog Muriel in a meadow behind my house. I remember that Saturday morning clearly. It was sunny, and the grass was wet from dew. It was such a beautiful morning that I never expected to find the strange thing I saw that day.

5. Discuss what not to do when writing the introduction paragraph. Students shouldn't use the words "setting" and "character," and they should hint at the conflict, not give away the story. This example demonstrates a poor introduction with weak word choices, syntax, and voice.
   - Let me tell you about when I got lost in the woods. The setting was a Saturday morning in the meadow behind my house. The characters were my dog Muriel and myself. We got lost, and then I met some miniature people living in a secret world.

6. To further demonstrate poor syntax, use the following sentences.
   - It was me and my dog Muriel walking in the woods that morning.
   - Muriel went behind my house Saturday morning, and she pulled me there, too.
   - We got lost in the woods, and then my dog and I couldn't find our way out.

7. Write the "correct" second paragraph.
   - It all began when Muriel woke me up at six a.m., making noises. I was tired when we went out, but I felt better soon because I got to see a pretty sunrise. For a while, Muriel and I walked in the wet grass enjoying the fresh air. Then Muriel got very excited and frantically pulled me into the woods.

8. When you are done with these paragraphs, TCUPSS them. Tell students that you will TCUPSS continuously from now on instead of saving a whole day for the process.

Day 4

Objective: Students will help write Paragraphs 3 and 4 from yesterday's plan.

Materials: Previously written plan and paragraphs.

1. Warm up by reviewing the plan and written paragraphs.

2. Remind students that Paragraph 3 will introduce the main conflict because it gives you three other paragraphs to deal with the problem.

3. Thinking out loud, write Paragraph 3. Continue using weak verbs.
   - Seconds later, we were deep in the woods. I was trying hard to hold onto Muriel, but she was running faster than I had ever seen her run. We reached a fallen tree and I leapt over it. But Muriel went under and her leash snapped. That's when I lost sight of her. I ran after her for a while until I realized I was lost. The trail was gone and I couldn't hear Muriel at all.

4. As you write Paragraph 4, remind students that this is where your characters' trouble gets more intense. Describe the complex syntax of Sentences 2 and 4. Sentence 2 ends with a quote. Sentence 4 combines two sentences, both with interesting syntax.

- After an hour of walking around without any luck, I heard noises. I went in the direction of the sounds, calling, "Muriel? Muriel?" Then, I swear I heard laughter. I stopped, a little scared, and at that moment, I saw tiny footprints in the dirt. I sat down to look at them and that's how I saw the tiny door in a tree. Well, of course I touched it, and a doll-sized person came out, shouting at me.

5. Discuss how the syntax could be different and simpler. The author could have written, "I called Muriel's name and walked over to the sound" for Sentence two. Sentence 4 could become "I was scared, so I stopped. Then I saw tiny footprints in the dirt." Discuss how these changes would affect the paragraph.

6. TCUPSS after you have completed these paragraphs. If time permits, you may invite a student to lead this process.

Day 5

Objective: Students will help complete the first draft.

Materials: Previously written plan and paragraphs.
1. Review the plan and the four paragraphs you have written.

2. Remind students this is the point where the characters get out of trouble and the story concludes. This is also where you go back to make sure you answered the Boss.

3. Thinking out loud, write these final paragraphs. Italicized sentences include complex syntax. Discuss how these sentences can be reworded and how rewording affects the paragraphs. Examples for a syntax discussion follow in Step 4.
   - Suddenly, he came at me and bit me. I felt the sting but didn't have time to do anything. Everything went black. *I fell, knowing I was fainting, but I could still hear.* I heard Muriel barking nearby. Plus, hundreds of miniature people were talking around me. I couldn't speak or move, but I felt the army of little people swarm over me. Then Muriel licked my face.
   - It didn't take long for the tiny people to get under me. I felt like I was on pins and needles as they raised me, but I was really on thousands of hands. I felt the people moving me like ants move things. *Twigs poked at me, leaves brushed my face, and my feet and head kept hitting tree trunks. The people were quiet, but the whole while I heard Muriel walking beside me. When I finally awoke, I was outside the woods with Muriel sitting at my feet.* No one believes the adventure I had in the woods, but I know what I saw when I got lost there. I will never go in those woods again.

4. To simplify the complex syntax of Sentence 3 in Paragraph 5, it could become "I fainted and fell to the ground. I could still hear." To alter the fourth through sixth lines of Paragraph 6, you might include the words

"I felt" before twigs, say "All I could hear was Muriel," and change "with Muriel sitting at my feet" to "near Muriel."

5. After writing these paragraphs, TCUPSS them, then read the complete story. Save the final draft for use during Week 8, Day 1.

WEEK 8 LESSON PLANS

Focus: Strong Verbs

Verbs can do more work than just help tell a story. They can make readers feel as if they're in the story. Students will learn how to bring their stories to life for readers with strong, active verbs.

Day 1

Objectives: Students will learn how to replace weak verbs with more active verbs and brainstorm ideas for a new narrative.

Materials: Previous week's narrative; Figure 5.2; prompt.

Note: Before class, make student copies of Figure 5.2 and create posters of chosen verbs. Also, post the following prompt.

- Everyone has been frightened before. Think about a time that you were terrified by something real or imaginary. Now tell a story about a time you were frightened.

  1. Review the definition of verbs, helping verbs, and infinitives. If desired, discuss gerunds.
     - Verb: A word used to show an action or indicate the existence of something.
     - Helping verb: Forms of "to be" that are part of a verb phrase such as "was going."
     - Infinitive: A verb phrase beginning with "to" that doesn't refer to a person or subject. For example: I want to go home. "To go" is the infinitive.
     - Gerunds: A noun form of a verb ending in "-ing."

  2. Display last week's narrative. Tell students that this is well written, but that it could be improved with stronger, more vivacious verbs. Discuss that Vivacious Verbs are just like vivacious people—they get noticed. Furthermore, they add Umph to writing and have more meaning than their weak counterparts.

  3. Ask students what they should look for when they TCUPSS for Umph. They should remember Rainbow Words, Awe-Inspiring Adjectives, and author's voice from previous lessons. Add that from now on, they should also look for Vivacious Verbs.

4. Point out the posters and pass out student copies of Figure 5.2, the Vivacious Verbs. Review the verbs together to clarify meaning. Allow volunteers to use some of the words in sentences.

5. With student help, read the narrative and underline all verbs. Point out the strong verbs in the essay: leapt, snapped, swarm, licked, poked, and brushed. Discuss they are strong because they help readers see action.

6. Model how to replace weak verbs in the first paragraph. Without student help and thinking out loud, exchange weaker verbs with more active verbs. Discuss why changing verbs sometimes requires a syntax change and why you left certain crucial "to be" verbs alone. Examples follow; italics indicate a change.
   - You*'ll* never *believe* what happened to me when I *got lost* in the woods. It *occurred* while I *was walking* my dog Muriel in a meadow behind my house. I *remember* that Saturday morning clearly. *The sun shone*, and the grass *sparkled with* dew. It *was* such a beautiful morning that I never *expected* to *discover* the strange things I *witnessed* that day.

7. Ask for student input in the next two paragraphs. Ideas follow.
   - Was trying: tugged; Was running: sprinted; Went: crawled; Ran: raced
   - Stopped: halted; Saw: spied, noticed; Sat: crouched; Touched: tapped

8. Now ask student volunteers to replace verbs in the last paragraphs. Ideas follow.
   - Came: lurched; Heard: detected; Were talking: jabbered
   - Felt: sensed; Moving: shuffling; Kept hitting: thumped; Sitting: relaxing

9. Point out your displayed prompt. Discuss the Boss, and then allow students to thoroughly brainstorm at least three ideas. Students may vote on their favorite idea to plan and write this week. Some examples follow: Lightning storm while alone; car accident; amusement park ride stops; noises during a power outage; shadows outside bedroom; wild animal chases you; graveyard.

10. Announce that this week will be a Students in Control Week. They will dictate what you write and you will not contribute ideas.

11. If time permits, allow a student volunteer to draw the tier cake on chart paper and begin the collaborative plan.

Day 2

Objectives: Students will plan and write the introduction of a narrative.

Materials: Brainstormed ideas from yesterday; verb sentences.

Note: Before class, post the verb sentences from Step 1.

Figure 5.2   Vivacious Verbs

See/Hear/Find			Feel/Touch/Put		Smell	Stand/Stop
Notice	Perceive	Sense	Heave	Knock	Sniff	Wait
Glimpse	Listen	Affect	Drag	Slap	Whiff	Halt
Examine	Snoop	Threw	Hit	Punch	Reek	Pause
Discover	Eavesdrop	Pat	Thump	Experience	Stink	Stall
Detect	Pay attention	Yank	Whack	Come across	Perfume	Rise
Spot	Overhear	Caress	Push	Struck	Detect	Remain
Witness	Pry/Spy	Finger	Haul	Wallop	Notice	Stay put
Visit	Heed	Stroke	Pull	Pound	Breathe	Freeze
Realize	Take note of	Handle	Tug	Stir	Inhale	Hover
Investigate	Attend to	Pat	Jerk	Upset		Hang
Observe		Tap	Tug	Mess up		

Taste/Eat	Walk/Move/Went		Talk/Speak/Say			Sit/Rest
Sample	Saunter	Bound	Chat	Shout		Stoop
Savor	Stroll	Hurdle	Gossip	Call		Bend
Sip	Shuffle	Hop	Chatter	Cry		Hunch
Lick	March	Bounce	Discuss	Scream		Crouch
Drink	Hike	Prance	Lecture	Bellow		Lean
Gobble	Stride	Strut	Babble	Screech		Support
Wolf	Pace	Sashay	Rant	Bark		Relax
Scoff	Toddle	Sway	Prattle	Bawl		Settle
Consume	Totter	Swagger	Rumor	Holler		Plop
Munch	Crawl	Frolic	Tattle	Roar		Drop
Chomp	Sway	Wriggle	Converse	Whisper		Splash
Devour	Lurch	Stomp	Yak	Murmur		Plunk
Gorge	Wobble	Storm	Chitchat	Sigh		Prop
Swallow	Stumble	Plod	Make conversation	Moan		Lounge
Nibble	Trip	Speed	Negotiate	Groan		Vegetate
Dine	Skip	Trudge	Deliberate	Growl		Slouch
Lunch	Jump	Traipse	Consult	Snarl		Slump
Breakfast	Mosey	Scramble	Articulate	Whimper		Situate
Gulp down	Meander	Lumber	Verbalize	Grunt		
Feast	Wander	Sneak	Address	Mumble		
Indulge	Hurry	Leap	Preach			
Inhale	Creep	Inch	Jabber			
	Race	Sprint				

Copyright © 2006 by Karen Donohue and Nanda N. Reddy. All rights reserved. Reprinted from *180 Days to Successful Writers: Lessons to Prepare Your Students for Standardized Assessments and for Life* by Karen Donohue and Nanda N. Reddy. Thousand Oaks, CA: Corwin Press, www.corwinpress.com. Reproduction authorized only for the local school site or nonprofit organization that has purchased this book.

1. Ask students to identify the verbs in the following sentences, and then suggest ways of changing the sentences to include Vivacious Verbs.
   - I went down the stairs in a hurry.
   - He was going to the library after school.

2. Review the prompt, chosen idea, and any work you've completed on the plan.

3. Remind students of the story structure and transition words.

4. Work quickly to flesh out the story with only student input.

5. Review the completed plan and post it.

6. Begin writing the introductory paragraph as your students dictate the sentences. Ask students to consider their word choices, voice, and flow whenever applicable.

7. TCUPSS when done.

Day 3

Objective: Students will complete Paragraphs 2, 3, and 4.

Materials: Previously written plan and introduction; verb sentences.

Note: Before class, post the verb sentences from Step 1.
1. Ask students to identify the verbs in the following sentences, and then suggest ways of changing the sentences to include Vivacious Verbs.
   - I saw him eat a whole pizza by himself.
   - The thief got away with over a million bucks.

2. Review the plan sheet and the introduction.

3. Prompt students to begin writing Paragraphs 2, 3, and 4.

4. When appropriate, refer students to the word choices posters and prompt them to edit their thoughts. Also, encourage them to think about the voice in the story and to add extra unplanned, descriptive sentences to flesh out the story.

5. Upon completion, TCUPSS the paragraphs. Focus strongly on Umph: Vivacious Verbs, Awe-Inspiring Adjectives, Rainbow Words, a strong voice, and details.

Day 4

Objectives: Students will complete Paragraphs 5 and 6, then edit.

Materials: Previously written plan and paragraphs; verb sentences.
1. Ask students to identify the verbs in the following sentences, and then suggest ways of changing the sentences to include Vivacious Verbs.
   - I felt sick to my stomach and wanted to go home.
   - Jean got a dog for her birthday, and we had fun with it.

2. Review the prompt and written paragraphs.

3. Prompt students to begin the writing. Guide them when necessary.

4. When done, read the work out loud and TCUPSS. Help students improve sentence structure, replace weak verbs, and add voice. Demonstrate how to make the story "pop" and come to life in places where it falls flat.

5. Ask volunteers to write the final draft on chart paper for display.

Day 5

Objective: Students will plan independently to a prompt.

Materials: Prompt; verb sentences.

1. Ask students to identify the verbs in the following sentences, and then suggest ways of changing the sentences to include Vivacious Verbs.
   - Ron and I went to the store to get milk and came back with donuts instead.
   - Sheryl didn't like the story because it was boring.

2. Display and read the following narrative prompt.
   - You get home from school and find a witch there instead of your family. Think about what could have happened and how the problem can be solved. Now write a story about finding a witch in your home.

3. Brainstorm ideas. For example, the witch could have eaten, kidnapped, tied up, or made an agreement with the family; the witch could be a babysitter, relative, or friend; the witch could have avoided the family and is there to kidnap the writer; the family could owe the witch something; the witch could be in trouble, lost, or hiding out in the house.

4. Tell students to draw the plan sheet and plan the prompt on their own.

5. Help students generate ideas and stay on track with the story structure. Remind them to write phrases, not complete sentences.

6. Ask students to share their plans afterward. Collect for grading.

WEEK 9 LESSON PLANS

Focus: Similes

Similes are fun tools for students. When used wisely, they can add a new dimension to student writing and act as a vehicle for "voice." However, if used poorly, "like" and "as" become distracting. Students will learn to use similes wisely to enhance their writing.

Day 1

Objective: Students will learn how to use similes to enhance their work.

Materials: Figures 5.3 and 5.4.

Note: Before class, make displays and student copies of Figures 5.3 and 5.4. Generate some poor and cliché similes for examples during Step 4.

Figure 5.3   ASk fOR LIKEly Similes

Similes

Feelings
Happy . . . like a well-fed baby
Sad . . . as a losing team
Angry . . . like fire ants
Confused . . . as a rat in a maze
Fun . . . like birthday parties
Bored . . . as a cow
Bold . . . like Tom Sawyer
Scared . . . as lost children

Senses
Looked <u>shiny like washed car</u>; <u>as filthy as a muddy pup</u>
Smelled <u>as good as fresh bread</u>; <u>like rotting compost</u>
Tasted <u>like food for Royalty</u>; <u>as good as burnt rubber</u>
Felt <u>as bumpy as a country road</u>; <u>like cold, hard steel</u>
Sounded <u>like a crow cawing</u>; <u>as if angels were singing</u>

Some Common Adjectives and Adverbs	
Silly as an elephant doing tricks	<u>sang</u> (terribly) <u>like a whining alleycat</u>
Crazy like a witch	<u>drove</u> as recklessly <u>as a blind driver</u>
Lovely as fresh morning dew	<u>spoke </u>(carefully) <u>like a politician</u>
Fresh like the butcher's meat	<u>danced</u> as beautifully <u>as a ballerina</u>
Lazy as a sloth in a tree	<u>dunked</u> (easily) like a professional
Trembling like grass in the wind	<u>walked</u> as quickly <u>as a kid on his way to a candy shop</u>

Copyright © 2006 by Karen Donohue and Nanda N. Reddy. All rights reserved. Reprinted from *180 Days to Successful Writers: Lessons to Prepare Your Students for Standardized Assessments and for Life* by Karen Donohue and Nanda N. Reddy. Thousand Oaks, CA: Corwin Press, www.corwinpress.com. Reproduction authorized only for the local school site or nonprofit organization that has purchased this book.

1. Return the plans students wrote last week. Briefly note general problems you might have encountered and general successes.

2. Tell students that this is your final week of guiding them through narratives. They will learn one final Umph tool before writing independently.

3. Point out the ASk fOR LIKEly similes poster, and ask students if they see something strange in the poster. They should note the odd lettering. Discuss that the lettering will remind them of two key words used in similes: AS and LIKE.

4. Tell students they use similes all the time when they compare two unlike things. Give a few verbal, cliché examples (e.g., She's as pretty as a picture; He shook like a leaf on a tree).

5. Discuss the poster's title further: ASk fOR "LIKEly" Similes. The title indicates that not all similes are good. Some are "unlikely." For example: fat as a chicken (are all chickens fat?); heavy as my backpack (not every reader knows you); she is like a ball stuck in a tree (confusing); silly like silly putty (silly putty isn't really silly); dumb as a squirrel (squirrels may be smart); mean as your little sister (not everyone has a mean sister).

6. Tell students similes that are confusing or too hard to understand won't work because students can't be next to their readers to explain them. With more sophisticated students, discuss overused similes, or clichés. Even though these are "likely," they are not the best choices because people use them too often (high as a kite, free as a bird, dumb as rocks, etc.). But with all other students, allow clichés for now.

7. Pass out student copies of Figure 5.3, ASk fOR LIKEly Similes, and discuss the similes. What unlike things can they be used to compare? Do they all use the words "like" or "as"? Discuss places where these particular similes wouldn't fit. For instance, "The dog was as filthy as a muddy pup" isn't the best choice because the sentence compares two similar things, dog and pup. However, "The baby was as filthy as a muddy pup" works better.

8. Discuss how similes can replace words completely. For instance, you don't need to say, "He spoke carefully like a politician." You may simply say, "He spoke like a politician." The simile provides the image of being careful.

9. Verbally use a few of the similes in complete sentences. After each sentence, discuss the two unlike things being compared. Ask student volunteers to offer sentences and cite the unlike items they are comparing.

10. Display Figure 5.4 and read Switched. Point out indentation, correct grammar and spelling, strong details and word choices, and the strong voice. Tell students that even though the story is good, similes would improve it.

11. Insert similes or replace words with similes in the first two paragraphs as follows.
    - It's true: It's true as the facts in an encyclopedia
    - Really fast: As fast as lightning hits
    - Raining out: Raining like the sky exploded
    - Were stuck: Were like prisoners
    - Annoying: As annoying as a fly buzzing near your ear
    - Flickered: Flickered like firecrackers

12. Ask student volunteers to insert similes near the italicized words or phrases in the third and fourth paragraphs, or they may replace words with similes. Examples follow.
    - Confused: Like a deer in headlights
    - Standing: Stiff as a statue
    - Gulped: Gulped like a nervous cartoon character
    - Fancy limo: Limo, fancy as fine jewelry
    - Dumb: Dumb as a box of rocks
    - Glitzy: Like a rock star on tour
    - Lonely: As lonely as a lost bear

13. Instruct students to choose two underlined words or phrases in the fifth and sixth paragraphs. They need to insert similes or replace words with similes at the locations. Provide a time limit and allow students to share their choices after completion. Examples follow.
    - Tripped: Tripped like a duckling learning to walk
    - Laughed: Laughed like hyenas
    - Poor Arnold: Poor Arnold, who was like a bug getting stomped on
    - Headache: An ache like a hammer had hit my head
    - Looked at me: Looked at me like she was seeing a ghost
    - Made fun of him: Talked about him like he was dirt

14. Review the many options students now have for Umph: similes, Vivacious Verbs, Awe-Inspiring Adjectives, and Rainbow Words.

Figure 5.4   Switched

This will sound like a tall tale, but *it's true*. I still can't figure out exactly how it happened, but one afternoon, while watching TV, I switched places with Arnold Baxter, my least favorite TV star. It was bizarre, and happened *really fast*. Read on to find out more.

It all started on a Friday afternoon when I was watching a "Baxter's World" marathon with my sister, Tina. It was *raining out*, so we *were stuck* inside. Arnold Baxter, a minor character who's *annoying* on the show, was up to his usual dumb pranks. I started making fun of him. The next thing I know, the TV *flickered*, and I was in Arnold Baxter's body, on the show's set!

I was *confused* and thought someone played a prank on me. I called for Tina, but she didn't answer. All I could see was Arnold Baxter's fake TV room, and I was Arnold, *standing* in it. Someone snapped his fingers at me and said, "You okay? We're done for today." I just shook my head and *gulped*. Then a strange lady kissed me on the cheek and led me to a *fancy limo*.

The lady, Arnold's mom, showed me into her fancy house and said, "Cheer up hon. It's not that kids don't like you. They just don't like your character." I couldn't believe Arnold knew kids thought he was *dumb*! In the house, I quickly figured out Arnold's life wasn't *glitzy*. He had chores, schoolwork with a tutor, and singing lessons. And he had no friends. His life was *lonely*.

The next day, as I was getting ready to act like Arnold on stage, I *tripped* and the other actors, the ones I liked, *laughed*. Right then, I felt sad for *poor Arnold*, and I wished I never thought those rotten things about him. That's when I felt a *headache*. I closed my eyes, and when I opened them, I was back on the couch next to Lisa.

Lisa *looked at me* and said, "What's with you?" She said I had been "out of it" for five minutes. But I swear I was inside Arnold Baxter's body, and I regretted that I *made fun of him*. I learned that I should never judge a book by its cover.

Copyright © 2006 by Karen Donohue and Nanda N. Reddy. All rights reserved. Reprinted from *180 Days to Successful Writers: Lessons to Prepare Your Students for Standardized Assessments and for Life* by Karen Donohue and Nanda N. Reddy. Thousand Oaks, CA: Corwin Press, www.corwinpress.com. Reproduction authorized only for the local school site or nonprofit organization that has purchased this book.

Day 2

Objectives: Students will complete a plan and write an introduction for a narrative.

Materials: Prompt.

Notes: A complete Rainy Day essay is provided during Week 17 if you need a reference.

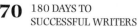

1. Warm up with a simile review. Ask students to make up similes for the following words: patient, rough, and tearful. Example answers could be: patient as a nurse; rough as a potholed road; tearful like a cranky baby.

2. Display the following prompt.
   - Everyone has dealt with a rainy day. Think about how you or your friends have spent rainy days. Now write a story about a rainy day.

3. Discuss that this is a realistic narrative without a provided conflict.

4. Tell students that you will plan the story and write the introduction paragraph collaboratively. Later, they will complete the stories independently.

5. Plan the narrative with student input. Refer back to the story structure and emphasize movement of time with transitions.

6. Brainstorm ideas and begin writing the introductory paragraph with student input.

7. TCUPSS when done, adding similes.

Day 3

Objective: Students will complete the story's middle.

Materials: Previously written plan and introduction.

1. Ask students to make up similes for the following words: gentle, funny, and stern. Example answers could be: gentle as a spring drizzle; funny as a monkey doing tricks; stern as a principal.

2. Review yesterday's plan and read the introduction. Note the similes.

3. Tell students they will be writing the story's middle, Paragraphs 2, 3, and 4, independently. Discuss that students should include strong adjectives, verbs, similes, and details. Also, discuss that they should try to make the pieces unique with personal voices.

4. Provide a time limit and allow students to write. Offer close assistance.

Day 4

Objective: Students will write Paragraphs 5 and 6.

Materials: Previously written plan and paragraphs.

1. Ask students to write similes for the following words: brave, loud, and yellow. Example answers could be: brave as a soldier; loud as a fire-cracker; yellow as a daffodil.

2. Review the plan, attending closely to Paragraphs 5 and 6.

3. Provide a time limit and ask students to complete the final paragraphs. As students work, provide close assistance.

4. After students are done, provide a time limit for TCUPSSing. Tell students to edit the story as a whole, focusing on similes, word choices, and voice.

5. When students are done, ask them to refer to the rubric and rubric posters. Review the requirements for the various grades and ask students to assign a grade to their stories.

6. Collect the stories, shuffle, and randomly read two or three. After reading the stories, refer to the rubric and discuss the scores they might achieve based on the categories.

7. Grade the papers, noting students' self-scores. Save the papers with both scores for a rubric lesson during Week 16, Day 4.

Day 5 (No Help Day)

Objective: Students will write a narrative story independently.

Materials: Narrative prompt.

Note: Format and present the following prompt as you did the pretests.

- Imagine waking up and finding out you've switched bodies with your best friend. How can this have happened and how can this problem be solved? Now write a story about switching bodies with your best friend.

  1. Tell students they will have a chance to plan and write a story on their own today, in one class period.

  2. Provide a time limit. You may break the time limit up into planning time, writing time, and editing and revising time.

  3. Provide the prompt and begin the test.

  4. When time is up, pick up student papers. Assess the test as you did your first expository test. If possible, acquire two teachers to grade the papers, with detailed scores according to rubric categories. Then use a tool such as Resource D to analyze student progress and problems. Determine your class's overall strengths and weaknesses to guide your future instruction.

6 Dressing Things Up: Independent Writing

Welcome to the second nine weeks of the school year! You have accomplished a lot in the first term. But until now you have done mostly modeling and guided writing. During this second quarter, you will begin to remove the scaffolding and let students write independently.

Students will further learn to use similes, metaphors, quotes, anecdotes, and sensory details to beef up their writing. They will begin to apply these skills easily to stories and essays, requiring less time to successfully complete each type of writing.

WEEK 10 LESSON PLANS

Focus: Metaphors

Students are ready to write independently and in a more sophisticated style. Mind-Bending Metaphors will allow them to add more style and complexity to their writing.

Day 1

Objectives: Students will learn how to write and use metaphors in their writing.

Materials: Figures 6.1 and 6.2.

Note: Make a poster of Figure 6.1. Make a display and student copies of Figure 6.2.

Figure 6.1 Mind-Bending Metaphors

Compare two things directly without using "like" or "as."

Example:	Meaning:
The campfire was a towering inferno.	It was a very big and hot fire.
We were helpless infants when we started the cooking class.	They didn't know what they were doing.
It was pouring buckets during the storm.	It was raining hard.
Mom was a raging beast when she saw the mess we had made in the family room.	Mom was *very* angry.
	The crowd was loud.
	The children were hungry.

Copyright © 2006 by Karen Donohue and Nanda N. Reddy. All rights reserved. Reprinted from *180 Days to Successful Writers: Lessons to Prepare Your Students for Standardized Assessments and for Life* by Karen Donohue and Nanda N. Reddy. Thousand Oaks, CA: Corwin Press, www.corwinpress.com. Reproduction authorized only for the local school site or nonprofit organization that has purchased this book.

1. Tell the students that today they will learn a new way that writers use their words to compare things. Direct student attention to Figure 6.1, Mind-Bending Metaphors.

2. Explain that a metaphor is related to a simile because it also compares unlike things. However, metaphors do not use the words "like" or "as." Briefly review similes with the following examples.
   - By the time I ate dinner at nine o'clock I was hungry like a bear out of hibernation.
   - I answered the phone quick as a wink because I was expecting Tony's call.
   - The quarterback was leveled flat as a pancake when the other player tackled him.

3. Further discuss the word "mind-bending" in the title. It indicates that metaphors cause readers to "bend their minds" or move away from traditional thinking. When two unlike things are compared directly without like or as, one object "becomes" the second in readers' minds.

4. Review the examples. Then ask students to identify the two unlikely things being compared.
   - The campfire is compared to a towering inferno.
   - The writer is comparing the characters to helpless infants.
   - The rain is compared to buckets full of water.
   - Mom is compared to a raging beast.

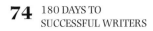

5. For the next two boxes in Figure 6.1, create metaphors to fit the meanings provided.

6. Make up two metaphors and write their meanings in the other spaces.

7. Display and pass out copies of Figure 6.2, My Room. Read the paper aloud. Discuss the score it might receive, possibly a three.

8. Model adding metaphors to Paragraph 1 using the examples that follow. When you are finished, read the paragraph aloud.
   • Change many to: truckloads of
   • Change bothers me to: is a thorn in my side

9. For Paragraphs 2 and 3 you will work as a whole group to add metaphors. Use student suggestions and read the new paragraphs aloud when complete. Some examples follow.
   • Change large to: a monster that practically takes over the room
   • Change I drive it really fast to: I am a maniac when I drive that car
   • Change in charge to: King of the castle
   • Change messy to: a junk yard

10. Now tell the students they will work independently to write metaphors for the italicized portions of Paragraphs 4 and 5. As students work, make up metaphors of your own.

11. When the students have completed the assignment, ask volunteers to share and allow them to compare their metaphors to yours. Discuss the paper's new score, likely a four.

Figure 6.2 My Room

Everyone has a favorite place. Hands down, my favorite place is my room. There are many reasons why I love being in my room. I'll tell you about the three biggest reasons. The first is that there are *many* fun things to do in there. Second, it is my room and no one bothers me when I'm in it. Third, my sister isn't there. She *bothers me*. Sit back and relax as I further explain why my room is my favorite place.

First, my room is loaded with fun stuff. I have a lot of super cool things to keep me occupied. For example, my T.V. is *large*. Then there are my toys. The best toy I have is my remote control car. *I drive it really fast*. Finally, I've got video games and a video game player in my room. Need I say more?

Second, it is my room, so I'm the boss in there. I am *in charge*. Nobody can come in if I don't allow it. Although sometimes my mom overrules me. But that's okay because she cleans up in there every once in a while. She says my room is *messy*. But I like it that way.

Third, and most important, it does not have my sister in it. She is *not friendly*. We fight a lot. My mom says *we argue too much*. I try to avoid her as much as possible and I keep a sign on my door that says, "No sisters allowed." I don't like it when she comes near my room.

In conclusion, my room is a great place. It is my *safe spot*. It is a fun place to be, it is where I'm in charge, and my sister can't get inside. What is your favorite place?

Copyright © 2006 by Karen Donohue and Nanda N. Reddy. All rights reserved. Reprinted from *180 Days to Successful Writers: Lessons to Prepare Your Students for Standardized Assessments and for Life* by Karen Donohue and Nanda N. Reddy. Thousand Oaks, CA: Corwin Press, www.corwinpress.com. Reproduction authorized only for the local school site or nonprofit organization that has purchased this book.

Day 2 (Copy Day)

Objectives: Students will plan and write part of an expository paper independently.

Materials: Prompt; metaphor sentences.

Note: Before class, display the sentences for metaphor work.

1. Display and read the following sentences. Guide students to improve the sentences with metaphors. Suggested changes follow.
   - "The kindergartner was lost in the crowded hall at her new school" may become "The kindergartner was a lost lamb in the crowded hall at her new school."
   - "I was excited to show my new bike to Amy" may become "I was a new puppy seeking attention when I showed Amy the new bike."

2. Display the following prompt.
   - Everyone has a favorite person. Think about who your favorite person is and why you like this person. Now tell why this person is your favorite person.

3. Ask the students the following questions.
   - What kind of prompt is this? (expository)
   - What shape plan will I draw? (pickle sandwich)
   - What does the Boss ask me to do? (tell about why that person is my favorite)

4. Now tell them you will make the plan and write the first two paragraphs with their help. Tomorrow it will be their turn to work; they will finish the paper by writing the remaining paragraphs.

5. Remind them that everyone will have the same plan to work from, so the papers will sound similar. However, they should use Rainbow Words, Awe-Inspiring Adjectives, Vivacious Verbs, ASk fOR LIKEly Similes, and Mind-Bending Metaphors to make their papers unique.

6. Draw the pickle sandwich as the students follow your lead. Be sure to choose a favorite person that most students will be able to relate to, like a mother or father. If you get too specific (e.g., Great Uncle Harry), the students may not be able to pull off the remaining paragraphs on their own. Your plan might look like this:
   - Introduction. Hands down, fave person is my mom: loving; supportive; loves me unconditionally; let me tell you more about fabulous mom
   - Paragraph 2. First of all, loving: gives lots of hugs; tells me she loves me; even loves all of my friends
   - Paragraph 3. Second, supportive: takes care of me growing up; calls me to see how things are going; sends me cards when I need a pick-me-up
   - Paragraph 4. The most important reason, loves me unconditionally: when I am bad; loves me when I am good; one time; she'll always be there
   - Conclusion. In conclusion, I've told you my mom is fave: she is loving; supportive; loves me unconditionally; wish you only knew my mom

7. Set a time limit on the plan.

8. The students should watch as you construct the first two paragraphs of the paper. Remind them that they will need to copy the paragraphs accurately. Example paragraphs follow.

   - Introduction. Hands down my favorite person is my mother. There are so many reasons why my mother bear of a mom is terrific, but I will discuss my top three. She gets such high marks because she is loving, supportive, and fun. Now let me tell you more about my fabulous mom.

   - Paragraph 2. First of all, my mom is a very loving person. She takes care of me like a mother bear. Ever since I can remember, she has given me lots of hugs for absolutely no reason. I can count on her to tell me she loves me even when I mess up and do something wrong. It isn't just me that she treats like gold; my friends are royalty at my house.

9. Locate the simile and metaphors and show the students why it is best not to overuse those techniques by inserting the following in Paragraph 2: "Ever since I can remember, she has been my safety blanket, always giving me lots of hugs for absolutely no reason."

Day 3

Objective: Students will complete an expository paper independently.

Materials: Previously written plans and paragraphs; metaphor sentences.

Note: Complete your model before class begins and display the sentences for metaphor work.

1. Display and read the following sentences. Guide students to improve the sentences with metaphors. Suggested changes follow.

   - "I searched the store for pink, sparkly sandals to match my new dress" may become "I was a fearless hunter on the prowl for pink, sparkly sandals to match my new dress."

   - "Mathias worked through the test quickly and with ease" may become "Mathias was a computer, quickly and easily spitting out answers to the test questions."

2. Review the plan.

3. Using the same plan, students will finish the essay by writing Paragraphs 3, 4, and 5. Students should include one or two original metaphors and TCUPSS their paragraphs as they complete them.

4. Display your model and point out your metaphors.

5. Allow students to compare their paragraphs to your model and share.

Day 4 (Pair Day)

Objectives: Students will edit a paper and identify similes and metaphors.

Materials: Previously written papers; highlighters; Figure 3.4.

Note: Before class, make student copies of Figure 3.4.

1. Tell the students that today they will be working with partners to TCUPSS their papers using Figure 3.4, the Checklist for Peer Editing. Remind them of the rules for peer editing.

2. They will read through their partners' paper to make corrections and highlight the similes and metaphors. Good similes and metaphors should be noted in the Umph section of Figure 3.4.

3. Examples of good similes and metaphors can be shared aloud toward the end of class and written onto a large piece of construction paper.

4. Assign publishing as homework. See "Preparing to Teach" in Chapter 1 for publishing ideas.

Day 5

Objective: Students will learn the pacing necessary to complete an essay under a time limit.

Materials: Prompt.

Note: Before class display the following prompt.

- Every classroom needs a pet. What kind of animal would make the best classroom pet? Now explain what animal would make a great classroom pet.

  1. Inform students that today they will watch you do all the work. You will demonstrate how to handle the pressure of writing under a time limit. Explain that this is important because all professional writers have deadlines.

  2. Set a time limit to plan and write the paper. Put a responsible student in charge of the timer. If you would like to limit planning time, ask the student to let you know when you should have completed your plan.

  3. Think aloud as you plan and write this paper. Your plan might resemble the following.

- Paragraph 1. Every classroom needs a pet, choose fish: easy to care; clean; quiet
- Paragraph 2. First of all, easy to care for: feed once a day; food is cheap; no walking or bathing; everyone helps
- Paragraph 3. Second, are clean: live in water; no hair; no feathers; change water; wash bowl
- Paragraph 4. Last, splashing noise: dogs, cats disturb; mice and hamsters make noise; squeaky wheels
- Paragraph 5. In summary, choose fish: easy to care for; clean; quiet

  4. Using your plan, write your paper. Keep the pace necessary to complete the paper and have time to TCUPSS.

  5. Ask the students for comments about the paper.

WEEK 11 LESSON PLANS

Focus: Quotations

Dialogue, when used properly, is a valuable writing tool. Students will learn to correctly include dialogue in their writing.

Day 1 (Pair Day)

Objective: Students will learn to use quotation marks to write dialogue.

Materials: Figure 6.3; dialogue sentences; name tags (optional).

Note: Make a display and student copies of Figure 6.3. If you are using nametags, label them in advance. Also, post the dialogue from Step 1 for correction.

1. Display and read the following dialogue.

Please pass the salt Jim said patiently.

Here you go Jim replied Shona as she reached for the salt.
Danielle screamed watch out. You are going to knock over your glass.
The glass fell over and shattered. Uh oh too late.

---

2. Ask the students to point out the exact words that came out of the person's mouth in each sentence. Ask volunteers to act out the dialogue. You may provide nametags if you desire.

3. Emphasize that if a person says something in writing, writers must put those exact words inside quotation marks. The first word spoken should be capitalized. The speaker's name, which is called a tag, and other non-spoken words are kept outside of the quotation marks.

4. Demonstrate these corrections for each sentence.

"Please pass the salt," Jim said patiently.

"Here you go, Jim," replied Shona as she reached for the salt.
Danielle screamed, "Watch out! You are going to knock over your glass!" The glass fell over and shattered. "Uh oh, too late."

---

5. As you model, point out that the speaker's punctuation is always included within the quotation marks.

6. Display and distribute copies of Figure 6.3, A Trip to Wild Waters. Model how to add quotation marks to the first paragraph.

Figure 6.3   A Trip to Wild Waters

Model

   Wow! We get to go to Wild Waters on Saturday, exclaimed Jim. He jumped up and down. I haven't been there in years. Aren't you excited?

   Yeah, Danielle said. I can't wait to see the animals. The zebra is my favorite. What is your favorite animal?

Pair and share

   Jim replied excitedly. It has got to be the alligator pit! I love watching all those scary alligators lying around with their mouths wide open. Their teeth are so large and crooked.

   You won't see me hanging around that place. Alligators are too much for me, declared Danielle. Jim, we'll have to find something else to see together.

   Jim's eyes lit up. Hey maybe we could go on that new roller coaster. What do you think of that?

Independent practice

   Danielle shouted, Wo-hoo! Definitely. I can never get enough of those thrill rides. I can't wait to go on that one that turns you all the way upside down. She wiggled her head and leaned it down, sticking her tongue out for emphasis. Then she grabbed her stomach and laughed. We'll have to eat lunch after we go on that one. I do not want to lose my lunch on a roller coaster.

   I agree, Jim said. Especially since a hamburger costs almost ten dollars there.

Copyright © 2006 by Karen Donohue and Nanda N. Reddy. All rights reserved. Reprinted from *180 Days to Successful Writers: Lessons to Prepare Your Students for Standardized Assessments and for Life* by Karen Donohue and Nanda N. Reddy. Thousand Oaks, CA: Corwin Press, www.corwinpress.com. Reproduction authorized only for the local school site or nonprofit organization that has purchased this book.

   7. Allow students to work in pairs and complete Paragraphs 2 and 3.

   8. Students will complete the final paragraphs independently.

   9. For homework, ask students to look in their library books for dialogue. They should list the patterns they find.

Day 2

Objectives: Students will plan and write half of a narrative paper independently.

Materials: Prompt; dialogue sentences.

Note: Before class, post the dialogue for correction.

   1. Display the following dialogue and lead students through the corrections.

   Shona asked Hey have either of you seen that new girl yet?

   I have! Can you believe how much she looks like Mrs. York?

   Oh, that's all I need. One hour a day of Mrs. York is plenty for me complained Jim.

2. Review the tier cake. Ask students to draw it and describe the story structure.

3. Display and read the following prompt.
    *   Imagine that you wake up one day, look out of your bedroom window, and you see a castle. Think about who or what might live in that castle. Now write a story about the day you woke up and saw a castle outside your window.

4. Brainstorm ideas. Ask students what comes to mind when they think of a castle. Why is there a castle suddenly outside their window? What characters could be found inside? What kind of problems could occur as a result of this castle appearing on their lawn?

5. Provide time for planning and observe student work.

6. After planning, instruct students to write Paragraphs 1, 2, and 3.

7. Remind them to use their resources to enhance their stories. Encourage them to use dialogue.

8. For homework, ask students to look for dialogue in the books they are reading. They should write down three or four sentences of dialogue between two speakers as it appears in the book.

Day 3

Objective: Students will finish writing a narrative paper independently.

Materials: Previously written plans and paragraphs; dialogue sentences.

Note: Before class, post the dialogue for correction.

1. Display the following dialogue and lead students through the corrections.

Jim weaved through the roaring crowd. What do you think the score is? He screamed into Danielle's ear.

She pulled back and rubbed her ear. How should I know? I am even shorter than you are.

Will you two just calm down! I am gazing at a sea of red and blue t-shirts, too. Let's just try to make the best of it until we can reach our seats Shona admonished.

---

2. Lead a discussion of the homework assignment. Students should have noticed that a new paragraph begins each time there is a new speaker. Make the necessary corrections in the paragraph above to reflect this pattern.

> Jim weaved through the roaring crowd. "What do you think the score is?" he screamed into Danielle's ear.
>
> She pulled back and rubbed her ear. "How should I know? I am even shorter than you are."
>
> "Will you two just calm down!" Shona admonished. "I am gazing at a sea of red and blue t-shirts, too. Let's just try to make the best of it until we can reach our seats!"

3. Review the prompt with the students and instruct them to read their plans and the paragraphs they wrote yesterday.

4. Allow the students to complete their stories.

5. Monitor student progress and provide assistance. Encourage them to use dialogue.

Day 4 (Pair Day)

Objectives: Students will TCUPSS with partners and identify correctly used similes, metaphors, and quotations marks.

Materials: Previously written narrative story; dialogue sentences; highlighters; Figure 3.4.

Note: Before class, make student copies of Figure 3.4. Also, post the dialogue for correction.

1. Display the following dialogue and lead students through the corrections.

> Oh yes! I love it when we have pizza squealed Danielle.
>
> What a treat said Jim it isn't even Friday. The gleeful pair excitedly made their way to their usual table by the window.
>
> I guess today's lunch made your day Shona commented. You two look like you just opened birthday presents.

2. Pair students to TCUPSS their partner's papers using Figure 3.4, the peer-editing sheet. Remind them of the peer-editing rules.

3. Monitor the students' peer editing as they work.

4. When TCUPSSing is complete, provide each student with a highlighter. The Students' task is to reread the story and highlight similes, metaphors, and correctly used dialogue.

5. Allow students to share the similes, metaphors, and quotes they found.

Day 5

Objective: Students will learn the pacing necessary to complete a timed narrative.

Materials: Prompt.

Note: Before class, choose a narrative prompt. You may use a prompt from Resource A.

1. Tell students that today you will do most of the work as they watch you write a narrative.

2. Choose a student to be in charge of the timer.

3. Display the prompt and begin planning.

4. Adhere to the time limit you set. Think aloud as you plan and write; be sure to include dialogue and other style devices you have taught.

WEEK 12 LESSON PLANS

Focus: Sensory Details and Skeleton Plans

Sensory details fill writing with imagery. This week, you will teach students how to use their five senses to enrich their writing. You will also teach them to plan their writing more efficiently.

Day 1

Objective: Students will practice their planning skills.

Materials: Prompt.

Note: Create a display of the prompt and fasten four sheets of chart paper to the board. You will model how to create four plans from one prompt.

1. Inform the students that today you will demonstrate skeleton planning. This is a plan with only the essential details, completed in about ten minutes.

2. Display the following prompt.
   - Everyone has a favorite season of the year. Think about your favorite season and why you like it. Now write to explain what your favorite season is and why you like it.

3. Put a student in charge of the timer.

4. Draw the pickle sandwich on one sheet of chart paper. Start by modeling a plan as if your response was spring. An example follows.
   - Introduction. Without a doubt, spring: warm weather; loads of flowers; spring break
   - Paragraph 2. To start off, weather is warm: after long winter; cool breezes; sun shines
   - Paragraph 3. Also, loads of flowers: faves wild flowers; remind me of Grandma's garden; smell

- Paragraph 4. The most important reason, spring break: no school; beach; friends; do whatever
- Conclusion. I wish spring all year, because: weather; flowers; spring break; can't wait

5. Ask the student helper to set the timer again.

6. Draw, plan, and model as if your response to the prompt was summer. An example follows.
   - Introduction. If you ask me, no better season than summer: no school; outdoor activities; vacations
   - Paragraph 2. First of all, no school: no homework; stay up late; sleep until noon; no cafeteria food
   - Paragraph 3. Second, outdoor activities: swim; bike or skate; beach
   - Paragraph 4. Finally, family vacations: road trip; new places; visit friends and family; don't see often; best place to go is . . .
   - Conclusion. Let me sum up, summer is best: no school; outdoors; vacations; can't wait

7. Model on a third plan for fall. An example follows.
   - Introduction. I know exactly, favorite season fall: a million reasons; top three: changing leaves; cooler weather; holiday; stick around . . .
   - Paragraph 2. To begin, changing leaves: colors; rake for money; jump in piles; mom doesn't like
   - Paragraph 3. Next, weather: nice change; jackets and sweaters; new boots
   - Paragraph 4. Finally, Thanksgiving holiday: turkey and stuffing; pumpkin pie; mom makes the best; see family
   - Conclusion. Ah, fall, feel it coming: love it because: changing leaves; cooler weather; Thanksgiving holiday; can't wait

8. Model a fourth plan using winter.
   - Introduction. Hands down, winter is my fave season: weather; holidays; winter break; sit back . . .
   - Paragraph 2. First, weather: snow; snow days; hot chocolate; cozy fire
   - Paragraph 3. Second, holidays: Christmas; family gathers; presents; turkey
   - Paragraph 4. Third, no school: winter break; no work; no homework; sleep in
   - Conclusion. Is it winter yet? Is my fave: can't wait; holidays; winter break; can't wait

9. Display the plans and discuss.

Day 2 (Pair Day)

Objective: Students will learn to use their five senses to enhance their writing.

Materials: Figure 6.4; previously written plans.

Note: Before class, draw and color large pictures of a nose, eye, hand, mouth, and ear. Then place the icons above the corresponding senses on a poster of Figure 6.4.

Figure 6.4 Sensory Details

Smell	Look	Feel	Taste	Hear
putrid	glassy	rough	salty	high pitched
flowery	narrow	smooth	sweet	soft
fresh	bright	rubbery	succulent	loud
freshly baked	shiny	slick	bitter	whisper
odorous	worn	wet	sour	scream
foul	dingy	slimy	lemony	scrape
soapy	fake	bumpy	spicy	screech
buttery	realistic	damp	saucy	rumble

Copyright © 2006 by Karen Donohue and Nanda N. Reddy. All rights reserved. Reprinted from *180 Days to Successful Writers: Lessons to Prepare Your Students for Standardized Assessments and for Life* by Karen Donohue and Nanda N. Reddy. Thousand Oaks, CA: Corwin Press, www.corwinpress.com. Reproduction authorized only for the local school site or nonprofit organization that has purchased this book.

1. Display Figure 6.4, the sensory details poster. Explain that good writers use their five senses when they write to help them connect to their readers.

2. Discuss each sense and guide students to add two or three words for each. Have the students write this list in their resource binders.

3. Review yesterday's skeleton plans.

4. Pair students and ask each pair to take out four sheets of paper. They should label them spring, summer, fall, and winter.

5. Instruct students to draw a nose, eye, hand, mouth, and ear on each page.

6. Students will write sensory details for each season on their papers. To prompt ideas, ask the following questions: What does the air smell like? What do you see around you? What do you feel? What do you eat during this season? What do you hear?

7. Choose one season and model. Some examples for summer follow.
   • Smell: chorine; strawberries; salty beach air
   • Taste: BBQ; lemonade; ice cream
   • Feel: burnt, peeling skin; grass under bare feet; sweaty
   • Hear: baseball game; mosquitoes; lawnmowers
   • See: bathing suits; sandcastles at the beach; kids in swings

8. Allow students to share sensory details when the pairs have completed the assignment.

Day 3 (Pair Day)

Objective: Students will use the skeleton plans to write expository papers with partners.

Materials: Previously written plans; brainstormed sensory details.

1. Review the plans.

2. Pair students. Instruct pairs to choose a plan and use the sensory details they brainstormed yesterday to enhance the paper.

3. Each pair should write an expository paper from the plan they chose.

4. Provide the time limit and monitor students as they work.

5. After writing, students should TCUPSS their papers, Monitor.

6. Provide time for sharing. Point out differences in the completed essays.

Day 4

Objective: Students will use a given plan to write an expository paper independently.

Materials: Previously created skeleton plans; brainstormed sensory details.

1. Instruct students to choose a different plan from the one they worked with yesterday.

2. Provide a time limit for students to complete this paper. Remind them to use sensory details they brainstormed.

3. Monitor students.

4. Ask volunteers to read their papers or favorite sentences aloud when completed.

Day 5 (No Help Day)

Objectives: Students will plan, write, and edit a timed expository paper.

Materials: Prompt.

Note: Before class, format and present the following prompt as you did the pretests.

- Everyone does fun things with their family. Think about something fun that your family does together. Now write about the fun things your family does together.

  1. Tell the students that today they will be writing to a prompt with a time limit.

  2. Pass out the papers and set the timer.

  3. Collect the papers and score them. Analyze for student growth and problems. Save this analysis for Week 14.

WEEK 13 LESSON PLANS

Focus: Hooks and Correcting Slang

All great writing must hook the reader. However, even an interesting paper can lose readers with poor grammar or slang.

Day 1

Objectives: Students will plan a narrative story and learn strategies to hook their readers.

Materials: Previously written papers.

1. Tell the students that today they will learn how to get their readers' attention by writing a strong hook. The hook is found at the beginning of a piece and gets the reader excited to continue the story. It can be a loud sound, a quote, or even a hint at the story's problem. Sometimes the writer uses an entire paragraph to hook their reader.

2. Display and read the following sentences.
   - Let me tell you about the day I lost my favorite thing in the world.
   - Let me tell you about the day I saw gigantic footprints in the grass.
   - Everyone does different things during their summer vacation and I spent mine having fun.

3. Tell them that at the time you wrote these introductory sentences you were trying to teach them the basics. Now they are ready to make their writing more interesting and exciting.

4. Show them how to rewrite the sentences. Example hooks follow.
   - "Oh no!" I shrieked. "My purse is gone!" That was my reaction the day I lost my favorite thing in the world.
   - Curiosity almost got the best of me on that sunny Monday morning.
   - Splash! I heard a lot of that this summer at the pool.

5. Display the following paragraph.
   - Everyone has acted in a way that made someone proud. I am no exception. It happened at school in the fourth grade. I'm going to tell you about the day I made someone proud.

6. Rewrite the paragraph to demonstrate how a writer can hook readers with an entire paragraph.
   - Cheers and claps bounced off of the gymnasium walls. My ears rang from the noise, but I didn't care one bit. It all happened back in fourth grade at an awards assembly the day I made someone very proud.

7. Instruct students to find three old papers from their resource binders that need exciting hooks or introductory paragraphs.

8. Allow the students to work on revising their hooks and paragraphs. Provide assistance.

9. Allow students to share the original and improved hooks.

Day 2 (Pair Day)

Objective: Students will practice using correct grammar.

Materials: Figures 6.5 and 6.6.

Note: Make a display of Figure 6.5. Also, make a display and student copies of Figure 6.6.

1. Tell the students that sometimes people use different speech depending on where they are. When they are with friends or family, they will most likely use casual or street talk.

2. Provide them with an example. If you were in the South, you might use "y'all" instead of "you all" when talking to friends. Another example would be using "yeah" instead of the more proper "yes" when answering a question.

3. Explain that while street talk may be acceptable on the playground, it is not a good idea to use in school, at work, or when writing anything. Discuss that the first S in TCUPSS is for Spelling and Sound. This means students should listen for and correct street talk in their writing.

4. Pass out copies of Figure 6.5, the street talk poster. Review it with students and make corrections.

5. Brainstorm other examples of slang and add them to the poster.

6. Distribute Figure 6.6, Found a Dog, a paper filled with slang. Read and discuss the score the paper might receive, most likely a two. Model how to edit the first paragraph with appropriate editing marks as students copy your changes.

7. Call on volunteers to help you correct Paragraph 2.

8. Pair students and instruct them to find and correct all the street talk in Paragraphs 3 and 4. Then review the paragraphs.

9. Instruct students to work independently on the final paragraph. Monitor their progress.

10. Review the corrections as a whole group and discuss the paper's possible new score, a three.

Day 3 (Pair Day)

Objectives: Students will plan and begin to write narratives with partners.

Materials: Prompt.

1. Tell the students that today they'll work with partners to begin narrative stories.

2. Review the importance of a good hook. Students should remember to hook their readers in the first line.

3. Pair students.

4. Display the following prompt.
   - How do you think you would feel if you were ten feet tall? Imagine a spell was cast upon you that made you ten feet tall for one day. Write about what happened to you the day you were ten feet tall.

Figure 6.5   Street Talk

Street Talk	Correction
I seen; he seen; she seen, they seen	I *saw*; he *saw*; she *saw*; they *saw*
They was; we was	They *were;* we *were*
Ya'll ain't	
They woulda; they would of; coulda; could of	
It don't; she don't; he don't	
It do; she do; he do	
Wuzzup; what up	
Cut off/out (the lights, the TV, etc.)	
Me and _____ (did something: ran, ate, etc.)	
I'm gonna; I'm fixin' to	

Copyright © 2006 by Karen Donohue and Nanda N. Reddy. All rights reserved. Reprinted from *180 Days to Successful Writers: Lessons to Prepare Your Students for Standardized Assessments and for Life* by Karen Donohue and Nanda N. Reddy. Thousand Oaks, CA: Corwin Press, www.corwinpress.com. Reproduction authorized only for the local school site or nonprofit organization that has purchased this book.

Figure 6.6   Found a Dog

> Set back and lit me tell ya'll about the time I done found a dog. It was my friend and me and we was in the park. It was Wednesday and we was playing basketball.
>
> In the middle of the game I was fixin' to run down the court and I seen a dog. I done stop and I called to it, what up dog? It came over. It was brown.
>
> We played awhile wit it and then I had a idea. Then I said lets take it home to show my folks it. My friend said OK. We moseyed on down to my house.
>
> My mom said that dog is stank but my dad said I could keep it if I walk it and feed it and clean up after it. I was happy. I gots a dog. I love the dog.
>
> Now ya'll knows about the time I found a dog. It was da bomb kind of day in me life, and I ain't never gonna forget it. Do you got a dog?

Copyright © 2006 by Karen Donohue and Nanda N. Reddy. All rights reserved. Reprinted from *180 Days to Successful Writers: Lessons to Prepare Your Students for Standardized Assessments and for Life* by Karen Donohue and Nanda N. Reddy. Thousand Oaks, CA: Corwin Press, www.corwinpress.com. Reproduction authorized only for the local school site or nonprofit organization that has purchased this book.

5. Instruct students to plan together and begin writing. Each student should write a copy of the narrative. Monitor their progress.

Day 4 (Pair Day)

Objective: Students will complete narrative papers with partners.

Materials: Previously written plans and paragraphs.

Note: Make student copies of Figure 3.4.

1. Tell the students that today they will work with their partners to finish the stories they started yesterday.

2. Allow the pairs time to review their plans and paragraphs. Students should then write the remaining paragraphs.

3. Monitor the students.

4. When the partners have completed their papers they will trade with another pair.

5. The students should then TCUPSS the papers using Figure 3.4, the peer-editing sheet. Tell them to especially look for an effective hook and the absence of street talk.

6. Ask volunteers to share these papers with the class.

7. Assign publishing as homework.

Day 5 (No Help Day)

Objectives: Students will plan, write, and edit narrative papers within a timed session.

Materials: Prompt.

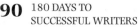

Note: Before class, format and present the following prompt as you did the pretests.

- Everyone has taught something to someone else. Think about a time you taught something to someone. Now tell about the time you taught someone something.

  1. Tell the students that today they will write to a prompt under a time limit.
  2. Pass out the prompt and set the timer.
  3. Monitor the students.
  4. Collect papers and score. Analyze for student growth and problems. You will use this analysis in the following weeks to provide individual assistance.

WEEK 14 LESSON PLANS

Focus: Timed Writing

All students will face writing deadlines. It is best to begin preparing them to think, plan, write, edit, and revise quickly now that they are adept at using style devices. This is a three-day week.

Day 1

Objective: Students will write to an expository prompt.

Materials: Prompt.

Note: Before class, make a list of individual weaknesses based on the timed writings you have scored.

1. Inform the students that today they will write to an expository prompt. It will be timed, but they can ask you for help if they get stuck or have a question.

2. Display the following prompt.
   - Many families have holiday traditions. Think about your favorite holiday tradition. Now write to tell about your favorite holiday tradition.

3. Review the prompt with the class. Remind them that they are permitted to use their resource binders and posters. Set the timer and allow students to begin.

4. Monitor the students. Provide individual help based on diagnosed student needs.

5. Collect papers, grade, and analyze.

Day 2

Objective: Students will write to a narrative prompt.

Materials: Prompt.

1. Tell the students that today they will write again to a narrative prompt under a time limit while you provide help. Display the following prompt.
   - You are a turkey and it is getting close to a holiday. What could you do to save yourself? Write a story about how you try to keep yourself from being part of dinner.

2. Review the prompt with the class. Set the timer and allow students to work.

3. Monitor the students. Provide individual help based on diagnosed student needs.

4. For homework, assign students to bring their address and the address of someone special.

Day 3

Objective: Students will write a friendly letter.

Materials: Envelopes; stamps (optional).

Note: Before class, write a friendly letter to your students on chart paper and post it.

1. Review the parts of a friendly letter using your display. Tell the students they are going to write friendly letters to special people in their lives whose addresses they should have brought in for homework.

2. Help students understand that they should inform the person why they are special in the body of the letter.

3. Allow the students to work on their letters. Monitor their progress and provide help.

4. Pair the students. Instruct them to TCUPSS the letters with partners. Next, have the students write final drafts before placing them in envelopes.

5. Teach students how to correctly address and stamp an envelope. Provide stamps if desired.

6. Collect the letters if they are to be mailed.

WEEK 15 LESSON PLANS

Focus: Anecdotes

Students have explored using extra details to strengthen the voice in their work. Now they will use anecdotes to further enrich their writing.

Day 1 (Pair Day)

Objectives: Students will plan with partners, and then write independently.

Materials: Prompt.

1. Inform students that today they will work with partners to plan for a prompt. However, they will write their essays independently.

2. Display the following prompt.
   - Everybody should know how to take care of a pet. Think about how you or someone you know cares for a pet. Now write about how to properly care for a pet.

3. Pair students and provide a time limit to plan. Monitor their work.

4. Instruct students to independently write their papers in the remaining time.

5. Provide assistance based on individual diagnosed needs.

Day 2

Objective: Students will learn how to use anecdotes in their writing.

Materials: Anecdotes poster; Figure 6.7.

Note: Make and display a poster of the following anecdote starters.

Anecdote Starters

Remember a specific time:

Just last week (year, month, summer, spring, etc.) . . .
I remember when . . .
Last Monday (or another day) . . .
Once . . .
I will never forget . . .

Give an example:

For instance . . .
For example . . .
Let me give you an example . . .

Remember a specific thing you do or did:

When I do that, . . .
Usually, I (or we) . . .
I usually . . .

Tell more specifically why you liked something . . .

I loved that because . . .
That was wonderful because . . .
We had the best time because . . .

---

1. Review the poster with the students. Explain that an anecdote, or a little story, is a simple and effective way to elaborate. Point out why it is called a little story; it is only one sentence long. Students simply need to choose an anecdote starter from the poster and finish the sentence.

2. Ask volunteers to practice using the starters. Examples follow.
   - I always have good luck. Just last week I was walking toward my locker and found a five-dollar bill.
   - My friend and I finally got to hang out alone. We had the best time because there were no little sisters around to bother us.
   - Lately, I've been changing my routine. I usually eat the crust of my pizza first, but today I started with the cheesy middle.

3. Display and distribute student copies of Figure 6.7, Reading Is Important. Read, and discuss the score the paper might earn, a four or five.

4. Model adding anecdotes to Paragraph 2. Examples follow.
   - Just yesterday I wrote an e-mail to my friend in California.
   - For example, she might not be able to pay her bills on time.
   - For instance, I wouldn't know what the president was up to.

5. Guide students to add anecdotes to Paragraph 3.

6. Instruct them to complete the remaining paragraphs independently. Allow students to share when they have completed the assignment. Discuss the paper's new score, a five or six.

7. See Week 23, Day 1 for an additional lesson on elaboration using this new tool.

Day 3 (Pair Day)

Objectives: Students will plan cooperatively and writing independently to a prompt.

Materials: Prompt; anecdote sentences.

Note: Before class, display the sentences for anecdote practice.
   1. Display the following sentences and guide students to add anecdotes.
      - Saturday we played with water balloons. We even _____.
      - I am the best daughter. One time I even _____.

   2. Tell the students that today they will plan with partners and then write independently. Remind students to make their own plans.

   3. Pair the students.

   4. Display the following prompt.
      - As you are walking back from lunch at school one day, you and a friend notice a doorway that you have never noticed before. Imagine what could be behind that door. Now tell about what you saw when you and your friend opened that mysterious door.

Figure 6.7   Reading Is Important

There is no doubt that **everyone** knows reading is important. It is one of the subjects we study from the day we start going to school. This is because reading is important to communicate, get a good education, and succeed with everyday tasks. Read on to find out more.

The first reason it is important to learn how to read is because that is how most people communicate. People write each other letters and e-mails to share information. Just yesterday, _____. My mom wouldn't be able to understand her mail if she didn't know how to read. For example, _____. Last, I wouldn't know what was going on around the world if I couldn't read the newspaper. For instance, _____.

The next reason reading is important is because you need it in order to learn. I need to know how to read to understand math. For example, _____. Also, if you can't read, you won't know how to write. Just the other day, while reading, I found a great word to use in my writing. It was _____. Reading is the only way to learn about Social Studies and Science. Last week, I read _____. I know that reading is the key to getting a good education.

The last reason is because you need to get along in the everyday world. You have to be able to read signs. For example, _____. Furthermore, you need to know how to read when you go to the store. If you couldn't read in a store, _____. Last, you need to know to read so that you can get a job. If I couldn't read, _____.

Now you know why it is important to learn how to read. You need it to communicate, get a good education, and do everyday tasks. I hope you'll never give up trying to be a good reader.

Copyright © 2006 by Karen Donohue and Nanda N. Reddy. All rights reserved. Reprinted from *180 Days to Successful Writers: Lessons to Prepare Your Students for Standardized Assessments and for Life* by Karen Donohue and Nanda N. Reddy. Thousand Oaks, CA: Corwin Press, www.corwinpress.com. Reproduction authorized only for the local school site or nonprofit organization that has purchased this book.

5. Allow them time to plan with their partners. Monitor their progress.

6. After planning, students should write their own papers. Remind them to use anecdotes. Provide assistance based on individual diagnoses.

Day 4

Objectives: Students will identify and correctly use anecdotes in a paper.

Materials: Previously written papers; highlighters.

Note: Before class begins, find the Pizza Fanatic essay from Week 3.
1. Review the anecdotes poster. Ask for a few examples of anecdotes using the starters.

2. Tell students you will add anecdotes to an old essay they helped you write before. Read Pizza Fanatic to the students. Ask them to help you insert anecdotes. Examples follow.
   • Paragraph 1. Just last week I ate pizza for breakfast.
   • Paragraph 2. My dad likes to put sardines on his pizzas.
   • Paragraph 3. We even send the pizza delivery person a Christmas card every year.
   • Paragraph 4. One time I even used turkey slices to make an interesting pizza.
   • Paragraph 5. I usually make a pizza once a week.

3. Explain that sometimes they might not have an experience related to what they are writing about. If this happens, it is perfectly acceptable to make something up. However, anecdotes they make up must be believable.

4. Instruct students to choose papers from their binders that could use a few anecdotes. Expository essays are easier to work with.

5. Provide time for the students to insert anecdotes and allow them to redraft their papers. Monitor the students. Provide assistance based on diagnosed needs.

6. Allow students to share the anecdotes they inserted.

Day 5 (No Help Day)

Objectives: Students will plan, write, and edit a narrative paper under a time limit.

Materials: Prompt.

Note: Format and present the following prompt as you did the pretests.
   • Everyone goes shopping during the holiday season. Think about a time that you were shopping during this time. Now tell a story about a time you were shopping during the holiday season.

1. Inform the students that today they will be writing to a prompt under a time limit.
2. Pass out the prompt and set the timer. Allow the students to plan, write, and TCUPSS.
3. Collect these papers to be scored and analyzed. Students with previously diagnosed weaknesses should have improved. If not, consider other interventions.

7 The Improvement Process: Diagnosing and Fixing Problems

This is the best time to reread the pretests your students took at the beginning of the year. You will be astounded at the progress they have made.

However, even with the thorough instruction you provided, your students are probably not perfect writers. Some students may struggle with creating quick plans, developing good ideas, or grammar. You may also face problems unique to your classroom. Now is the time to fix these problems.

WEEK 16 LESSON PLANS

Focus: Grammar and Using a Rubric

Grammar lessons need to be taught constantly in innovative ways to break students of poor grammar habits. Students also need opportunities to self-reflect with rubrics to improve their writing.

Day 1 (Pair Day)

Objective: Students will practice TCUPSSing to correct grammar.

Materials: Figure 7.1.

Note: Make a display and student copies of Figure 7.1.

Figure 7.1   Choice of Pet

Grab a char and set down and I can tell you about the pet I pic. A mice. Frist, mouse is quite. Next, very fun last we learn a lot about our mouse. Now grab a coke and popcorn and find a nise place to seat and listen to my story.

The first reason why I chose a mouse for my class pet. Because mouse are quite. It will not disturb me. Like one time I had one but at night it did't wake me up. Also a mouse don't makes lots of noise becaue sleeps lot. Only if it give it cheese, them the mouse wood sqeaks last, we can by our mouses and it will be quite so we can finish the whole book.

Then, mouse will be fun for watching it fun the flor. We could watchit cartwheels and watch it run around to get his exercise. And we can pet it sof fur. An we can take turns filling it an that's fun. The class would love to play with the mouse so we should have one.

Third, a mouse is good for learning. We got really smart because of our mouse. We learnd about fur is made of cells even seen an ex-ray of the bones and seen the gross blood an gut. We be amazed if we knew all facts about mouses.

Conclusion. So now you see why I pic that. It is cool to have a classroom pet all of the time. What pet would you want for a class pet?

Copyright © 2006 by Karen Donohue and Nanda N. Reddy. All rights reserved. Reprinted from *180 Days to Successful Writers: Lessons to Prepare Your Students for Standardized Assessments and for Life* by Karen Donohue and Nanda N. Reddy. Thousand Oaks, CA: Corwin Press, www.corwinpress.com. Reproduction authorized only for the local school site or nonprofit organization that has purchased this book.

1. Pair students and tell them they will practice TCUPSSing using a paper filled with errors.

2. Display and pass out student copies of Figure 7.1, Choice of Pet. Read and discuss its possible score, a one or two.

3. Pair students and monitor their work. Encourage them to use appropriate editing marks when making corrections.

4. When the students have completed this task, ask volunteers to provide the corrections. Correct your display as students provide answers. Discuss the paper's new score, a two or three.

Day 2

Objectives: Students will plan and write an expository paper from a given plan.

Materials: Prompt.

Note: Today the students will make a plan for an expository prompt. Then, you will collect their plans and pass them back in random order.

1. Display the following prompt.
   - Most people remember a gift that they received on a special occasion. Think about a special gift you received. Now write to tell about the best gift you ever received and the occasion on which you received it.

2. Allow students to plan. Tell them to make it neat and a bit more detailed than a skeleton plan because you are going to collect it and give it to another student.

3. Provide a time limit as students plan. When planning is complete, collect the papers.

4. Shuffle the plans and pass them out.

5. Provide time for students to write their papers from the given plans. Monitor.

6. Collect the papers. Discuss the process and the importance of a legible plan. Also ask students what it was like to write about someone else's experiences. Were they more creative? Did they choose words with more care?

Day 3 (Pair Day)

Objective: Students will practice using the rubric.

Materials: Rubric; rubric posters; Figures 7.2–7.6; student essays from Week 9.

Note: Before class, prepare your rubric and rubric posters as you did during Week 5. Make displays of Figures 7.2 through 7.6. Students will also need their Rainy Day essays from Week 9, Day 2.

1. Review the rubric and rubric posters.

2. Display and read Figure 7.2, Rainy Day Score 1. Have students predict its score. They can do this by holding up their fingers.

3. Scrutinize this paper using the rubric and assign points for each subcategory. Compute the score and compare to student guesses.

4. Repeat with the remaining Rainy Day essays, Figures 7.3 to 7.6.

5. Pass back students' rainy day essays from Week 9. Ask students to compare their predicted scores to actual scores and to scrutinize their papers according to the rubric categories.

6. Ask the following questions.
   a. Did you receive a fair grade?
   b. What helped you earn the score you received?
   c. What prevented you from earning a higher score?
   d. Ask volunteers to read their papers and have classmates guess their scores.

Figure 7.2   Rainy Day Score 1

> Let me tell you my story about a bad rain storm. One day it was rainin bad. I was scared It rain all day.
>
> Few grammatical and spelling errors. Insufficient amount of writing.
>
> Score: 1

Copyright © 2006 by Karen Donohue and Nanda N. Reddy. All rights reserved. Reprinted from *180 Days to Successful Writers: Lessons to Prepare Your Students for Standardized Assessments and for Life* by Karen Donohue and Nanda N. Reddy. Thousand Oaks, CA: Corwin Press, www.corwinpress.com. Reproduction authorized only for the local school site or nonprofit organization that has purchased this book.

Figure 7.3   Rainy Day Score 2

It was raining alot at home. Now let me tell you my story about a bad rain storm.

One day it was raining so bad and it was ice coming with the rain and it was coming down bad. It was hitting the house loud.

I was scared I was crying because the rain was raining hard. I felt water hitting the howse. I was cold as ice and rain.

Then a big peace of ice hit the ground it was muddy and there was mud slung on the howse. The ice hit the car and I broke a windo out.

Finally I went outside to play in it for a long time. I wasn't scared any more. I went with myself and stepped in mud. I drove my dirt bike in it.

Now you can see why I like when it rained once I wasn't scared anymore. It rain all day long in the summer and ice come with the rain sometimes.

This paper has good organization but it feels unfinished. It has poor grammar, poor word choices, and lacks support.

Score: 2

Copyright © 2006 by Karen Donohue and Nanda N. Reddy. All rights reserved. Reprinted from *180 Days to Successful Writers: Lessons to Prepare Your Students for Standardized Assessments and for Life* by Karen Donohue and Nanda N. Reddy. Thousand Oaks, CA: Corwin Press, www.corwinpress.com. Reproduction authorized only for the local school site or nonprofit organization that has purchased this book.

Figure 7.4   Rainy Day Score 3

Are you here to listen to my fantastic rainy story? Well if you are sit down and relax and I'll tell you about this wonderful day in April. The birds were feeding their young and cherping away. The flowers were blumming and bees were pollinating the rose bushes. Casey and I were in the middle of all of this when we made the best of a rainy day.

The day started off boring. I had nothing to do so I called Casey. She answered and after we had a chat we agree to have her come over to my house. Once when she came over we ended up sleeping in the tent and telling goess stories, but we were just going to hang out this time.

Just a short wile later I herd the door bell and it was Casey. It was a lovly spring day, so she wanted to play outside. It started raining, but we desided to take our bikes for a ride anyway.

Minets later we were free as could be. Casey is my best friend in the hole universe so I was happy. We rode down the street but I couldn't see her because she was fast and the faster I went the more water splashed my face. It was imposible to see were I was going. All of the sudden I hit a rock and my bike skidded. I fell flat on me face.

Casey helped me brush myself off. I was ok but we started heading home. Thankfuly the crunching, blue rain died down and we made it safely back home. When we got there she said, "Let's stay in the next time it rains!" And we played Monopoly instead and it was a blast!

Now you should know what I did on that day when the birds were singing, flowers were blumming, but it was raining hard. We learned a great lesson that it's better to stay dry at home.

This story gets off topic a bit and has some poor grammar, but it generally answers the Boss. The score would improve with a better hook, flow, and more relevant details.

Score: 3

Copyright © 2006 by Karen Donohue and Nanda N. Reddy. All rights reserved. Reprinted from *180 Days to Successful Writers: Lessons to Prepare Your Students for Standardized Assessments and for Life* by Karen Donohue and Nanda N. Reddy. Thousand Oaks, CA: Corwin Press, www.corwinpress.com. Reproduction authorized only for the local school site or nonprofit organization that has purchased this book.

Figure 7.5 Rainy Day Score 4

"Mom, I'm so bored!" That is what I said to my mom when it started raining. I was at home, and it was just mom and me. The problem was that it was raining.

When it first started to rain, I thought, "Oh boy, this is going to be a joy." I asked my mom I wanted to go outside and splash around. But she said no, that I'd get a cold. In other words, she'd get mad at me if I played in the rain. She told me to go read a book or take a nap.

Seconds later, I got an idea. "I know what we can do. We can go get popcorn and soda and watch a movie!" Mom agreed, so I got the drinks and she popped the buttery corn. This was going to be a blast!

After that we picked out a movie called *Where the Heart Is*. It is a really good movie, but a little sad. We cried big crocodile tears while munching on our popcorn and slurping soda.

Later, when the movie was over and we had stopped crying, we realized the rainstorm was over. We put everything away and went to the park for a picnic. We saw a rainbow and mom let me splash in some puddles. When we came home, I took a bath and then I fell asleep in front of the TV.

The moral of the story is, if you think hard you can make a rainy day a blast. Just like I did with my mom. I thought it was going to be boring, but it was not at all. It was fun. Would you do the same?

Good organization and details. This writer has a strong voice and there are few grammatical errors. This could be improved with more details, better hook and flow, and more original ideas.

Score: 4

Copyright © 2006 by Karen Donohue and Nanda N. Reddy. All rights reserved. Reprinted from *180 Days to Successful Writers: Lessons to Prepare Your Students for Standardized Assessments and for Life* by Karen Donohue and Nanda N. Reddy. Thousand Oaks, CA: Corwin Press, www.corwinpress.com. Reproduction authorized only for the local school site or nonprofit organization that has purchased this book.

Figure 7.6 Rainy Day Score 5

What luck! As soon as I started watching my favorite TV show, it began to rain and we also lost all power at our house. Mom and dad usually like black outs, but not me. I didn't enjoy that dark afternoon one teensy weensy bit, at least not at first. Stick around and I'll tell you the tale of how I spent my rainy evening in May.

It all started after a long, hard day at school. I got home, looking forward to just sitting in front of the TV. I love watching "Tiny Toons" but I got home too late. So I watched "Barney," and I noticed that it had started to rain like mad. Not too long after that my favorite show, "Even Stevens," came on. I was excited until the TV started blinking on and off.

Seconds later, I was sitting in pitch-black darkness. There wasn't any electreecity! I wanted to scream out in anger. I heard soft voices and footsteps as my parents crept around the kitchen. Then I heard a plate drop and pots banging. "Where are all the candles?" my mom shouted. I got up to help mom but bumped into dad as he was feeling his way like a blind man. He laughed, then banged around looking for a flashlight like a lost puppy.

Just when Dad found the flashlight, I heard a booming sound like fireworks. I screamed. Thunder crashed all around and I saw a crooked line of lightening through the window. The lightening lit up the sky. I couldn't believe it was so dark at 5:30 in the afternoon.

Dad thought it was the perfect time for a few spooky tales. Moments later my little family was hudled around the kitchen table telling ghost stories like we were at a campfire. My dad tells great stories. Once he scared me so bad that I had to sleep with the light on for a whole week! We had such a great time that when the power came back on, I was sorry.

Author's voice is strong, few errors and good organization. More originality and tension would help this paper earn a 6.

Score: 5

Copyright © 2006 by Karen Donohue and Nanda N. Reddy. All rights reserved. Reprinted from *180 Days to Successful Writers: Lessons to Prepare Your Students for Standardized Assessments and for Life* by Karen Donohue and Nanda N. Reddy. Thousand Oaks, CA: Corwin Press, www.corwinpress.com. Reproduction authorized only for the local school site or nonprofit organization that has purchased this book.

Day 4

Objective: Students will write to a prompt under a time limit.

Materials: Prompt; sticky notes.
1. Remind the students of yesterday's lesson.

2. Pass out sticky notes. Ask students to write two or three things that they need to focus on as they write to an expository prompt today.

3. Display the following prompt.
   • Everyone dreams about what they'll be when they grow up. Think about what you want to be. Now explain what you want to be and why.

4. Set the timer and allow students to write.

5. Monitor and provide assistance to help students reach the goals listed on their sticky notes.

6. Ask students to put their sticky notes on their papers. Collect, grade, and analyze for conferences next week. Also, respond to students' sticky notes.

Day 5

Objective: Students will write to a prompt under a time limit.

Materials: Prompt; sticky notes.
1. Pass out sticky notes.

2. Ask students to write two or three things that they need to focus on as they write to a narrative today.

3. Display the following prompt:
   • Imagine you are at the beach digging in the sand. As you dig, you hit something hard with your shovel. Think about what you might have hit. Now write a story about the time you were digging at the beach and hit something hard with your shovel.

4. Set the timer and allow students to write.

5. Monitor and provide assistance to help students reach the goals listed on their sticky notes.

6. Ask students to put their sticky notes on their papers. Collect, grade, and analyze for conferences next week. Respond to students' sticky notes.

WEEK 17 LESSON PLANS

Focus: Clarifying Problems

Students have trouble truly seeing the errors they consistently make. They need lessons that help them visualize their problems clearly.

Day 1

Objectives: Students will publish their work and conference with the teacher.

Materials: Figure 3.4; sticky notes; previously written student essays; publishing materials.

Note: Today you will hold individual conferences, spending a few minutes with students to discuss strengths, weaknesses, and what they need to be working on; you should aim to conference with half of your students today. Keep a stack of sticky notes with you to make notes for students to keep in their binders. Also, make student copies of Figure 3.4 and decide how students will publish their work. See "Preparing to Teach" in Chapter 1 for publishing ideas.

1. Inform the students that today they will work with partners to TCUPSS papers using Figure 3.4, Checklist for Peer Editing. Then they will publish.

2. Return the expository essay from Week 16, Day 4.

3. Provide materials and instructions for publication.

4. Pair students and allow them to TCUPSS their partners' papers and publish.

5. Hold individual conferences as the students work.

Day 2

Objectives: Students will publish their work and conference with the teacher.

Materials: Figure 3.4; sticky notes; previously written stories; publishing materials.

Note: Follow the procedures from the previous day to complete your conferences.

1. Inform the students that today they will work with partners to TCUPSS papers using Figure 3.4, the Checklist for Peer Editing. Then they will publish.

2. Return the narrative from Week 16, Day 5.

3. Provide materials and instructions for publication.

4. Pair students and allow them to TCUPSS their partners' papers and publish.

5. Complete your individual conferences as the students work.

Day 3

Objective: Students will write a collaborative essay including errors they consistently make.

Materials: Prompt.

1. Identify and discuss problems your students are consistently experiencing. They may be the following: lack of details, irrelevant details, poor syntax, grammar, overuse of style devices, lack of organization, monotonous sentence structures, poor focus, lack of voice, poor word choice, lack of flow and transitions, and dull introductions or conclusions.

2. Explain that today you will purposely make mistakes in an expository essay. Focus on the top five problems your students make in essays.

3. Display the following prompt.
   - Everybody has a favorite day of the week. Think about which day of the week you like best. Now write to explain which day of the week is your favorite.

4. Make a skeleton plan using student suggestions. If the problems relate to organization, focus, or details, you may begin making them now. As you make the errors, point them out.

5. Use student suggestions to write the essay and continue to point out the flaws.

6. You will correct this paper on Day 5.

Day 4

Objective: Students will write a collaborative story including errors they consistently make.

Materials: Prompt.
   1. Follow the procedures from the previous day using the following narrative prompt.
      - Imagine finding a strange object in your backyard. Think about how it could have gotten there and what might happen when you touch it. Now write a story about finding a strange object in your backyard and what happened when you touched it.

Day 5

Objective: Students will correct consistent errors.

Materials: Previously written papers.
   1. Display and read the Favorite Day essay from Day 3.

   2. Correct the errors using student suggestions.

   3. Repeat with the Strange Object story from Day 4.

   4. Reread the papers. Discuss how you fixed the problems.

WEEK 18 LESSON PLANS

Focus: Elaboration

Adding extra details, anecdotes, sensory details, metaphors, and similes is often a challenge for students, especially when writing under a time limit. Continuous practice helps reinforce its use.

Day 1

Objective: Students will learn how to elaborate a previously written paper.

Materials: Scissors; tape; markers; Figure 3.1.

Note: Before class, you will need to locate Figure 3.1, the corrected version of I'm Special from Week 3. You will be physically cutting this paper apart during the lesson to add details.

1. Before class, write the following sentences on strips of paper to be inserted in the essay.
   - Not to boast, but there is no one in the world like me. (To replace hook)
   - I am also one of the best friends a person could ask for. (To insert after "good son and brother")
   - My parents strut around, proud as peacocks. (To insert after "grades")
   - Even though there are a few of us, we can cause quite a ruckus. (To insert after "skateboards")

2. Display and read I'm Special.

3. Using the rubric, grade this paper. It would probably earn a three or four, especially if it included common grammar errors students make. This is because the paper is flat and could use elaboration.

4. Tell the students they will elaborate to help make the paper earn a higher score.

5. Discuss techniques including anecdotes, adding details, using sensory details, rewording flat or dull sentences, and adding similes or metaphors.

6. Point out a spot in the paper where more elaboration could be added. Tell them there is not enough room so you'll show them how to add space. Cut the original story and insert the elaboration, using tape to fasten the pages together.

7. Repeat this process with your other prewritten sentences for Paragraphs 1, 2, and 3.

8. Guide students to add elaboration to Paragraphs 4 and 5.

9. Read the final paper and rescore. Discuss how the score improved.

10. Display this paper for reference during tomorrow's lesson.

Day 2 (Pair Day)

Objective: Students will practice elaborating.

Materials: Student papers from Week 2; scissors; tape.

Note: Before class, locate Week 2's essay on summer vacation. Make copies for group use.

1. Explain that they will work in small groups to do the same cutting and pasting activity you modeled yesterday.

2. Group students. Pass out copies of the summer vacation essays and other materials.

3. Allow the groups to work as you monitor.

4. Collect the papers for use tomorrow.

Day 3

Objectives: Students will share and discuss elaboration techniques.

Material: Yesterday's papers and teacher model.

Note: Before class, rewrite the summer vacation essay to include the following elaborations.

- In intro after "summer": I was a slug and I vegged out with my friends this summer.
- After "swimming": so much so that my hair turned minty green.
- After "money": I scored a whole new wardrobe this summer.
- After "fishing and swimming": I caught an enormous fish that fed the whole family that night.

1. Display and read the original essay.

2. Using the rubric, determine its score. It would score a three or four because it uses simple sentences.

3. Now read the essay with your improvements and rescore. It should improve by a point.

4. Allow students to share their elaborations.

Day 4

Objective: Students will practice elaborating.

Materials: Student papers; scissors; tape.

Note: Students will locate papers of their choice to elaborate today.

1. Explain that students will independently apply the cutting and pasting activity to papers they choose from their binders.

2. Allow students to work as you monitor.

Day 5

Objectives: Students will plan and write to a narrative prompt under a time limit.

Materials: Prompt.
1. Tell the students that they will have a chance to practice their elaboration techniques.

2. Display the following prompt.
   - Imagine that you were swimming in the ocean one day and you felt something brush up against your leg. Think of what it might have been. Now write a story about when something brushed up against your leg as you swam in the ocean.

3. Set the timer and allow students to work. Monitor and provide help.

4. Collect and save these papers for Week 19, Day 1.

WEEK 19 LESSON PLANS

Focus: Conferencing and Self-Reflection

For the improvement process to be effective, students need direct feedback from the teacher. They need to analyze and reflect on their growth and weaknesses.

Day 1

Objective: Students will score their own papers.

Materials: Rubric; rubric posters; student papers from Week 18, Day 5.

Note: Use Resource E or a similar tool to help students score their own papers. If using Resource E, students will need one slip. Copy and cut the slips before class. If you use another tool, adjust the procedures to fit.
1. Review the rubric and scoring posters. Tell the students that today they will practice using the rubric to score their own papers.

2. Pass out student papers from last week.

3. Distribute and explain how to use the scoring slips. Students should write their names and indicate they are scoring narrative papers on the slips.

4. Students should analyze their papers and assign themselves scores in each category indicated on the scoring slips. They may use the rubric and rubric posters to help them.

5. When they are finished, they should give the paper an overall score by subtotaling and averaging (dividing by six if using Resource E).

6. Collect and score the students' papers according to each rubric category; you may also use scoring slips. Compare with student scores and save for tomorrow's lesson.

Day 2

Objective: Students will increase the score of an existing paper.

Materials: Teacher and student scored papers from Day 1.

1. Return the student papers and allow students to examine them along with their scoring slips.

2. Ask them to write down two to three things they need to do to improve their scores. Allow volunteers to share what they need to do to improve their scores.

3. Guide the class to brainstorm ways to develop the papers.

4. Instruct students to work independently to improve their papers. Talk with students to resolve great discrepancies in scores.

5. Use this opportunity to work closely with struggling writers.

Day 3

Objectives: Students will publish their work and conference with the teacher.

Materials: Previously written papers; publishing materials.

Note: Decide how the students will publish their work and prepare all materials before class.

1. As the students work to publish their work from the previous day, meet with students individually. Discuss their strengths and weaknesses. Use their papers to show them specific examples. Make notes on sticky pads for the students to use during Days 4 and 5.

Day 4

Objective: Students will complete a timed writing using notes made at their conferences.

Materials: Prompts.

Note: Students will complete timed writings over the next two days. Give half the students the expository prompt; the other half will get a narrative. Use the following prompts.

- Expository: Everyone has dreams. Think of something that you have always wanted to do but haven't. Now explain what it is that you have always dreamt of doing.
- Narrative: Most people have built something once. Think about something you built. Now tell about a time you built something.

1. Tell students they will complete timed writings over the next two days, but not everyone will get the same prompt today.

2. Ask students to retrieve and review their conference notes.

3. Pass out the prompts. Set the timer. Monitor and provide help based on diagnosed needs.

4. Collect the papers when time is up.

Day 5

Objective: Students will complete a timed writing using the notes made at their conferences.

Materials: Prompts.
1. Follow the same procedures from Day 4. Students who wrote an expository yesterday will write a narrative today.

WEEK 20 LESSON PLANS

Focus: Organization

Organization includes elements such as transition words, indentation, focus, flow, and relevant details. Even if students master other skills, lack of organization will ensure low scores on tests.

Day 1

Objective: Students will review expository formatting by going backward from an essay to a plan.

Materials: Figure 7.7.

Note: Make a display and student copies of Figure 7.7. As students work, meet with students who are struggling with organization in a small group.
1. Announce that it is Backward Day.

2. Distribute student copies and display your copy of Luckiest Kid (Figure 7.7). Read the paper aloud. Discuss its possible score, a four.

3. Draw a pickle sandwich as students draw theirs. Plan the first paragraph with student help.

4. Students will then work individually to complete the plan as you work with struggling students. Review when completed.

Figure 7.7 Luckiest Kid

> If I won a million dollars I would be the luckiest kid ever! I know exactly what I'd do. After I got over the shock, I would go out and spend some money. The first three places I would visit are the toy store, the bike shop, and Burger King. Now sit back and let me tell you about what I would do if I won a million dollars.
>
> The first thing I would do is go to the biggest toy store in town. I would take the shopping cart and run down every aisle. Toys would pile up in my cart. I would get all the really awesome video games I've always wanted. I would especially look for a shiny, black remote control car, the ones that are as fast as rockets. Those are my favorite.
>
> The next thing I would do is hit the bike shop. I would buy the fanciest bike in the whole shop. It would be a flaming red ten-speed with a horn, compass, and a basket. I would show off my bike to the whole neighborhood. It would feel amazing to own that fantastic bike.
>
> The last thing I would do is head for Burger King. That is my favorite place to eat in the whole world. I would order all the hamburgers and fries I could gobble down; and you can bet that's a lot because my mom says my stomach is a bottomless pit! I would even pay for all the other people in the store. After all I could afford to be generous.
>
> I promise you this, if I were ever to win a million dollars I would do everything I just wrote about. I would buy all the toys I wanted, get a super bike, and eat everyday at Burger King. What would you do if you won a million dollars?

Copyright © 2006 by Karen Donohue and Nanda N. Reddy. All rights reserved. Reprinted from *180 Days to Successful Writers: Lessons to Prepare Your Students for Standardized Assessments and for Life* by Karen Donohue and Nanda N. Reddy. Thousand Oaks, CA: Corwin Press, www.corwinpress.com. Reproduction authorized only for the local school site or nonprofit organization that has purchased this book.

Day 2 (Pair Day)

Objective: Students will review narrative formatting by going backward from a story to a plan.

Materials: Figure 7.8.

Note: Make a display and student copies of Figure 7.8. As students work, meet with students who are struggling with organization in a small group.

1. Tell the students that today will be another Backward Day; they will be working with a narrative.

2. Distribute student copies and display your copy of Figure 7.8, Behind the Barn Doors. Read the paper aloud and discuss its possible score, a four.

3. Draw a tier cake as students draw theirs. Use student input to plan Paragraphs 1 and 2.

4. Students will then work individually to complete the plan as you work with your small group. Review when completed.

Figure 7.8   Behind the Barn Doors

I couldn't believe my eyes. That is how I felt one day not too long ago. One day when I was all alone walking on a deserted country road I had a terrific adventure. I came across a door that was usually locked. However, on this day it was wide open. Lend me your ears and I'll tell you all about that day.

It all started when I was walking to my friend's house at dusk. The light was quickly fading and I tried to hurry. I couldn't get a ride so I had to walk a mile to her house. The road was completely empty and lonely. The only noises I heard were crows in the distance.

A few minutes later I came across an old rust colored barn. It looked ancient and it was falling apart. I had passed that old barn millions of times and the door was always locked. However, on this day it swung wide open. I felt confused and curious about why that would be.

Moments later I decided to investigate. I slowly crept up to the door. I saw that it was pitch black inside. There wasn't a thing moving inside. I felt so terrified I was shaking like a leaf.

My adventure continued as I got to the door. As I walked through it, I screamed so loud. I just knew everyone in the world heard me. I couldn't believe my eyes. It was a gigantic pea-green metal space ship. The outside was covered with pictures of aliens. I figured it must have been their captain. I felt weird standing there staring at the green and slimy one-eyed aliens standing around it, but I couldn't help it.

Immediately I took off and didn't stop running until I reached the safety of my friend's house. When I told her about it she did not believe me. I had to prove it to her so I dragged her back to the barn. To my disbelief the barn was empty. I'll never know where those aliens came from or if they were ever really there. Now my friend thinks I am crazy. It was such a crazy adventure. Have you ever come across a door that was usually locked?

Copyright © 2006 by Karen Donohue and Nanda N. Reddy. All rights reserved. Reprinted from *180 Days to Successful Writers: Lessons to Prepare Your Students for Standardized Assessments and for Life* by Karen Donohue and Nanda N. Reddy. Thousand Oaks, CA: Corwin Press, www.corwinpress.com. Reproduction authorized only for the local school site or nonprofit organization that has purchased this book.

Day 3 (Pair Day)

Objective: Students will complete an expository essay by planning and writing in pairs.

Materials: Prompt.

Note: Work in a small group with students who are struggling with expository writing while the others work in pairs. Display the following prompt.

- It is important to take care of our environment. Think about why it's important to take care of the air, water, and land around us and consider the things you do to take care of these resources. Now explain why it's important to take care of the environment.

  1. Pair students. Inform them that they will work in pairs to complete an expository today.
  2. Read the prompt, brainstorm, and allow students to work. Work with your small group.
  3. When the papers are complete, allow time for pairs to share.

Day 4 (Pair Day)

Objective: Students will complete a narrative by planning and writing in pairs.

Materials: Prompt.

Note: Work in a small group with students who are struggling with narratives while the others work in pairs. Display the following prompt.

- Sometimes kids get in trouble at school. Think about a time you got in trouble at school. Now tell the story about a time you got in trouble at school.

  1. Pair students. Tell the pairs that they will complete narratives today.
  2. Read the prompt, brainstorm, and allow students to work. Attend to your small group.
  3. When students are done, allow time for sharing.

Day 5 (No Help Day)

Objective: Students will complete a practice test.

Materials: Prompt.

Note: Format and present the following prompts as you did the pretests. Students struggling with narrative writing should write a narrative, and those working on expository should write an expository.

- Expository: Most people have hosted a party at least once. Think about how you would plan for a party. Now explain how you would plan for a great party.
- Narrative: Everyone has been to a party. Think of the best party you have been invited to. Now write a story about the best party you have ever been to.

  1. Tell students they will have a chance to complete a prompt on their own today.
  2. Pass out the papers and set the timer.
  3. Collect the papers when time is up. Use these papers to assess student progress.

WEEK 21 LESSON PLANS

Focus: Planning Difficult Prompts

Students sometimes have trouble writing to prompts that are boring, confusing, require a vivid imagination, or require specific life experiences. They need to learn strategies to deal with these kinds of prompts.

Day 1

Objective: Students will brainstorm for difficult expository prompts.

Materials: Prompts.

1. Explain that students may face difficult prompts. They need to be prepared to write even if they have little interest in the topic.

2. With each prompt you review today, use the same strategy. First, you will read the prompt with the class. Ask them why they feel this is difficult.

3. Give some ideas you would use. Allow volunteers to offer additional suggestions and list these.

4. The following are boring prompts.

   • Prompt: Eating healthy is important. Think about why it is important to eat a healthy diet. Now explain why it is important to eat healthy foods.

Why is this difficult? Don't know very much about nutrition, disagree with the statement, don't like healthy food, think there's not much to write about healthy food, etc.

Ideas: So you can live a long life, you might get overweight, junk food causes serious health problems, doctors are expensive, you feel tired and sluggish if you eat poorly, eating well gives you energy, you can play sports, fast food and junk food are expensive, etc.

   • Prompt: Knowing how to read is important. Think about why it is important to know how to read. Now explain why reading is so important.

Why is this difficult? Not sure what the right answer is, can only think of one reason, the topic is boring, etc.

Ideas: To communicate, get a good job, earn money, go to college, follow directions, read food labels, order from a menu at a restaurant, read important papers you get in the mail, so you won't get lost going somewhere, to read the newspaper and know what is going on, so you can use a computer and the Internet, to read birthday cards from friends.

5. The following are confusing expository prompts that could be mistaken for narratives.

   • Prompt: Have you ever thought about what it might be like to be the teacher for a day? Think about whether you would like to be the teacher for a day. Now explain why you would or would not like to be the teacher for a day.

Why is this confusing? This prompt gets kids thinking about being the teacher for the day and all the things they would do. Some might be fooled and start writing a narrative about the time they were the teacher for the day. Review the key words in the Boss. Point out that it asks them to explain why or why not. This indicates they need to list things.

Ideas: Yes—you get to be in charge, get to do what you want, can do cool lessons, are allowed to eat lunch in the classroom, earn money. No—you might have discipline problems, hate grading work, have to teach all day long, have to stay late at school.

- Prompt: Have you ever thought what it's like to be a fish? Think about what it would be like to be a fish. Now explain what you could do if you were a fish.

Why is this confusing? Here students may start fantasizing about turning into a fish and get sidetracked into writing a story. Really this prompt is about knowing what kinds of things fish are capable of doing. They will have to use their knowledge of fish to write to this prompt.

Ideas: Swim in deep water, see things that humans cannot, breath with gills, eat live food, lay eggs, live in coral reefs, dodge sharks and fishermen, swim in a school, and migrate.

- Prompt: Surprise! You have just won a free trip to a place of your choice. Think about where you would go on your free trip. Now explain why you would choose that place.

Why is this confusing? This prompt starts off sounding like a narrative. The catchy No-Brainer sentence could throw the students off the right track.

Ideas: Bahamas—sunny beaches, fancy hotels, great food. Six Flags—wild rides, games, amusement park food. A ski lodge—skiing, campfires, sledding, and snowshoeing.

6. Ask the students what they learned. If time permits, discuss additional prompts that might be difficult.

Day 2

Objective: Students will brainstorm ideas for difficult narrative prompts.

Materials: Prompts.

1. Use the same strategy for brainstorming that you used in yesterday's lesson.

2. Remind students that there are two main types of narrative stories: realistic and imaginary. Explain that some prompts could be either realistic or imaginary depending on which way they choose to write them. Remind them that the rule is that all narratives must have a problem and show passing of time; however, problems don't have to be exciting.

3. The following realistic prompt is about something that could really happen. This might not be a true story, but it is possible.

   • Prompt: Imagine that you found a $100 bill one day. Think about what you would do with that money. Now write a story about what you did when you found a $100 bill one day.

Why is this challenging? Students may get confused and plan to write about three things they would do with their $100 bill. With a few word changes, this prompt could easily be an expository. Discuss the "expository" wording: Describe what you would do if you found a $100 bill? Point out that the Boss says to write a story about what you did with the money. That means you should pretend that you have already found it and are telling what happened that day. Further, students could have unrealistic expectations of $100. Discuss the types of things that money could realistically purchase. Discuss unrealistic purchases also.

Ideas: The writer could have found it at the mall, on their way home from school, at an amusement park, or on the playground. Events might include finding the owner, visiting lost and found, spending it on presents for others, donating it to charity, or putting it in the bank. Or the finder could spend it selfishly and then endure some punishment or guilt.

Example: Finding it at an amusement park, buying a lot of junk food, ride tickets, etc. In the end, throws up, gets sick for days, wishes they never found the money or had given it to lost and found.

---

4. Tell the students that there is a specific kind of realistic narrative that is called a personal narrative. These seem like they would be the easiest kind because they ask the writer to tell about something that has really happened to them. However, the difficulty comes when the student has not experienced the scenario given in the prompt. When this happens they should make something up or think hard about how they could make it fit to something they have experienced.

- Prompt: Everyone needs help sometimes. Think of a time that you needed help. Now tell about a time you needed help.

Why is this difficult? Students may have trouble thinking of something on the spot that they have needed help with. Or they may believe the thing that they needed help with makes for a boring or short story. They may think the prompt is more difficult than it is.

Ideas: Remind them that they can write about a time they needed help with anything, and that they could embellish the story with a few made-up anecdotes. It could have been help with homework, a school project, fixing a bicycle, cooking something, or choosing a present for someone. Brainstorm ideas and discuss how you'd write stories for these ideas.

---

5. Explain that imaginary prompts are ones that ask you to make believe. They can be difficult because they require a vivid imagination, but they usually do not want you to go over the top.

- Prompt: One morning you wake up but you are not in your bed. Think about what it would be like to wake up in a strange place. Now write about waking up in a strange place.

Why is this difficult? This could be a scary thought for most students and elicit uncomfortable or traumatic thoughts during the writing. Or students could write about waking up in an outrageous place and then find it difficult to end a bizarre fantasy story.

Ideas: The setting could be a space ship, the fictional world of a book or movie, a slumber party, a new bedroom in a new house with new parents, or even as far fetched as an alternate universe. To end, the writer could wake up from a dream, solve a puzzle, find a way back home, or find the key or door that led them to the new setting in the first place.

---

6. Review what the students learned today.

Day 3 (Pair Day)

Objective: Students will work in small groups to plan for two expository prompts.

Materials: Prompts.

Note: Students will use chart paper today.

1. Choose two challenging prompts or use prompts from this week.

2. If using this week's prompts, remind students of the various ideas they discussed, but challenge them to come up with original approaches to the prompts.

3. Divide the class into groups of three or four students.

4. Display the prompts.

5. Groups will draw their plans on chart paper and share with the class.

Day 4 (Pair Day)

Objective: Students will work in small groups to plan for challenging narrative prompts.

Materials: Prompts.

1. Choose two challenging narrative prompts or the ones you worked with earlier in the week.

2. Follow the procedures from yesterday.

Day 5 (Pair Day)

Objective: Students will write in pairs to a challenging prompt.

Materials: Prompts.

Note: Before class, retrieve the prompts you used this week. Number each of the prompts and post them on the board. Then write numbers on slips of paper and place in a hat. Let student pairs choose a number from the hat. The pairs will have to write to the corresponding prompt.

1. Point out the numbered prompts on the board. Pair students and allow each pair to draw a number from the hat.

2. Set the timer and allow pairs to plan and write. Monitor their progress.

3. Allow volunteers to summarize their papers.

WEEK 22 LESSON PLANS

Focus: Common Grammar Problems

Common grammar problems include run-on sentences, dialogue, and spelling. These basic errors confuse the reader and are important to address before the state test.

Day 1 (Pair Day)

Objectives: Students will repair run-on sentences, incomplete sentences, and lack of sentence variety.

Materials: Figure 7.9.

Note: Make a display and student copies of Figure 7.9.

Figure 7.9   Won a Game

Wow, I can't believe I won was what I thought after I finished the three legged race with my best friend Patty at my school's field day last March. Piece of cake. And I didn't even want to do it cause I lost at the egg tosses and jump roping and tug of war and I even tried my hand at the whistling contest without winning even third place. So first place I couldn't believe.

It started a hot day in March after lunchtime so I was stuffed and that's probably why I didn't do so hot at the jump roping or tug of war. Huff puff, huff puff. Out of breath in like five seconds. I told Patty let's do something real easy like egg tosses or horseshoes and we thought that egg tosses would be a breeze because it's just throwing a little old egg around. Super easy. I tossed and Patty caught but she didn't catch real good cause we were out. Like the second ones out and man were we bummed out because like after that we thought we wouldn't win a thing.

Later I decided to try the scavenger hunt because Mrs. Nelson was in charge of that. Hah, I thought this would be a breeze then I found out she wanted us to find things like ants and round pebbles and stuff that we had to go digging around in the ground like gophers or something. Not me, no way. Like I want dirty nails. Left that quick as a wink.

So the whistling contest. At least that's clean. Whistled real good I thought. But this boy Terry whistled like some kind of bird in a tree or something and Sue whistled a million different ways so I thought for sure I'd get third place cause I could whistle some songs but I got fourth place after Anne. Cause she could do car sounds, like who cares. Double bummer.

That's why three legged shocked. Patty dragged me over there and I was screaming no the whole time and I couldn't believe Mr. Tiller when he said we won and I still can't believe it really. So keep trying. I mean look at me I won so what you waiting for, go compete and win too.

Copyright © 2006 by Karen Donohue and Nanda N. Reddy. All rights reserved. Reprinted from *180 Days to Successful Writers: Lessons to Prepare Your Students for Standardized Assessments and for Life* by Karen Donohue and Nanda N. Reddy. Thousand Oaks, CA: Corwin Press, www.corwinpress.com. Reproduction authorized only for the local school site or nonprofit organization that has purchased this book.

1. Explain that poor grammar can ruin student work even if students have the most vivid imaginations, know the pickle sandwich and tier cake formats by heart, and use the best words.

2. Display your model and pass out student copies of Figure 7.9, Won a Game. Discuss its possible score, a three.

3. Tell the students that today you will start looking at run-on and incomplete sentences. Explain that run-ons are sentences that have no punctuation marks. They "run" together, leaving the reader confused and out of breath. Run-ons are the opposite of incomplete sentences. Explain that incomplete sentences leave readers confused, feeling that something is missing and unsure of what the sentence is about.

4. Read the first paragraph and emphasize when you are out of breath or confused.

5. Model breaking up the run-ons and fixing the incomplete sentences. Remember to vary sentence structure by creating compound sentences (combining two sentences), starting with gerunds (-ing words), and writing prepositional phrases (a "setting" statement). Have the students follow along with you and make the corrections on their copy.

6. Use student suggestions to make appropriate changes to Paragraph 2. Ask students for a variety of suggestions. Then choose the "best sounding" sentences. This will emphasize the value of varied sentence structure.

7. Pair students and instruct them to correct the sentences in Paragraphs 3 and 4. Monitor.

8. Review the paragraphs.

9. Assign the students to correct Paragraph 5 independently.

10. Review the corrected paragraph and discuss its new score, a four or five.

Day 2 (Pair Day)

Objectives: Students will repair and add dialogue to a narrative paper.

Materials: Figure 7.10.

Note: Make a display and student copies of Figure 7.10.
1. Tell students that today you will work with dialogue. Remind them that dialogue can add a lot of pizzazz to a narrative story if used correctly. However, it can be overdone. A story with too much dialogue can be very hard to read. They also need to be careful with punctuation marks.

2. Display and pass out student copies of Figure 7.10, Lost Something. Read and discuss its possible score, a three or four.

3. Model making corrections to Paragraph 1.

4. Reread the corrected paragraph and emphasize its improvements.

5. Use student suggestions to make appropriate changes to Paragraph 2. This paragraph has too much dialogue. Point out why this is problematic and model cutting out the unnecessary dialogue.
   • Pair students. They should fix the dialogue problems in Paragraphs 3 and 4. Monitor their progress.

6. Review the paragraphs.

7. Assign students to complete Paragraphs 5 and 6 independently.

8. Review the corrections and the paragraph's new score, probably a five.

Figure 7.10 Lost Something

Have you seen my necklace? I asked frantically. I looked around the store and Catherine, the storeowner, said no honey. Not me, my mom said, glancing through the dress rack. I couldn't believe I lost my favorite necklace and was in shock. What am I going to do? I cried. It was thick and gold and it sparkled like treasure. Read on to hear what happened the day I lost something.

It all started one sunny Saturday. Come on mom! I cheered as I bounced into the store. Wow I exclaimed when I saw the Barbie doll on the shelf. I was immediately attracted to her jet-black hair that touched the tip of her toes. Can't I get her mom? I tried hard to convince her, but I was unsuccessful. Mom replied firmly no. Fine, I'll look at colorful costume jewelry I said.

At the jewelry counter, I wanted to try on a hundred different necklaces. I found one with gorgeous, sparkling gems. May I try this one on I asked Catherine. I went to fasten it around my neck and that's when I discovered my own necklace was gone. I screamed oh no. I immediately started looking for it, crying I've got to find it!

Some time later I let out a frustrated sigh, ughh why haven't I found it. I looked in the cold, crowded girl's bathroom. I was depressed because it was a present from my grandma, and it was real gold. I saw Joan from school. She asked what in the world are you looking for? I explained, and she got on her knees to help me look. Other people in the store started to help, too.

Out of the blue mom said, are you sure you even had it on? That's when I remembered I took a bath and left it on my dresser at home. I felt so embarrassed because I had all those people looking for it. I shouted out never mind, it's not lost, and everyone stopped looking.

I decided not to look at necklaces anymore. I realized the one I had meant a lot to me and I said to my mom I'll never forget to put it on again. Have you ever lost anything?

Copyright © 2006 by Karen Donohue and Nanda N. Reddy. All rights reserved. Reprinted from *180 Days to Successful Writers: Lessons to Prepare Your Students for Standardized Assessments and for Life* by Karen Donohue and Nanda N. Reddy. Thousand Oaks, CA: Corwin Press, www.corwinpress.com. Reproduction authorized only for the local school site or nonprofit organization that has purchased this book.

Day 3 (Pair Day)

Objective: Students will practice TCUPSS.

Materials: Figure 7.11.

Note: Make a display and student copies of Figure 7.11.

1. Tell student that today they will TCUPSS an expository paper. This paper includes incorrect dialogue, run-on sentences, incomplete sentences, street talk, spelling errors, and capitalization and punctuation errors.

2. Display and pass out student copies of Figure 7.11, Class Rules. Discuss its possible score, a one.

3. Follow the procedures from yesterday.

Figure 7.11   Class Rules

One rule I'm fixin' to add to my classroom rules is this check out more than one book. Why because it makes us be more smart. an my second reson it helps us got AR prazes. last it make us good reader. Read on to heard more.

The first reason. Be more smart. We be more smart if we can read mor books. I told the libearain 2 books ain't enough. It isn't dat much. Some kids should get even more. And teachers will be proud of us if and when we read more. Last the tests. We pass the tests if we can read more books. So don be mean and lets check out more books.

My second reason why I choose more books. AR tests. Kids can get more point and more prize if they get to read more books so they should get to check out as many as they wan that way they can even get to be on TV for gettin a lots of points. Then my mom wood say good job.

Finly, more books will get good readers. We will get beter grads and pass our reading class. Then we will do better and techer will be prowd a us and say you can have a pizza party in the class. We can evn get on AB oner roll. So why not let us read more we will get beter.

As you can see good grads, AR point and smart. Thas why I choice this rule. Let us check out more books.

Copyright © 2006 by Karen Donohue and Nanda N. Reddy. All rights reserved. Reprinted from *180 Days to Successful Writers: Lessons to Prepare Your Students for Standardized Assessments and for Life* by Karen Donohue and Nanda N. Reddy. Thousand Oaks, CA: Corwin Press, www.corwinpress.com. Reproduction authorized only for the local school site or nonprofit organization that has purchased this book.

Day 4 (Pair Day)

Objective: Students will practice TCUPSS.

Materials: Figure 7.12.

Note: Make a display and student copies of Figure 7.12. A corrected version can be found in Week 23, Day 4.

Figure 7.12   My First Bike

Theirs a frist time for evything we do. This's when I first learned how to rode my bike it was with my dad, my sister, and me.

It all start on christmas morning I got one big present. When I opened it my eyes sawed a new green and black bik. Yeah, I screemed, now we have to learn you how to ride said my dad.

A few min. later I felt scard a little bit. Suddently I hear somone yell from in back of me get on the bike. My dad give me a push down. I run into a tre and it hurts, but I"m ok.

Later on that daye I leanred to us the breaks. I also learn how to stir an go strate. Then we had to go start agin, and, test some skills. I would of give up but my dad said no way.

That afternoon I didn't have to get push. Down the hill we go I almost hit the three again. I'm at the bottom. I made the breaks go eeeeeeeeeeee. Wow, I ain't even fall I said real happy.

Finally I learn to ride me bike. I never forget that day or how to ride my bike. Now told you, you tell the first time you learn to do something for the frist time?

Copyright © 2006 by Karen Donohue and Nanda N. Reddy. All rights reserved. Reprinted from *180 Days to Successful Writers: Lessons to Prepare Your Students for Standardized Assessments and for Life* by Karen Donohue and Nanda N. Reddy. Thousand Oaks, CA: Corwin Press, www.corwinpress.com. Reproduction authorized only for the local school site or nonprofit organization that has purchased this book.

1. Display and pass out student copies of Figure 7.12, My First Bike.

2. Discuss its possible score, a one.

3. Follow the procedures from Day 2.

Day 5 (No Help Day)

Objective: Students will complete a practice test.

Materials: Prompt.

Note: Format and present the following prompt as you did the pretests.
  - Everyone learns to swim sometime. Think about the first time you went swimming. Now write a story about the first time you went swimming.

    1. Tell students that they will write to a prompt on their own today. Remind them of the grammar problems they reviewed this week.
    2. Pass out the prompt and set the timer.
    3. Monitor students and collect the papers when time is up. Grade and analyze these papers.

WEEK 23 LESSON PLANS

Focus: Style, Voice, and Elaboration

Writers seeking a high score must make their papers stand out. To create unique works, students need to use style devices, incorporate their own voices, and elaborate.

Day 1

Objective: Students will review anecdotes.

Materials: Figures 7.13, 7.14, and 7.15.

Note: Make a display and student copies of Figure 7.15. Using Figures 7.13 and 7.14 as a guide, make a large paper doll out of poster board. On the doll's body write the words, "Dress Me Up." Then make a hat with a face, shirt, skirt, and shoes to go on the doll, preferably out of different colored paper. Write "Senses" on the hat and draw the sense icons on the face; write "Awe-Inspiring Adjectives, Vivacious Verbs, and Rainbow Words" on the shirt; write "Anecdotes" and include some starters on the skirt; finally, write "Similes" on one shoe and "Metaphors" on the other.
  1. Tell the students the focus of this week is elaboration.

  2. Display the Dress Me Up Doll without the hat and face, shirt, skirt, or shoes. It may seem silly, but this paper doll will help students remember to "dress up" their writing or elaborate.

3. Tell them that for the next three days you will add new articles of clothing to the doll. Each of these will have an elaboration technique written or drawn on it.

4. Attach the skirt to the paper doll and review anecdotes. Remind them that an anecdote is a little story that can be used to "dress up" their writing.

5. Display and pass out Figure 7.15, A Bad Day.

6. Model adding anecdotes to the first paragraph with blanks as students follow along. As you model, think aloud of an anecdote that doesn't fit. Tell students such an anecdote would make the writing worse, not better.

7. Guide students through the second paragraph.

8. Pair students and allow them to work on Paragraphs 3 and 4.

9. Students should dress up Paragraphs 5 and 6 independently.

10. Allow students to share anecdotes.

Figure 7.13   Dress Me Up Doll 1

Figure 7.14 Dress Me Up Doll 2

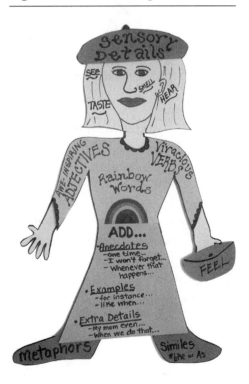

Figure 7.15   A Bad Day

Bad days happen to everyone. This is a known fact and I am no exception to the rule. I am going to describe the worst day of my young life. Read on to find out about my horrific day.

It was way back on my eighth birthday. I remember it like _____. I woke up early to the sound of crackling thunder and lightning. I was dreaming about _____

_____. I guess this should have given me a clue about what the rest of the day would bring. Still, I tried to remain cheery. I usually _____ _____ on my birthday.

I bounced down the hall to breakfast where I thought I'd find _____ _____. Instead, I discovered the table empty except for a box of cereal and a note. It was awful because _____. The note said, "Gone to work early. You'll have to eat and get yourself to school. Love-Mom." I felt _____.

After a dismal breakfast I headed to school. I hoped _____. When I got there, _____. What was going on here! My birthday is usually _____.

At the end of the day I had _____, _____ , and _____. I didn't think this many things could go wrong to just one person.

In the end, I decided that next year I'll _____. Looking on the bright side, at least my worst day is over. Now I'm just going to _____ and _____.

Copyright © 2006 by Karen Donohue and Nanda N. Reddy. All rights reserved. Reprinted from *180 Days to Successful Writers: Lessons to Prepare Your Students for Standardized Assessments and for Life* by Karen Donohue and Nanda N. Reddy. Thousand Oaks, CA: Corwin Press, www.corwinpress.com. Reproduction authorized only for the local school site or nonprofit organization that has purchased this book.

Figure 7.16   A Secret Garden

I couldn't believe my eyes. Flowers of every color greeted my eyes, even _____ flowers. I had untangled my _____ ball from a thick mass of vines, and that's when I stumbled upon the secret garden behind Grammy's house. I heard _____ and saw _____ there. You'll never believe how wondrous this place was.

It all started when I visited Grammy last summer. Her house was full of things to do, especially the attic, which was _____. But I got tired of the _____ attic and played outside where it was _____. Grammy's yard always smelled like _____ and there was a _____ swing set there, so I liked it. But one day, my ball got stuck in some _____ vines. As I dug it out, I discovered a _____ door.

I pushed and shoved, and the door creaked open. At first I felt _____ and I didn't want to go in. But then I heard _____. I crawled in and was amazed to find _____, _____, and _____. Then I heard a small voice _____ hello. I looked around and saw a tiny fairy. She was _____.

"I was wondering how long it'd take you to find this place," she said. She showed me her little home, which was a _____. It smelled like _____. She said she'd be my secret friend and we spent the day _____. The rest of that summer, we had fun _____ and _____ in the garden.

I didn't want to leave Grammy's that summer and wish I didn't. I never did see my friend again. But I will never forget her and the wonderful times we had in our secret garden.

Copyright © 2006 by Karen Donohue and Nanda N. Reddy. All rights reserved. Reprinted from *180 Days to Successful Writers: Lessons to Prepare Your Students for Standardized Assessments and for Life* by Karen Donohue and Nanda N. Reddy. Thousand Oaks, CA: Corwin Press, www.corwinpress.com. Reproduction authorized only for the local school site or nonprofit organization that has purchased this book.

Figure 7.17   Finding Treasure

> "Clank, clank," my shovel bounced off of a *hard* object. It happened one *glorious* summer day as I busily *dug* in the sand. My family and I *were at* Miami Beach on vacation.
>
> I was digging a *big* hole. I had *gotten down* about three and a half feet when my shovel *hit* against something *solid*. I thought of calling my dad, but I knew he wouldn't take me seriously. Even if he did, I was sure he would tell me to leave it alone and that it was just junk.
>
> I was *curious*. I couldn't just *walk* away. "What could it be?" I wondered aloud to myself. Thoughts of buried treasure *crept* into my cluttered head. There was only one way to *find* out. I decided to *dig* out that hard object no matter how long it took me or how *hard* it was to get out.
>
> There was much more sand to *throw* out of my hole. This task was certainly not *easy!* I had to lift the *heavy* shovel over my head to get the sand out of the hole. After much tugging and struggling, I freed the *stubborn* object. To my delight I realized that it was in fact an *old* chest. Of course it was locked! It didn't take long to *break* the *rusty* lock, thanks to my *trusty* steel shovel.
>
> I *paused* a moment before opening the *heavy* lid. I had to prepare myself for anything. I was *worried* that I'd be *disappointed*. When I finally got the *courage* to raise the lid and peer inside I was not at all disappointed. There were *shiny* gold pieces inside. I almost *passed out* from all the excitement. I had to do a double take and *rub* my eyes!
>
> Needless to say, this changed the rest of my beach vacation. We ate at all the *gourmet* restaurants and went on *shopping sprees* everyday! I even got to purchase a *big beach house*. From now on we'll be staying there during the summers instead of *smelly* hotel rooms. That chest changed my life and I'll never forget when I was digging at the beach that summer day.

Copyright © 2006 by Karen Donohue and Nanda N. Reddy. All rights reserved. Reprinted from *180 Days to Successful Writers: Lessons to Prepare Your Students for Standardized Assessments and for Life* by Karen Donohue and Nanda N. Reddy. Thousand Oaks, CA: Corwin Press, www.corwinpress.com. Reproduction authorized only for the local school site or nonprofit organization that has purchased this book.

Day 2

Objective: Students will add sensory details to a paper.

Materials: Figure 7.16.

Note: Make a display and student copies of Figure 7.16.

1. Attach the hat and face icons to the Dress Me Up Doll. Review sensory details.

2. Display and pass out student copies of Figure 7.16, A Secret Garden.

3. Tell students you will improve this paper by including sensory details. However, emphasize that they should not include pointless sensory details and that too many images can reduce the quality of their writing. Demonstrate overuse and misuse when you model the first paragraphs.

4. Follow the same procedures as you did in the previous lesson.

Day 3

Objective: Students will add similes and metaphors to a paper.

Materials: Figure 7.17.

Figure 7.18   Learning to Ride

There is a first time for everything we do. This is a story about when I first learned how to ride my bike. I was with my dad and my sister.

It all started one Christmas morning. I got one big present. When I opened my eyes I saw a new green and black bike. "Yeah," I screamed.

"Now we have to teach you how to ride," my dad said.

A few minutes later I felt a little bit scared. Suddenly I heard someone behind me yell, "Get on the bike." My dad gave me a push and I accidentally ran into a tree. It hurt, but I was ok.

Later on that day I learned to use the brakes. I also learned how to steer and go straight. Then I had to go back and test my skills. I would have given up if my dad hadn't said, "No way."

That afternoon I didn't need a push. Down the hill I went. I almost hit the tree again. At the bottom, the breaks went, "Eeeeeeeeeeee."

"Wow, I didn't even fall," I said happily.

I had finally learned to ride a bike. I'll never forget that day or how to ride my bike. Now I've told you about my first time on a bike. Have you learned something for the first time?

Copyright © 2006 by Karen Donohue and Nanda N. Reddy. All rights reserved. Reprinted from *180 Days to Successful Writers: Lessons to Prepare Your Students for Standardized Assessments and for Life* by Karen Donohue and Nanda N. Reddy. Thousand Oaks, CA: Corwin Press, www.corwinpress.com. Reproduction authorized only for the local school site or nonprofit organization that has purchased this book.

Note: Make a display and student copies of Figure 7.17.

1. Attach the shirt and shoes to the paper doll. Review Awe-Inspiring Adjectives, Rainbow Words, Vivacious Verbs, LIKEly Similes, and Mind-Bending Metaphors.

2. Display and pass out student copies of Figure 7.17, Finding Treasure. Discuss its possible score, a four or five.

3. Follow procedures from the previous day to replace adjectives and verbs and add similes and metaphors. Places where changes can be made easily are italicized.

4. As you model, come up with an "unlikely" simile and a confusing metaphor to emphasize that similes and metaphors should only be used if they make sense. Also, demonstrate how to "overuse" adjectives and rainbow words.

Day 4

Objective: Students will elaborate a previously written paper.

Materials: Figure 7.18.

Note: Make a display and student copies of Figure 7.18.

1. Display and pass out student copies of Figure 7.18, Learning to Ride.

2. Follow procedures from Day 1, utilizing all possible elaboration techniques. Encourage students to improve voice and sentence structure and to add support. Students may work on this paper in pairs, then share their varying results.

Day 5 (No Help Day)

Objective: Students will complete a practice test.

Materials: Prompt.

Note: Format and present the following prompt as you did the pretests.

- Everyone has had to do something that is hard to complete. Think about something that was difficult for you. Now explain what it was and why it was hard for you.

1. Tell students that they will write to a prompt on their own today employing all the skills they practiced this week.

2. Pass out the prompt and set the timer.

3. Collect papers, grade, and analyze.

8 Timers and Deadlines: Preparing for a Test

It is time to make final preparations for your state writing test. The lessons in this chapter will help your students improve their test-taking skills through independent and cooperative work. Complete the lessons during the four weeks preceding the test or adjust their order to fit your school calendar.

Consider increasing parental support for the test with events that teach parents what the test will cover. Team up with your Parent Teacher Organization to hold a Writer's Night Out. Draft a letter to parents explaining that the test is approaching and ask them to support their children by attending the meeting. At the meeting, explain details related to the test, demonstrate what is expected of their children, and describe ways parents can help. It is useful to show example prompts, the plan sheets, and sample papers.

WEEK 24 LESSON PLANS

Focus: Reviewing the Basics

As the test draws near, students need to review the writing process. This includes planning, writing, editing, and revising.

Day 1

Objectives: Students will practice skeletal planning, begin using the new spelling lists, and start the handwriting homework assignment.

Materials: Marathon prompts; Spelling List 1; handwriting practice paragraph.

Note: If desired, make changes to the spelling list and make student copies. Find four model essays and stories you have saved. Type the papers and make copies for students; assign one paragraph each night to be copied in the students' best handwriting. By the end of each week, your students will have copied an entire essay. Also, before class, make a display of the marathon prompts from Step 4.

1. Inform students that for the next four weeks they will do some additional homework to prepare for the test. Their spelling list will be modified to include words they may use in their writing, and they will practice their handwriting with a short paragraph each night. Poor handwriting can and will affect their scores on the state test. Their writing must be neat and easy for the scorers to read.

2. Pass out the spelling list and the first paragraph of this week's handwriting paper.

> Spelling List 1: first, finally, reason, favorite, mansion, limousine, trampoline, excellent, secret, clothes, since, animal, friend

3. Tell the students that today they will practice skeleton planning with a marathon.

4. Ask the students to get out four sheets of paper. Explain the following marathon procedure. Tell them that you will display a prompt and set a timer for about ten minutes. They will make a plan for this prompt. After the time is up, you will reveal a new prompt and set the timer again. This process will continue until they have plans for all four prompts.

Marathon Prompts

- Soccer, basketball, and softball are sports many of us enjoy. Think about a sport that you enjoy watching or playing. Now explain why you enjoy watching or playing this sport.
- One day your teacher was absent and your substitute was a famous basketball star. School was very different that day. Before you write, think about what happened that day. How was it different from a normal school day? Now tell a story about the day a famous basketball star was your substitute.
- Everyone has jobs they do around the house. Think about the jobs that you are responsible for at home. Now explain what jobs you do at home.
- Everyone has competed in a game before. Think about a time you competed in a game. Now tell a story about a time you competed in a game.

5. Set the timer and reveal the first prompt. Follow the marathon procedure. Monitor the students.

6. Allow students to share their ideas. Save the plans for use during Week 27, Day 1.

Day 2

Objective: Students will revise and edit paragraphs from previous work.

Materials: Previously written papers; handwriting homework.

1. Ask students to find an old paper that could use elaboration. This is most likely something they wrote earlier in the year.

2. Instruct students to trade papers with a partner. Students need to correct errors and add elaboration as needed to their partners' papers.

3. Monitor and allow students to share when they are done.

4. Pass out the handwriting homework.

Day 3 (No Help Day)

Objective: Students will plan and write to a narrative prompt along with the teacher.

Materials: Prompt; handwriting homework.

Note: Today you will plan and write to the same narrative prompt as the students. Format and present the following prompt as you did the pretests.

- Everyone has done something for the first time. Before you write, think about a time you did something for the very first time. Now write about that time and your experience doing something for the first time.

1. Explain that you will also be writing to the prompt today.

2. Distribute the prompt, set the timer, and write as students write.

3. When time is up, share your paper. Ask the students to save this paper for tomorrow's lesson.

4. Pass out the handwriting homework.

Day 4 (Pair Day)

Objective: Students will TCUPSS with partners, looking specifically for elaboration.

Materials: Previously written papers; Figure 3.4; highlighters; handwriting homework.

Note: Make student copies of Figure 3.4.

1. Ask the students to retrieve their papers. Display your copy.

2. Explain that today they will trade papers with partners and highlight their peers' use of elaboration. They will also recommend new ways for their partners to elaborate.

3. Model by TCUPSSing your own paper.

4. Pair the students. Pass out highlighters and Figure 3.4, the Checklist for Peer Editing. Monitor the students.

5. After TCUPSSing, students should write final drafts with suggested elaborations.

6. Collect papers and save for tomorrow.

7. Pass out handwriting homework.

Day 5 (Pair Day)

Objectives: Students will read and score their papers with partners.

Materials: Previously written papers; rubric and rubric posters; self-scoring slips; handwriting homework.

Note: Use Resource E or a similar tool for student self-scoring. If using the resource, copy and cut apart the scoring slips before class. Use your rubric and posters or Resources B and C.

1. Randomly pass out student papers and the scoring slips. Review how to use the slips.

2. Ask students to use the rubric and rubric posters to score the papers they have received.

3. After scoring, collect the papers.

4. Read papers randomly and allow students to guess their scores. Discuss ways authors could have improved their scores.

5. Pass out the handwriting homework.

WEEK 25 LESSON PLANS

Focus: Writing Papers From Given Plans

When writing from a provided plan, students often focus more on the "bigger picture" regarding writing and, as a result, their creativity becomes unleashed.

Day 1

Objective: Students will write expository papers from a given plan.

Materials: Figure 8.1; handwriting homework; Spelling List 2.

Note: Make student copies of Spelling List 2 and Figure 8.1. Prepare this week's handwriting practice.

Spelling List 2: guess, strange, beautiful, pretty, cousin, awesome, wonderful, great, know, where, were, million, treasure

---

Figure 8.1   A Quieter Cafeteria

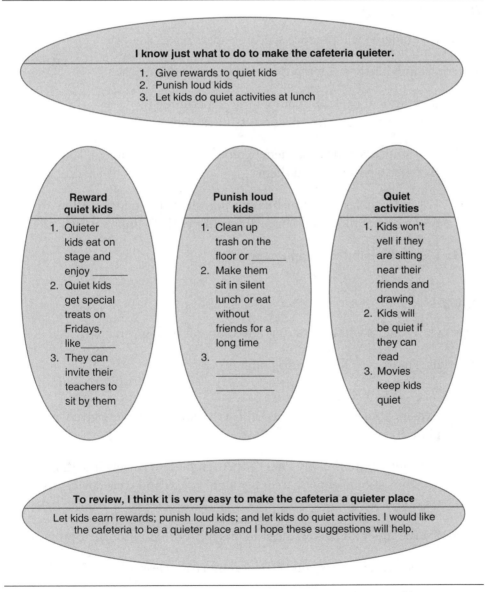

Copyright © 2006 by Karen Donohue and Nanda N. Reddy. All rights reserved. Reprinted from *180 Days to Successful Writers: Lessons to Prepare Your Students for Standardized Assessments and for Life* by Karen Donohue and Nanda N. Reddy. Thousand Oaks, CA: Corwin Press, www.corwinpress.com. Reproduction authorized only for the local school site or nonprofit organization that has purchased this book.

1. Explain to the students that today they will write essays using a plan that you have already made for them. Pass out Figure 8.1, A Quieter Cafeteria, and review it with the class.

2. Remind the students that they will have to elaborate or their papers will be the same.

3. Set the timer. Monitor their progress.

4. Collect these papers and save for tomorrow's lesson.

5. Pass out handwriting homework and Spelling List 2.

Day 2 (Pair Day)

Objective: Students will practice scoring papers using a rubric.

Materials: Previously written papers; rubric and rubric posters.

Note: Make student copies of your rubric or Resource B.
1. Review the rubric and pass out student copies.

2. Pair students and allow them to score each other's papers. They may use the rubric posters to aid them.

3. When the pairs have finished scoring, share the papers. Allow them to discuss what they could have done differently to improve their scores.

4. Distribute handwriting homework.

Day 3

Objective: Students will write a narrative paper from a given plan.

Materials: Figure 8.2; handwriting homework.

Note: Make student copies of Figure 8.2.
1. Explain that today students will write stories using a given narrative plan.

2. Pass out Figure 8.2, My First CPR Attempt, and review it with the class. Students should employ their personal voices and style devices to create unique essays.

3. Set the timer and allow the students to work. Monitor their progress.

4. Collect these papers and keep for tomorrow's lesson.

5. Pass out handwriting homework.

Figure 8.2 My First CPR Attempt

Hook: She just dropped, right before my eyes. No one knew what to do . . .		

Character(s)	Setting	Conflict
Me, bus driver, friends, Jenny	After school on the bus, Valentine's Day	Jenny fainted, I had to do CPR for the first time

It all started . . .	Seconds later . . .
• Tired, after school • Valentine's Day, too much chocolate • Loud, laughing with friends • Jenny dropped	• Bus pulled over, driver panicked . . . • "Who knows CPR?" • Nervous, just learned it • Never tried it
After a minute . . . • I spoke up • Jenny looked bad • Paramedics would take five minutes • Pulse, listened, pumped, breathed hard • Everyone was silent	**Suddenly . . .** • Jenny coughed • Too weak to talk, she had too much sugar • Paramedics showed up • I saved her life

If I didn't try something, even though it was my first time, someone could have died. I feel proud of my first CPR attempt.

Copyright © 2006 by Karen Donohue and Nanda N. Reddy. All rights reserved. Reprinted from *180 Days to Successful Writers: Lessons to Prepare Your Students for Standardized Assessments and for Life* by Karen Donohue and Nanda N. Reddy. Thousand Oaks, CA: Corwin Press, www.corwinpress.com. Reproduction authorized only for the local school site or nonprofit organization that has purchased this book.

Day 4 (Pair Day)

Objective: Students will practice scoring their papers using a rubric.

Materials: Previously written papers; rubric and rubric posters.

Note: Make student copies of your rubric or Resource B.

1. Review the rubric and pass out student copies.

2. Pair the students and allow them to score each other's papers. They may use the rubric posters to aid them.

3. When the pairs have finished scoring, share the papers. Allow them to discuss what they could have done differently to improve their scores.

4. Pass out handwriting homework.

Day 5 (No Help Day)

Objective: Students will write to an expository prompt under a time limit.

Materials: Prompt; handwriting homework.

Note: Format and present the following prompt as you did the pretests.
- Everyone has a special person in his or her life. Think about someone who is special to you. Now tell who that person is and why the person is special to you.

1. Pass out the prompt and set the timer. Allow students to work.

2. Collect papers, grade, and analyze.

3. Pass out handwriting homework.

WEEK 26 LESSON PLANS

Focus: Cooperative Writing

As the test approaches, students become more aware of their weaknesses. They are open to learning from their peers.

Day 1

Objectives: Students will make plans for a given prompt and then trade with peers to write.

Materials: Prompt; Spelling List 3; handwriting homework.

Note: Make student copies of Spelling List 3 and prepare this week's handwriting practice.

> Spelling List 3: does, tomorrow, special, still, steal, dollars, surprise, listen, people, girl, important, with

1. Explain to the class that today they will create plans from the following prompt.
   - Imagine that you accidentally get locked in the classroom one night. Think about what might happen to you when you have to spend the night in your classroom. Now write a story about the time you were locked inside of your classroom overnight.

2. Set a timer and allow the students to create their plans. Remind them to be neat.

3. When students have completed their plans, collect and redistribute.

4. Direct students to use the plans they have been given to write.

5. Collect the papers for use in tomorrow's lesson.

6. Pass out handwriting homework and Spelling List 3.

Day 2 (Pair Day)

Objectives: Students will TCUPSS and share their papers.

Materials: Previously written papers; handwriting homework.

1. Begin class with a recap of yesterday's activity.

2. Hand out student papers. Tell the students that they will now work with partners to TCUPSS these papers and then share their work with the class.

3. Pair students. Monitor as they TCUPSS.

4. Allow them to share.

5. Pass out handwriting homework.

Day 3 (Pair Day)

Objective: Students will write to a prompt with partners.

Materials: Prompt; handwriting homework.

Note: The prompt for today's lesson can be tricky for some students. You may want to discuss it with them before you allow them to write.

1. Post the following prompt and ask a student to read it aloud.
   - You have just won a contest that makes you a millionaire for the day. Think about what you would do if you were a millionaire for the day. Now tell what you would do if you won that contest.

2. Ask students why this prompt is confusing. Some students might think it is narrative because they are pretending that they have won a contest; this may falsely encourage them to tell a story.

3. Pair students and allow them to collaborate on their plans and essays.

4. Collect these papers for use in tomorrow's lesson.

5. Pass out handwriting homework.

Day 4 (Pair Day)

Objectives: Students will TCUPSS and share papers with the class.

Materials: Student papers written on Day 3; handwriting homework.

1. Begin the class with a review of yesterday's lesson.

2. Pass out student papers. Tell the students that they will now work with partners to TCUPSS these papers and then will share their work with the class.

3. Pair students. Monitor as they TCUPSS.

4. Allow them to share.

5. Pass out handwriting homework.

Day 5 (No Help Day)

Objective: Students will write to a narrative prompt under a time limit.

Materials: Prompt; handwriting homework.

Note: Format and present the following prompt as you did the pretests.

*   Everyone has had something funny happen to them. Think about something funny that has happened to you. Now tell about the time something funny happened to you.
    1. Pass out the prompt and set the timer. Allow students to work.
    2. Collect papers, grade, and analyze.

WEEK 27 LESSON PLANS

Focus: Studying for the Test

Believe it or not, your students are ready for a standardized state test. They will write one last time this week before the test. If desired, prepare materials for the review game on Day 5.

Day 1

Objective: Students will write papers from plans of their choice.

Materials: Marathon plans; Spelling List 4; handwriting homework.

Note: Before class, make student copies of Spelling List 4 and prepare this week's handwriting practice. Make study guides, or use Resources F and G. Retrieve plans from the marathon during Week 24, Day 1.

> Spelling List 4: always, thought, bought, feel, breakfast, remember, mysterious, noticed, diamond, something, because, went

1. Tell students that today will be the last day they will have to write before the big test.

2. Inform them to choose their favorite plan from the marathon and write a paper from that plan.

3. Pass out plans and allow them to use their resource binders. Provide help as needed.

4. Save time for the students to share their work at the end of class.

5. Pass out handwriting homework, Spelling List 4, and study guides. Encourage students to study them each night.

Day 2

Objective: Students will read and discuss quality expository papers.

Materials: Example expository papers; handwriting homework.

Note: Today you will share expository papers with the class. Before class, locate and make display copies of as many quality expository examples as you can find.

1. Display and read examples to the students. Remind them how they can learn from hearing and discussing other writers' work.

2. As you share papers, ask students to list their strengths and allow them to guess their scores.

3. Pass out handwriting homework.

Day 3

Objective: Students will read and discuss quality narrative papers.

Materials: Example narrative papers; handwriting homework.

Note: Today you will share narrative papers with the class. Before class, elocate and make display copies of as many quality narratives as you can find.

1. Follow the procedures from Day 2.

Day 4 (Pair Day)

Objective: Students will review for the writing test.

Materials: Handwriting homework; chart paper; markers.

Note: Fasten ten sheets of chart paper to the walls in a manner that will facilitate this lesson. The students will rotate around the room and write on these sheets. Write one of the following categories on the top of each sheet.

- Expository; Narrative; TCUPSS; Parts of a prompt; Elaboration; Awe-Inspiring Adjectives; ASk fOR LIKEly Similies; Mind-Bending Metaphors; Vivacious Verbs; Rainbow Words.

1. Point out the categories listed on the charts. Explain that students will rotate around the room to write one thing they know about each category.

2. Divide the class into ten groups. Pass out markers to each group and place groups at the charts.

3. Monitor students as they write at each chart and review after all groups have visited each chart. If desired, provide a time limit at each chart.

4. Pass out handwriting homework.

Day 5

Objective: Students will play a game to review for the state writing test.

Materials: Trivia game board; question cards; timer; handwriting homework.

Note: Before class make a writing trivia game board. You can use pocket and index cards glued on a poster board. Develop questions that the students can answer.

1. Explain the rules. One student from the first team will stand and chose a category from the game board. Pretend to be the game host and read the question aloud. Set a timer. If that student answers correctly before time runs out, the first team earns a point. Otherwise, the second team has a chance to answer the question, as well as their own question. Play should continue until all the questions have been answered correctly.

9 Beyond Tests and Essays: Applying Expository Writing Knowledge

Expository, narrative, expository, narrative—have you grown tired of this repetition yet? It is understandable if you have. Though repetition was crucial to teaching your students the fundamentals, working only with basic expository and narrative structures can become tedious and is not realistic. It's time for your students to apply their knowledge to more exciting and pragmatic writing tasks.

AN OVERVIEW OF THE PROJECTS

Depending on your circumstances, you either have approximately nine weeks of school left or you're only halfway through the year. As such, this chapter and Chapter 10 are not organized by week with daily lesson plans; they are organized according to projects. This chapter features expository-related projects, while Chapter 10 features narrative-related projects.

Adapting the Original Framework

During the upcoming weeks, your students will call upon the writing knowledge they've accumulated to tackle journalism, subject reports, and poetry in the expository realm and chapter stories, plays, autobiographies, and more poetry in the narrative realm. The transition will be easy if you are prepared for the following changes.

You will continue to follow the model-guide-independence-assessment-reteach paradigm as best as you can. While you cannot feasibly allow students to redo projects based on assessment, you should assess long projects periodically and help students solve problems throughout projects. If you repeat projects, confer with students so that they know their strengths and weaknesses the second time around.

You will introduce new writing tasks by modeling examples using modified planning sheets. For example, the pickle sandwich for some journalism articles features one top bun, five pickles, and a "square" pickle.

You will shorten the process of guidance and expect independence quickly. However, students will receive your support throughout each project; every day is treated as a "help day."

Students will continue to use all of the stylistic tools they learned, and they will edit using TCUPSS. However, they may write several drafts and will learn to combine aspects of narrative and expository writing to complete each project. They will also explore different, more authentic avenues of publication.

Rubrics will be modified at times. While there are many small differences between how you have been teaching and how you will continue, the main change is that your students' works will now resemble published works—a great testament to their writing ability.

Planning the Remaining School Year

Review the projects and lessons in this and the remaining chapters closely before moving forward. Projects are not in a "must follow" order, so feel free to skip around and interchange them. Each of the three expository and four narrative projects takes one to two weeks to complete as presented, but they can be extended to cover over eighteen weeks altogether. If your time is limited, immerse your class in a few projects they find interesting. If you have more time, follow suggested ideas to extend some projects or repeat others with different topics after assessment. You may also introduce "advanced" skills from Chapter 11.

EXPOSITORY-RELATED PROJECTS

Expository-related projects include newspaper writing, subject reports, and some poetry. Before presenting the lessons, discuss that most "real life" writing includes aspects of both expository and narrative writing. The writing may more closely resemble one genre, but will usually contain elements of the other. For example, newspaper articles might be formatted according to expository writing: listing main points and supporting information. However, there is often a narrative element involved since articles usually follow one event with a time structure.

Project 1: Journalism

In teaching newspaper writing, you will model how to write editorials, news stories, and feature stories. You will also demonstrate interviewing.

Prior to introducing this project, collect newspapers from your community. Try to find high school or middle school issues, as well as suitable alternative papers. Cut out articles that are appropriate for your classroom to use as examples during the lessons.

You may extend this project to publish a grade level or school newspaper. If you choose to do this, you will need to assign groups of students to complete different sections and provide opportunities for research. You should also further discuss terminology, including banner, circulation, copy editor, budget, deadline, dummy, and publisher. Finally, you will need to acquire resources, including enough paper, ink, and computers to produce sufficient issues for the entire school or grade level. To make the project easier, collaborate with other teachers to publish the newspaper. Your administrator and a local press can also be invaluable resources if you pursue this larger project.

Introducing Newspaper Journalism

Objectives: Students will learn the basics of newspaper writing and categorize articles as news, sports, lifestyle, editorial, and business stories.

Materials: Sample newspapers and articles.

Notes: Collect sample newspapers with appropriate articles before class.

Newspaper Terminology

Assignment: The article, or story, a newspaper reporter must research and write.

Byline: The reporter's name, written below the headline at the top of the article.

Business: The section of the newspaper that discusses money or finances, local and large national companies, and job or work issues.

Column: An article that is published in a regular position in a newspaper that gives the opinions of a columnist, a reporter who writes on an ongoing topic.

Copy: The final draft of the article. Reporters aim for "clean copies," final drafts without mistakes.

Dateline: Found near the byline, this tells the setting of the story, for instance a city or street, but not necessarily the date.

Editor: The person who supervises the newspaper.

Editorial: Opinion articles written by the editor, reporters, and newspaper readers. Reviews and columns are not called editorials, but technically fit the definition.

Feature article: An article that is not "breaking" news or time sensitive. It includes information readers want to know, but usually can be printed at any time of the year. These articles can be found in the lifestyle, travel, food, business, or leisure sections of the newspaper.

Headline: The title of the story that tells what the story is about. More important headlines are printed in larger font.

Interview: A question and answer session with someone who will be quoted in an article.

Lifestyle: A section of the newspaper with articles that relate to entertainment, daily living, hobbies, and local events. This section usually contains feature articles.

News article: A time-sensitive article about something important that occurred. The topic usually must be written about immediately or it becomes "old" quickly.

Reviews: Opinion articles on books, movies, concerts, CDs, video games, and other events or items of interest to readers.

Sports: The section of the newspaper that reports on local, national, and worldwide sporting events.

Story: Used synonymously with "article" in the newspaper world.

1. Announce to your class that they will become journalists and spend some time working on journalism, or newspaper writing. Discuss that this type of writing is a lot like expository, with a few differences. Ask students what they know about newspapers and journalism. Complete a KWL (Know, Want to Know, and Learn) chart if desired.

2. Discuss the newspaper terms.

3. Pass out examples of newspapers and have your students tell you how the papers are generally organized. They should find the major headline news in the first section—these are often time-sensitive news articles and can include local, state, national, and world news. Point out leisure or lifestyle, sports, business, weather, editorials, and advertisements, including the classifieds. Some newspapers also include sections on food, local events, home, and travel.

4. Discuss that you will focus on news articles and feature articles found on the front page and in the lifestyle, sports, editorial, and business sections of the newspaper. Read examples of headlines found in each of these sections. Discuss how the headlines tell what the article is about.

5. Read the list of school-related headlines below in random order. Have students identify the proper category of the article. Reviews are considered editorials.
   - News articles: Mrs. Martinez's class grows gigantic tomatoes; New teacher moves in; Vandals tag playground equipment; Art classes plan to paint a ten-foot mural; Spring Fling was a hit.

- Lifestyle: Easy ways to keep your room clean; How to not fall behind when you're sick; Does tutoring help grades; Learn to speak up in class; Teachers share their favorite childhood memories; Future cooks share easy after-school treats.
- Editorial: The best teacher at the school; Worst videogames this season; Books you shouldn't miss; Why pizza should be served every day; Say no to the new bus rules; There should be a C honor roll.
- Sports: Tigers hammered at track meet; Cheerleaders win state championship; Croquet, the new after-school craze; Techniques to win a race; Get more exercise every day.
- Business: Fundraising ideas; Sno-cone prices skyrocket; How much does it cost to run a school; Library fines—how to prevent them; How kids can earn extra cash—tips from teachers; Save up for that new toy in just one month; Featured kid business: Jenny's lemonade stand.

6. Have volunteers brainstorm headlines for the different categories. Discuss.

7. Ask students to write headlines on slips of paper. Collect the slips and return in random order. Ask students to read their headlines and identify their categories.

8. Save the headlines for use during the Mini Newspaper lesson.

Editorials, Part I

Objectives: Students will learn the definition of an editorial; they will learn how to plan and write an editorial.

Materials: Examples of editorials; Figures 9.1 and 9.2.

Note: Before class, make display copies of Figures 9.1 and 9.2. If you prefer to model your own editorial topic for Step 15, prepare it in advance. Also, find appropriate examples of editorials in newspapers to use as examples.

1. Tell students they will begin writing editorials because they are most like expository essays.

2. Review the definition of editorial. Discuss that editorial means viewpoint and that newspapers editors and journalists try to present most of the news fairly, from more than one viewpoint. However, they write editorials about serious topics that people argue about. Emphasize that editorials are often pure opinion, so readers often disagree with them and write "letters to the editor" in response; these are also called editorials.

3. Discuss that you will focus on the more serious editorials in this lesson and save reviews and column-type articles for later.

4. Pass around sample editorials you clipped from newspapers' editorial sections. Discuss the format. Editorials can read like personal essays, where private examples are included and the author's voice is clear.

Journalists often state an opinion, discuss the opinion they disagree with, and then explain why they disagree.

5. Brainstorm examples of age-appropriate editorial subjects with students. Examples follow.
   - School uniforms—should kids wear them?
   - Recess—a waste of time?
   - Year-round school—does it keep kids smarter?
   - The dress code—too strict?
   - School rules—too many, too strict, unfair?
   - Reduced time in PE, art, and music classes—unfair?
   - Bullies—is there a way to deal with them?
   - After-school sports teams or clubs—not enough, more girl teams?

6. Ask volunteers for their opinions on the topics and encourage opposing viewpoints. If there are no opposing opinions, offer some. Tell students an editorial is only good if someone can disagree. You may discuss how editorials are related to debates.

7. Point to the pickle sandwich. Tell students that sometimes an editorial topic will give you enough to write an entire five-paragraph essay. Those times, you can plan your editorial using the traditional plan sheet. Other times, you may only have one or two things to say—so, you'll need only one or two pickles in the pickle sandwich. If you have only one thing to say, you'll need one extra large pickle in the sandwich and very strong supporting details.

8. Display and read Figure 9.1, The Awful Truth About State Tests.

9. Discuss the author's voice and opinion. Is the author young or old? How do you know? Is the opinion clear? Do you understand the opinion?

10. Tell students you're going to "work backward" to plan this editorial.

11. Ask students how many pickles they need. They should see that the editorial has one main opinion—the tests are too stressful—and two supporting paragraphs. The first supporting paragraph deals with the author's personal experience of stressing out and the second deals with basing student progress on one stressful experience.

12. Draw a modified plan using two pickles. In the introduction bubble, write the main opinion along with the opposing opinion. Tell students you must include the opponent's main point since that is what you are arguing against.
    - Example: Tests are best at finding out what kids know.

13. In the first pickle, use brief words to write the first reasons the author cites.
    - Example: stressed about time; couldn't eat or sleep; stuck with inaccurate score

14. In the second pickle, write the reasons the author cites in the second supporting paragraph.
    - Example: tested just once; can't retake; doesn't consider grades in school

15. Tell students you will plan an editorial in class about school uniforms. Your complete editorial will be Figure 9.2, A Little Uniformity (and Learning) Please.

16. Draw a plan with two pickles. Tell them that you are writing to support uniforms and will write in a student's voice. Tell them your opinion will be that uniforms do not violate students' right to free speech, but rather lack of uniforms violate students' right to learn. Discuss the meaning of the word violate and the concept of "free speech" if necessary.

17. Write your main opinion: street clothes can be distracting and not having uniforms violates students' right to learn. Then write the opposing opinion in the same bubble: students complain that uniforms violate their right to free speech.

18. Write your two main supporting opinions. Example: street clothes—cliques; street clothes—inappropriate.

19. Write your supporting ideas:
    - Cliques: choosing friends based on clothes; worrying about fashion, not school; name brands cause problems.
    - Inappropriate clothing: street clothes not proper for school; teachers focus on clothes, not class; students miss school.

20. Write the opinion, following the example. Your students probably disagree with your editorial, but they will get the point.

Figure 9.1   The Awful Truth About State Tests

Everyone makes a big deal of state tests. Teachers think those tests are the best ways to find out what kids know, and they often put students in groups according to test scores. Sometimes teachers even use the scores to decide who should pass or fail at the end of the year. All of that should stop because state tests are too stressful to show what students know.

Let me begin by saying that I'm a smart kid and that I failed my state test because of stress. I simply freaked out while taking it. I was so afraid I'd run out of time during our reading test, I wasted a gazillion minutes watching the clock. I couldn't concentrate because all I cared about was that ticking clock. Second, the test made me so nervous, I hardly slept the night before and I couldn't eat. As a result, I was tired and hungry during the test. Of course I couldn't do my best with all that pressure. So even though I love to read and am really good at it, according to the test, I'm a poor reader. Now I'm stuck with an awful test score for the rest of my life.

That takes me to what state tests show. Teachers and politicians are always saying the tests show what students know. But how can a test possibly do that if it tests a kid just one time? What if someone has a bad day, like I did? What if a kid just fought with her best friend? What if a student's dog just died? Kids can't do well if they're not having a good day, yet

(Continued)

Figure 9.1 (Continued)

the test happens on just one day. Tests don't consider that even smart people mess up some-times. I messed up on testing day even though I normally get straight A's in school, and I can't change my score. Is that fair? Of course not. Furthermore, imagine what it's like on test day: seats are separated, timers are ticking, and proctors march around like drill sergeants. Some kids can't handle that kind of pressure. That's why state tests shouldn't be the end all of a kid's life.

As you can see, everyone makes too big a deal about state tests. If you don't believe me, spend a day in my place. You'll see very quickly how stressful these tests are. Plus, when you get judged on just one test, you'll understand how totally unfair the process is.

Copyright © 2006 by Karen Donohue and Nanda N. Reddy. All rights reserved. Reprinted from *180 Days to Successful Writers: Lessons to Prepare Your Students for Standardized Assessments and for Life* by Karen Donohue and Nanda N. Reddy. Thousand Oaks, CA: Corwin Press, www.corwinpress.com. Reproduction authorized only for the local school site or nonprofit organization that has purchased this book.

Figure 9.2 A Little Uniformity (and Learning) Please

Most students complain when their schools even think about adopting uniforms. These kids argue that uniforms would violate their right to free speech. Well, I am a student, and I disagree with that viewpoint. If my school doesn't adopt uniforms, it will be violating my right to learn. Street clothes have become too distracting for school.

For starters, students fight and pick on each other every day because of clothes. Kids form cliques and choose friends based on clothes instead of personality. They judge each other's outfits every day. This forces students like me to constantly worry about clothes instead of worrying about what's important, schoolwork. Furthermore, it's not fair to kids who can't afford name brands. Those kids automatically get left out of groups even though they're fun and cool. Uniforms would change all of this. Students would focus on schoolwork instead of how they look.

Also, popular clothes are not always appropriate for school. See-through lacy blouses, mini skirts, baggy pants that show underwear, tank-tops, bandanas, the list goes on and on. Students should not be wearing these things to school, and yet they feel like they have to fit in. Teachers are forced to stop teaching so they can deal with dress codes, and that keeps the other kids (like me) from learning. Sometimes kids are even sent home because of clothing issues, so obviously their right to learn is violated. If schools enforced uniforms, inappropriate clothing and dress code violations would be less of a problem.

It's clear to me. Students have a right to learn, and this right is being violated because we're so caught up in dress codes, popularity contests, and fitting in. Uniforms would erase a lot of these issues and get students back to doing what they're supposed to be doing: learning!

Copyright © 2006 by Karen Donohue and Nanda N. Reddy. All rights reserved. Reprinted from *180 Days to Successful Writers: Lessons to Prepare Your Students for Standardized Assessments and for Life* by Karen Donohue and Nanda N. Reddy. Thousand Oaks, CA: Corwin Press, www.corwinpress.com. Reproduction authorized only for the local school site or nonprofit organization that has purchased this book.

Editorials, Part II

Objectives: Students will plan and write their own newspaper editorials.

Materials: Figures 9.1 and 9.2; previously generated list of editorial suggestions.

Note: Be prepared to pair students up in Step 3 if you choose to do so.

1. Review the definition of an editorial and the two samples (Figures 9.1 and 9.2). Remind students that when they write editorials, they need to make their voices clear and to support their opinions with strong, convincing reasons.

2. Review your age-appropriate list of editorial subjects. Tell students they could write an opinion based on one of those or respond to the samples.

3. You may pair students up for this lesson according to their interests or writing levels. Instruct students to draw plan sheets for their topics. Tell them it can look like the original pickle sandwich if they have three major opinions about a topic. Remind them that if they do not have three opinions, it will have fewer pickles.

4. Monitor students' work and offer suggestions.

5. Remind students to TCUPSS when done. Allow students to read their work out loud.

6. Students may write final drafts and publish them in a newsletter for the class, grade level, or school. Students may also choose to submit them to an existing newspaper.

7. Grade the editorials using the traditional expository rubric.

8. Repeat the lesson if desired, focusing on relevant, timely topics. If appropriate, encourage interested students to send their work to local newspapers.

Interviews and Feature Articles, Part I

Objectives: Students will learn how to plan and conduct an interview to write a feature article.

Materials: Figure 9.3; a subject to interview.

Note: You will model the interview process thoroughly by planning and conducting an interview in front of the students. Make plans with an interviewee well in advance. Draft the interview questions the night before the meeting. After the interview, you will model how to write an article from the notes, most likely the next day. You should prepare the completed article before class following Figure 9.3, Janitor Bob: An Everyday Hero. You may choose to do a separate lesson using only the Janitor Bob example before modeling the process.

1. Discuss that interviewing people is a natural part of journalism. News stories and feature articles often require interviews with experts, witnesses, celebrities, people who have done outstanding things, and award, sport, or contest winners. Journalists also interview everyday people who have something to teach the world.

2. Explain that within the context of school, interviewees for a feature article might be the following: contest or award winners; student

teams; teachers who are new, newly married, award winners, or new parents; a student who did something unique or noteworthy; "everyday heroes"; the principal; classes that are doing interesting projects; and even students who went on interesting field trips or vacations.

3. Tell the class that you have arranged for an interviewee to stop by your room. Discuss whom you chose, why you chose that person, and when you expect the person to arrive.

4. Tell students that you will plan the interview before the interviewee arrives.

5. Draw a modified pickle sandwich consisting of at least five small pickles and one square pickle between the buns—six pickles in all. Tell students that you will write your interview questions inside the pickles.

6. Write the interviewee's name in the introduction bun, as well as the main reason you are interviewing this person. Then write a few phrases showing what you already know about this person in this top bun.
   a. Janitor Bob. Reason for the interview: To find out more about this important person.
   b. Examples of things you know: He's friendly; he's at school before, during, and after school; kids call him JB.

7. Discuss at least five main questions to ask the interviewee. Write these questions inside the small oval pickles. Examples follow for Janitor Bob.

   - Tell us about your family. What are your favorite things about your job? What are your favorite sports and hobbies? What did you want to be when you were a kid? What are some things you wished kids knew about you?
   - Tell students that your square pickle is for a question that you will ask other people about the interviewee. You'll include the best quotes in the article. In the Janitor Bob example, you'd ask other students their opinions of the man.
   - You might write, "What do you like about Janitor Bob?"
   - Before the interviewee arrives, have your students take out blank sheets of paper. Explain that the plan sheet was for the questions; the blank sheets are for notes.
   - Students should take notes on the interviewee's answers to the five questions while you also take notes. You will compare notes after the interview.
   - Welcome your interviewee.
   - Begin the interview with Question 1 and take notes as the person speaks. If a question is not answered fully, probe for a more thorough answer. Model positive body language and appropriate wait time for answers.
   - Number your questions out loud ("Question 2") to prompt your students to organize their notes.

8. After the interview, compare notes with your students, filling in gaps.

9. Assign the following homework or "recess work" in pairs. Students should ask peers, teachers, or other relevant people outside of the classroom the "boxed pickle" question.

10. Review your notes from the interview. Ask students to share the best quotes they got during their "boxed pickle" assignment. Vote on one or two to use.

11. Tell your students you are going to organize the notes to make a great feature article. This means you may not write the article in the order of your notes. You might have to switch things around to make the story interesting.

12. Start with the things you already know to set a premise for the rest of the article; write an introduction based on this information. Use the article on Janitor Bob to guide you.

13. Model the rest of your feature article. As you model, remember that your main goal is to show students how to weave dry information into a creative story. You are showing them how to move beyond the strict structure of a plan sheet.

14. When you are done, demonstrate how to write a headline, byline, and dateline for this piece. TCUPSS and read the completed piece. Discuss what students learned.

Figure 9.3   Janitor Bob: An Everyday Hero

The Man Behind the Mop

Wright Elem. School—You see him before school, during school, and after school. You see him in the cafeteria, on the playground, and in the hallways. Students shout out, "Hey JB" when they see him, and Janitor Bob always waves and smiles back. One student even said, "I wish JB was my teacher. He's always so nice." But who is Janitor Bob? Is he just a friendly face with a mop? No way. Janitor Bob is a father, a builder of models, and a football player.

After school, you might find JB (he likes the nickname) at home playing with his four boys. His kids are all too young for school right now, but his twins (Eric and David) will be starting kindergarten right here at Wright Elem. next year. JB likes to build models, so he does this often with his kids. JB has built model airplanes, ships, and cars with his kids. He even put in motors to make them work.

We asked JB if he'd mind bringing in some of his models to share with students. He said, "Of course I don't mind!" That's because JB loves working at our school, and he loves the students. "My job is great. I really have fun here, and the kids are great," JB said. His favorite thing about his job is being around the students.

This isn't surprising considering that JB was a great student himself. When he was growing up, he was a model student. "I always listened. I was really quiet and I did *almost* everything my teachers asked me to do," he laughed. "I did *everything* the coach asked me to do." JB wanted to be a football player when he was a kid, and he worked hard toward this goal. Eventually, he played football in high school. But his dream of playing professional football never came true.

(Continued)

Figure 9.3 (Continued)

> "That's ok," JB said about his lost dream. "I'd have broken a bunch of bones if I played football. I wasn't ever big enough. I'm happy where I am." The thing JB wants to tell kids is to "put in your all, no matter what you do." He said, "I put my all into football, and I'm still a darn good player. I put my all into making models, that's why they turn out good. And I put my all in my job here." He didn't have to tell us that last part. We already knew. JB is the best janitor in this neck of the woods, and we are glad to finally get to know this man behind the mop.

Copyright © 2006 by Karen Donohue and Nanda N. Reddy. All rights reserved. Reprinted from *180 Days to Successful Writers: Lessons to Prepare Your Students for Standardized Assessments and for Life* by Karen Donohue and Nanda N. Reddy. Thousand Oaks, CA: Corwin Press, www.corwinpress.com. Reproduction authorized only for the local school site or nonprofit organization that has purchased this book.

Interviews and Feature Articles, Part II

Objectives: Students will plan interviews, interview partners, and then write interview articles.

Materials: Teacher model written during Interviews and Features, Part I.

Note: Before class, plan to pair students up with partners they may not know well. Also, create a display of the article you modeled during Part I.

1. Explain to students that they will interview classmates.

2. Announce the pairs, but do not allow the pairs to get together yet. Label students A and B as you put them in pairs.

3. Have your students plan interviews of their partners alone. They should consider what they know and what they want to know about their interviewees. They should come up with five major questions, with a sixth question in a "square pickle" for friends and classmates of the interviewee.

4. Provide time limits and allow the pairs to start interviewing each other. Students labeled A could interview first, followed by the B partners.

5. Monitor students.

6. Separate the partners, and then allow time for "mingling" so that students can get quotes for their square pickles.

7. Ask students to start writing their interview articles from notes, following your model. Display a copy of your example as a reference.

8. Monitor student progress and offer assistance. Students will need time to organize the information in a creative manner, so it will take much longer to write this first draft.

9. Instruct students to TCUPSS their completed articles and write final drafts.

10. Remind students that journalists normally create several drafts and make many changes before publication. For a more authentic experience, allow students to complete several drafts with your input or guidance.

11. Allow volunteers to read their interview articles out loud. Students may possibly publish these in a class book with pictures of interviewees.

12. You may grade these articles according to the traditional rubric. However, keep in mind that interviews are only as good as their interviewees. Students with poor interviewees might be at a disadvantage. You may also grade your students' interviewing skills by collecting their notes. You can create a rubric to do this, giving points for the quality of questions, the depth of the interview, and student ability to convert interview answers into an article.

Breaking News Articles

Objectives: Students will learn how to plan and write a news article.

Materials: Figure 9.4.

Note: Before class, review Figure 9.4, Big Spill Turns School Into Water Park.

1. Tell students you will model a "breaking news" article on a make-believe story. You will pretend that a water main burst at your school, flooding the cafeteria and the playground.

2. Draw a modified plan sheet with two top buns, three large regular pickles, and one large square pickle. List the words who, what, where, when, why, and how in the top bun.

3. Tell students that news stories always start out by stating the most important information in the first paragraph, which is done by answering the five w's and h. That is why you have two top buns.
   - Discuss the who: Janitor Bob discovered the problem; what: the school was flooded; where: cafeteria, parking lot, and playground; when: discovered at 5:30 a.m. yesterday morning; why: water main broke; how: unknown.

4. In the second "introduction" paragraph, you will list the main points of the story: the cafeteria shut down; the playground turned into a lake; students got a water park.

5. Transfer the main points into the three regular pickle tops, then list brief "facts" pertaining to each point. Examples follow.
   - Cafeteria shut down: kids made breakfast; local pizza place donates pizza.
   - Playground is a lake: workers pumped noisily all day; no schoolwork got done; parents picked up kids early.
   - A water park: racing paper boats, water slides, water soccer.

6. Reserve the final square pickle for student quotes and other interview notes. Examples: "The whole school was flooded as far as I could see," "I like cooking so it was kind of fun," "It was like listening to a lawnmower all day," and "We could hardly get anything done."

7. Demonstrate how to write the headline, dateline, and byline.

8. You may then read the completed article or model the process of turning facts into an interesting article as you "recreate" the article. You may also write the final article with a different voice and style to demonstrate how two different articles can be written from the same information.

Figure 9.4   A Big Spill Turns School into Water Park

Bookville, FL—Janitor Bob wondered if he was still sleeping and having a nightmare when he drove up to Wright Elementary School yesterday morning. At five-thirty in the morning, he was the first one at school, and he was surprised to find his pickup truck in a foot of water by the time he reached his parking space. "The whole school was flooded as far as I could see," the janitor said. "I just sat there and stared. I didn't know what to do."

Eventually, he did figure out what to do. He called the principal, called the water department, and waded toward the water main behind the cafeteria. Water was gushing from a broken pipe directly into the cafeteria kitchen. When Janitor Bob reached the cafeteria, he saw floating chairs and tables and ruined food! Bags of soaked bread and containers of food were submerged under water. Janitor Bob immediately realized the cafeteria would be useless and that he was in for a tough day.

Indeed, the cafeteria had to be shut down. The principal encouraged students to stay home, but it was too late. Many students arrived at school anyway. The lunch ladies set up a stand outside the front office stacked with food that Janitor Bob and others rescued from the cafeteria. "This is your cafeteria today, and you're the cooks," Mrs. Culinart, the cafeteria supervisor, announced as students lined up to assemble their own breakfast sandwiches. "I like cooking, so it was kind of fun," Seymour Ayes, a fourth-grade student said. For lunch, the students chomped on free pizza, donated by the local pizza place. That was a big hit.

Throughout the day, workers pumped water out of the cafeteria area into the school playground and fixed the water main. "It was like listening to a lawnmower all day," Mrs. Arthur said of the noisy pumps and workers. "We could hardly get anything done," Anita Storey, a second grader, added. Indeed, for a Monday, very little work got done. Many parents took their students out of school early when they heard the news, and the noise and water were very distracting. After a while, Principal Grator allowed the remaining students to go out and play—in their new water park that is. It was a warm day, so students enjoyed splashing and frolicking in the water. They raced paper boats, they turned the playground equipment into water slides, and they invented a "water soccer" game.

Today, everything has been restored. You would never have guessed that Wright Elementary School was practically submerged just one day ago. The playground has dried up, the cafeteria is up and running (and sparkly clean), and Janitor Bob is taking the day off. But students at Wright Elementary School will never forget the day their school felt like it was sitting in a lake.

Copyright © 2006 by Karen Donohue and Nanda N. Reddy. All rights reserved. Reprinted from *180 Days to Successful Writers: Lessons to Prepare Your Students for Standardized Assessments and for Life* by Karen Donohue and Nanda N. Reddy. Thousand Oaks, CA: Corwin Press, www.corwinpress.com. Reproduction authorized only for the local school site or nonprofit organization that has purchased this book.

A Mini School Newspaper

Objectives: Students will cooperate to plan, research, and write news or feature articles.

Materials: Sample newspapers; student-generated list of headlines from Introducing Newspaper Journalism.

Notes: Prior to this lesson, visit classrooms around the school to make a list of newsworthy topics. Also, prepare for Step 9 by contacting applicable teachers, school workers, and administrators. Plan to pair students according to their choices; you may ask students to make choices toward the end of a school day before the project begins.

1. Tell students they will put together a mini school newspaper. Students will pair up on assignments, and each pair will complete two articles. You, the editor, will decide which articles you will publish in the newspaper.

2. Discuss that your mini newspaper needs a name. You may hold a naming contest, allowing all students to submit one name, or brainstorm names.

3. Brainstorm article topics for your students to choose from. Discuss newsworthy things that are happening around the school and read the list of headlines students came up with to prompt ideas.

4. Instruct students to write their name and their top three choices for articles to work on. Have students number their choices in order of preference and turn them in. You will use the choices to assign students into pairs or groups for the articles.

5. Before continuing with the lesson, review your students' top three requests, then assign your students into pairs or groups to complete two articles, possibly a news article and a feature article. Mark one of the two articles as the main assignment and the other as extra credit.

6. Figure out what your students will have to do to complete the articles: Will they need to conduct interviews, use the Internet, or be outside of the classroom? Plan the logistics. You may issue hall passes, arrange for interviewees to visit your classroom, stagger the Internet use, etc. Plan for all possible problems.

7. Group or pair your students. Assume the fictional role of the newspaper editor handing out team assignments. Discuss that the first article is the most important; the second article is extra credit if they complete the first with time to spare.

8. Review the newspaper articles checklist. Discuss how each aspect factors into grading.

9. Instruct your teams to plan first. Provide a time limit to complete this process, and monitor students closely. Offer hints and advice.

10. As students complete plans, you may allow teams to describe their plans to the class.

11. After planning, students should begin the research process, which will vary with each article. You may allow students to use computers, watch TV, read magazines and newspapers, interview subjects, conduct research in the library, etc. Remind students to take notes. To help this process run smoothly, impose time limits and be sure interviewees, media specialists, etc., are aware of the project.

12. After researching, students should begin organizing their notes and writing their articles. Provide assistance.

13. Monitor progress. Some students will complete their first assignment quickly. Instruct those to edit and revise before moving on to their extra credit assignment.

14. Other students may get bogged down with planning, research, or writing and may not get to the second assignment. Others will require more research time than their peers. Reassure those students that their first assignment matters most and help those students get the research done quickly.

15. Some students might not have found enough information for their main articles, so may not be able to complete them. Discuss that this sometimes happens to real journalists. Reassign their extra credit assignment as their main one.

16. Provide time for students to polish their articles and gather art, if desired. Remind them of the headline, byline, and dateline.

17. After students submit articles and they have been graded, students may complete another final draft to publish, attending to layout.

18. Publish the newspapers by stapling and making enough copies for all students.

19. Set aside time for students to share articles with each other and read the newspaper.

Newspaper Articles Checklist

☐ Identify assignment as news or feature article.
☐ Draw modified pickle sandwiches to plan the project. Two top buns with 5 Ws and an H for news stories, square pickles for quotes.
☐ Take notes: Research facts, conduct interviews, and visit the site.
☐ Organize notes and write a draft.
☐ Write a headline, byline, and dateline.
☐ Review and TCUPSS the article to write a final draft.

Project 2: Subject Reports

Subject reports will require you to teach rudimentary research skills and how to access research materials. Materials include, but are not limited to, encyclopedias, nonfiction books, magazines, the Internet, and experts. You might need to reorganize your classroom schedule to accommodate available library and computer lab times to teach your students how to use these materials.

As presented, the project should take about two weeks. However, you may extend it by allowing students to publish their works into mini nonfiction books. Also, consider having students create hands-on projects to accompany their paper projects. For instance, they may create dioramas, scientific demonstrations, performances, interviews or lectures with experts, a slide show or photo collage, a video, or bring in objects related to their projects.

Introducing Subject Reports

Objectives: Students will read a sample outline of a report, learn how reports are organized, and generate ideas of report topics.

Materials: Figure 9.5.

Note: Before beginning this project, you may use the outlined material in Figure 9.5 to create one or more sample pages of a subject report. Also, if you plan to extend the activity to include a hands-on display or project, plan to demonstrate one for racecars. For a simple demonstration on speed and aerodynamics, collect straws and bottle caps of various sizes. Attach the straws to the varied bottle caps (use glue or make holes in the caps) to create "racecars," and prepare an incline (a board and book will do). Time each racecar across a level surface after letting it go down the incline and measure its distance. Compare.

Figure 9.5   Racecars and Racing, An Outline

1. History
    a. Horses, farmers, and horsepower
        – Chea's Pass Fairground and track
        – 1877 Wyoming International Racing Arena
    b. Store bought cars
        – 1900s, first cars
        – 1922 Chea's Pass first invitational auto race
        – 1920s–1930s Hundreds of racetracks all over country
        – Racing and bootlegging
    c. 1947 NASCAR standards
        – Rules for stock cars
        – System for winning
        – Modifications based on dirt tracks
    d. 1957 Bobby Allison at the Montgomery International Speedway
        – Pit Crew
        – Sponsorship

2. Types of cars and tracks
    a. CART and Formula 1
        – Car bodies, speeds, and specs
        – Champ cars
        – Rules for racing (fewer templates than NASCAR)

(Continued)

Figure 9.5 (Continued)

---

    b. NASCAR stock racing
       – Short track (e.g., Bristol)
       – Super speedway (e.g., Talladega, Daytona)
       – Car bodies, speeds, and specs
       – Rules for racing (hundreds of templates)
    c. Drag racing
       – Tracks
       – Car bodies, speeds, and specs
       – Rules for racing (two cars at a time)

3. The anatomy of a car
    a. Frame and body
       – Firewalls
       – The English Wheel
    b. Engine design and speed
       – Turbocharger vs. supercharger
       – Racecar vs. streetcar
    c. Tires
       – Nitrogen-filled
       – Threadless double tube design
    d. Aerodynamics
       – The Bernoulli effect
       – Drag and design

4. Safety
    a. Rollcage (materials and design)
    b. Window nets (purpose and materials)
    c. Roof flaps (purpose and design)
    d. Wraparound seat and 5-point seatbelt harness
    e. Foam-filled fuel cells in fuel tanks
    f. Lexan windshields

5. The future
    a. Concept cars
    b. Tracks, rules, and speeds
    c. Safety

Copyright © 2006 by Karen Donohue and Nanda N. Reddy. All rights reserved. Reprinted from *180 Days to Successful Writers: Lessons to Prepare Your Students for Standardized Assessments and for Life* by Karen Donohue and Nanda N. Reddy. Thousand Oaks, CA: Corwin Press, www.corwinpress.com. Reproduction authorized only for the local school site or nonprofit organization that has purchased this book.

1. Tell students they will begin working on individual subject reports and discuss a possible time frame.

2. Display and review Figure 9.5, the detailed outline of a report on racecars. If you wrote any sample pages, share those.

3. Ask students if they think the writer knew all of the information before she started writing the outline or report. They should realize that the writer probably "looked up" much of the information.

4. Discuss that students will not make outlines for their reports. Instead they will use modified plan sheets. However, they will not be able to fit all of their information on a pickle sandwich, so the plan sheet will be used as a brainstorming tool to begin the research.

6. To facilitate grading, allow students to turn in first drafts of each section (along with notes) as they are completed.

7. Review and grade students' work according to a rubric modified as follows.

8. Add "research skills" to the rubric as a seventh category. Award up to six points for the category based on the following subcategories (each worth two points). Divide your total rubric's points by seven to find the average.
   - Student used a variety of resources and cited them.
   - Student found relevant data, took good notes, and paraphrased.
   - Student organized the data in a meaningful, interesting way.

9. As you grade each paper, offer advice and catch overlooked mistakes. You may keep graded sections until all five are completed, then return the full reports to students.

10. After students have completed five sections, allow them to create polished final drafts and illustrate their work. Provide old magazines for clipped art.

11. Students should bind their final product and share their reports with each other. If students prepared hands-on projects, schedule due dates so that students have time to present those. You may grade these projects separately based on their creativity, relevance to the subject report, and complexity.

Project 3: List Poetry

Poetry is not normally thought of as expository writing. However, list poems are somewhat expository as they tell stories through organized lists of images or emotions and do not adhere to a time sequence. You will read examples of such poetry to your students, then lead them as they write poems. Although poetry is not normally "planned," you will teach your students to organize their thoughts and think up images before they write their poems.

You may incorporate these lessons into a longer poetry unit. Allow your students to write several versions of the three suggested forms, combine them with narrative-type poetry, and teach other forms such as haiku, sestina, acrostic, diamante, and cinquain. Students may publish "books" of their poetry, compile a class book, create greeting cards with their work, or decorate the classroom with poster-sized illustrated poems. Encourage interested students to copy their poems into poetry journals where they may write future poems. You may also allow students to memorize and recite their poems in front of the class. Finally, students may stage poetry readings of their original poems during a parent night.

Personal List Poem

Objective: Students will hear examples of expository poetry, then plan and write their own poems.

5. Draw a modified pickle sandwich with five pickles to show what a brief plan of Figure 9.5 would look like. List the topic in the introduction bun: racecars. List the main sections of the report in the pickles: history, types of cars and tracks, how a racecar is built, safety, and the future.

6. Under the main sections, list the following main points.
   - History: Horses, store bought cars, NASCAR rules.
   - Types: CART, NASCAR, and drag.
   - The anatomy of a car Frame, engine, tires, and aerodynamics.
   - Safety: Rollcage, seat and belts, window nets and roof flaps, fuel tank, and windshield.
   - Future: Concept cars, safety changes, rules and track changes.

7. Discuss that the five sections deal specifically with racecars. Most topics have a history, but very few are related to speed and building a car. Explain that if you were writing about cheerleading, you might include these sections: history, training, stunts and tricks, chants, and competitions.

8. Ask students to brainstorm categories for golf, bicycles, and dolls. Sample answers follow.
   a. Golf: History, famous golfers, building a golf course, clubs and other tools, tournaments and prizes, the rules, how to play, miniature golf, golf around the world, the business of golf, golf attire, women and golf.
   b. Bicycles: History, the inventors, styles, old vs. new, bike games, extreme racers, the Tour de France, famous bikers, biking laws, bikes as transportation, bikes as toys, biking around the world, biking for exercise, biking tools and clothing.
   c. Dolls: History, dolls around the world, famous or trendy dolls, doll collecting, porcelain dolls, making a doll, dolls for boys, figurines, dollhouses.

9. Brainstorm to generate a list of subject topics that interest your students. Some general categories and topics follow.
   a. Sports: Baseball, basketball, football, swimming, gymnastics, skiing, skateboarding, rollerblading, running, racing, hockey, karate, lacrosse.
   b. Hobbies: Stamp collecting, go-carts, video games, reading, art, piano, knitting, cards, hula-hoops, folk or street games, ballet, saltwater tank.
   c. Jobs: Acting or singing, magician, doctor, software engineer, fashion designer, model, judge, movie producer or director, firemen, soldiers, CIA and FBI agents.
   d. People: The President, the Pope, Oprah, Michael Jordan, Shirley Temple.
   e. Places: Africa, space, the ocean, rainforests, Hawaii.
   f. Animals: Dinosaurs, snakes, pets, desert creatures, whales, ants.

g. History: The Civil War, kings of England, the Dark Ages, the 1960s.
h. General interest: Trucks, toys, computers, music, dancing.

10. Discuss why very specific topics might be difficult to research and write about. Also, discuss why very vague topics are also poor choices.

11. Instruct your students to take out three sheets of paper. They will choose three ideas for subject reports in the order of their preference; the only off-limit topic is racecars since that is your example. Students are to plan each report idea on separate sheets of paper by drawing modified pickle sandwiches and thinking of at least five subsections related to each topic. They can list more, if desired, and then narrow down the subsections during research.

12. Tell students that you will review their choices and help them decide which subjects will be easiest to research. The others will be "backups" in case there isn't much information on the first topic. If they cannot think of five subsections, the topic might not be comprehensive enough. If there are many more than five (ten to twenty), the topic may be too broad.

13. Monitor students closely as they generate topics and plans. If you want your students to create a hands-on project, demonstrate yours. Then allow students to brainstorm at least one project for each of their three ideas and write these on the backs of their plans.

14. Have students turn in plans. Check over subjects and subsections to decide which topics will be easiest to report on. Help students choose a topic that they will find a great deal of information on. Then indicate which of the subjects should be their second choice.

Research

Objectives: Students will learn the different methods of research, conduct research for reports, and take notes from references.

Materials: Library and computer lab; encyclopedias, magazines, and nonfiction materials; racecar materials.

Note: Before class, gather reference materials a person might use to research racecars. Also, prepare to teach research skills. Many English books include valuable lessons.

1. Remind students of Figure 9.5, the outline on racecars. Show students materials the author of your sample report might have used: nonfiction books on racecars; encyclopedia articles; racing magazines; and Internet search results. Discuss the need to use more than one source to write a meaningful report.

2. Discuss the types of research tools available and how to use them: Encyclopedias, nonfiction books, the Internet, magazines, newspapers, and experts.

3. Review skills related to research: Alphabetization of guide words and phrases; looking up people and authors by last names; using an index; using a search engine online; library database searches of subjects; library call numbers; conducting an interview; taking notes, paraphrasing, quoting sources, and listing source information; ruling out poor sources and extraneous information; organizing facts.

4. After teaching research basics, allow your students to prepare for their research. Return their approved plans. Have students turn over their plans and make a list of research tools they hope to find.

5. Have students take out five blank sheets of paper and write one category on each sheet. These sheets will be used to take notes as they locate information. Discuss that students must list the name of the source, author, and page number (if applicable).

6. Tell students they don't have to fill the sheets. These are notes and can be in list order. Emphasize that the notes need to be relevant to the subcategory. For example, if "history of tuba playing" is a subsection, you won't include information about what a tuba player has to do if he wants to join the marching band.

7. Take students to the library or other reference source. Help them gather their references and monitor their note taking.

8. Provide adequate time for students to complete their research. Students may do some of it on their own as homework if they have access to resources.

Writing Subject Reports

Objectives: Students will use notes to write subject reports, edit and revise their work to create polished final drafts, and illustrate final work.

Materials: Students' notes from research; old magazines with illustrations.

1. Review the sample material on racecars if necessary.

2. Tell students they will use their research notes to write their subject reports.

3. Instruct them to return to their modified plan sheets. Using the notes they gathered, they will write the main points they want to cover on the plan sheet in the order they prefer. Discuss that this is the process of organizing their facts.

4. Monitor students' progress closely, giving advice and hints.

5. After planning, students should begin working on the first drafts of their subject reports. They should work on one section at a time, TCUPSSing and polishing them.

5. Draw a modified pickle sandwich with five pickles to show what a brief plan of Figure 9.5 would look like. List the topic in the introduction bun: racecars. List the main sections of the report in the pickles: history, types of cars and tracks, how a racecar is built, safety, and the future.

6. Under the main sections, list the following main points.
   - History: Horses, store bought cars, NASCAR rules.
   - Types: CART, NASCAR, and drag.
   - The anatomy of a car Frame, engine, tires, and aerodynamics.
   - Safety: Rollcage, seat and belts, window nets and roof flaps, fuel tank, and windshield.
   - Future: Concept cars, safety changes, rules and track changes.

7. Discuss that the five sections deal specifically with racecars. Most topics have a history, but very few are related to speed and building a car. Explain that if you were writing about cheerleading, you might include these sections: history, training, stunts and tricks, chants, and competitions.

8. Ask students to brainstorm categories for golf, bicycles, and dolls. Sample answers follow.
   a. Golf: History, famous golfers, building a golf course, clubs and other tools, tournaments and prizes, the rules, how to play, miniature golf, golf around the world, the business of golf, golf attire, women and golf.
   b. Bicycles: History, the inventors, styles, old vs. new, bike games, extreme racers, the Tour de France, famous bikers, biking laws, bikes as transportation, bikes as toys, biking around the world, biking for exercise, biking tools and clothing.
   c. Dolls: History, dolls around the world, famous or trendy dolls, doll collecting, porcelain dolls, making a doll, dolls for boys, figurines, dollhouses.

9. Brainstorm to generate a list of subject topics that interest your students. Some general categories and topics follow.
   a. Sports: Baseball, basketball, football, swimming, gymnastics, skiing, skateboarding, rollerblading, running, racing, hockey, karate, lacrosse.
   b. Hobbies: Stamp collecting, go-carts, video games, reading, art, piano, knitting, cards, hula-hoops, folk or street games, ballet, saltwater tank.
   c. Jobs: Acting or singing, magician, doctor, software engineer, fashion designer, model, judge, movie producer or director, firemen, soldiers, CIA and FBI agents.
   d. People: The President, the Pope, Oprah, Michael Jordan, Shirley Temple.
   e. Places: Africa, space, the ocean, rainforests, Hawaii.
   f. Animals: Dinosaurs, snakes, pets, desert creatures, whales, ants.

g. History: The Civil War, kings of England, the Dark Ages, the 1960s.

h. General interest: Trucks, toys, computers, music, dancing.

10. Discuss why very specific topics might be difficult to research and write about. Also, discuss why very vague topics are also poor choices.

11. Instruct your students to take out three sheets of paper. They will choose three ideas for subject reports in the order of their preference; the only off-limit topic is racecars since that is your example. Students are to plan each report idea on separate sheets of paper by drawing modified pickle sandwiches and thinking of at least five subsections related to each topic. They can list more, if desired, and then narrow down the subsections during research.

12. Tell students that you will review their choices and help them decide which subjects will be easiest to research. The others will be "backups" in case there isn't much information on the first topic. If they cannot think of five subsections, the topic might not be comprehensive enough. If there are many more than five (ten to twenty), the topic may be too broad.

13. Monitor students closely as they generate topics and plans. If you want your students to create a hands-on project, demonstrate yours. Then allow students to brainstorm at least one project for each of their three ideas and write these on the backs of their plans.

14. Have students turn in plans. Check over subjects and subsections to decide which topics will be easiest to report on. Help students choose a topic that they will find a great deal of information on. Then indicate which of the subjects should be their second choice.

Research

Objectives: Students will learn the different methods of research, conduct research for reports, and take notes from references.

Materials: Library and computer lab; encyclopedias, magazines, and nonfiction materials; racecar materials.

Note: Before class, gather reference materials a person might use to research racecars. Also, prepare to teach research skills. Many English books include valuable lessons.

1. Remind students of Figure 9.5, the outline on racecars. Show students materials the author of your sample report might have used: nonfiction books on racecars; encyclopedia articles; racing magazines; and Internet search results. Discuss the need to use more than one source to write a meaningful report.

2. Discuss the types of research tools available and how to use them: Encyclopedias, nonfiction books, the Internet, magazines, newspapers, and experts.

3. Review skills related to research: Alphabetization of guide words and phrases; looking up people and authors by last names; using an index; using a search engine online; library database searches of subjects; library call numbers; conducting an interview; taking notes, paraphrasing, quoting sources, and listing source information; ruling out poor sources and extraneous information; organizing facts.

4. After teaching research basics, allow your students to prepare for their research. Return their approved plans. Have students turn over their plans and make a list of research tools they hope to find.

5. Have students take out five blank sheets of paper and write one category on each sheet. These sheets will be used to take notes as they locate information. Discuss that students must list the name of the source, author, and page number (if applicable).

6. Tell students they don't have to fill the sheets. These are notes and can be in list order. Emphasize that the notes need to be relevant to the sub-category. For example, if "history of tuba playing" is a subsection, you won't include information about what a tuba player has to do if he wants to join the marching band.

7. Take students to the library or other reference source. Help them gather their references and monitor their note taking.

8. Provide adequate time for students to complete their research. Students may do some of it on their own as homework if they have access to resources.

Writing Subject Reports

Objectives: Students will use notes to write subject reports, edit and revise their work to create polished final drafts, and illustrate final work.

Materials: Students' notes from research; old magazines with illustrations.

1. Review the sample material on racecars if necessary.

2. Tell students they will use their research notes to write their subject reports.

3. Instruct them to return to their modified plan sheets. Using the notes they gathered, they will write the main points they want to cover on the plan sheet in the order they prefer. Discuss that this is the process of organizing their facts.

4. Monitor students' progress closely, giving advice and hints.

5. After planning, students should begin working on the first drafts of their subject reports. They should work on one section at a time, TCUPSSing and polishing them.

6. To facilitate grading, allow students to turn in first drafts of each section (along with notes) as they are completed.

7. Review and grade students' work according to a rubric modified as follows.

8. Add "research skills" to the rubric as a seventh category. Award up to six points for the category based on the following subcategories (each worth two points). Divide your total rubric's points by seven to find the average.
   - Student used a variety of resources and cited them.
   - Student found relevant data, took good notes, and paraphrased.
   - Student organized the data in a meaningful, interesting way.

9. As you grade each paper, offer advice and catch overlooked mistakes. You may keep graded sections until all five are completed, then return the full reports to students.

10. After students have completed five sections, allow them to create polished final drafts and illustrate their work. Provide old magazines for clipped art.

11. Students should bind their final product and share their reports with each other. If students prepared hands-on projects, schedule due dates so that students have time to present those. You may grade these projects separately based on their creativity, relevance to the subject report, and complexity.

Project 3: List Poetry

Poetry is not normally thought of as expository writing. However, list poems are somewhat expository as they tell stories through organized lists of images or emotions and do not adhere to a time sequence. You will read examples of such poetry to your students, then lead them as they write poems. Although poetry is not normally "planned," you will teach your students to organize their thoughts and think up images before they write their poems.

You may incorporate these lessons into a longer poetry unit. Allow your students to write several versions of the three suggested forms, combine them with narrative-type poetry, and teach other forms such as haiku, sestina, acrostic, diamante, and cinquain. Students may publish "books" of their poetry, compile a class book, create greeting cards with their work, or decorate the classroom with poster-sized illustrated poems. Encourage interested students to copy their poems into poetry journals where they may write future poems. You may also allow students to memorize and recite their poems in front of the class. Finally, students may stage poetry readings of their original poems during a parent night.

Personal List Poem

Objective: Students will hear examples of expository poetry, then plan and write their own poems.

Materials: The Real Me, Take It or Leave It.

Note: Before class, write the poem you will model, if desired, and make a display of the sample.

The Real Me, Take It or Leave It

Jeans and t-shirts crumpled on my floor—
That's me.
Half-eaten moldy pizza under my bed—
It's mine.
I don't iron. I don't scrub.
I've got a ring around my tub.
Yes, I'm a slob—take it or leave it.

Math, science, reading, art—
I'm good at it all.
A's and B's and never C's,
I'm just plain smart.
You need your hard drive rewired?
I'm your gal.
That's right, I'm a messy geek—take it or leave it.

You can count on me to make chicken soup
When you get sick with the flu.
I never forget birthdays,
I give good advice,
And friends come to me
Whether they want to laugh or cry
Cause I'm a friendly sloppy nerd—take it or leave it.

You might be surprised
To hear I'm almost a rock-n-roll star.
I'm a whiz at the guitar.
And I have a great band.
The songs we write
Would blow your mind.
So if you need entertainment,
You know where to go.
To me, your jolly, untidy rockin' geek—take me or leave me.

---

1. Display and read The Real Me, Take It or Leave It.

2. Tell students this poem was planned with a pickle sandwich. The author described four main traits: she's messy, smart, a good friend, and a great guitar player. She gave details related to each trait.

3. Create a modified pickle sandwich with four pickles and work backward to plan it.
   a. Messy: un-ironed clothes on floor; moldy pizza on bed; no cleaning
   b. Smart: all subjects are easy; all A's and B's; good at fixing computers
   c. Good friend: make chicken soup; remember birthdays; give advice; friends like to talk
   d. Guitar player: good at guitar; in a band; write music; fun to watch

4. Discuss how such a bland plan sheet can create a fun, interesting poem. Ask students why the poem isn't as boring as indicated by the pickle sandwich. They should realize word choice is the biggest reason. Point out good word choices.

5. Discuss the poem's form: does it rhyme, does it have rhythm, and is there some sort of pattern? Tell students that this is called free verse. They are allowed to include patterns, rhyme, or rhythms, but are not required to. If they choose to incorporate rhyme and rhythm, they can include as much or as little as they wish. The poems need not be structured.

6. Create a pickle sandwich and instruct students to draw their own. Tell students you will model a personal poem as they work on theirs individually. You will write free verse poems describing yourselves in ways people may not be aware of. Emphasize that they shouldn't feel that they have to follow the sample. Encourage students to be honest; good poems don't lie.

7. Brainstorm a list of four traits that students might not know about you and instruct your students to do the same.

8. To prompt ideas, you can list a few "example" traits: bad cook; clean freak; funny; deep thinker; ice skater; scared of babies; singer; actress; baton twirler; popsicle house builder; big sister; jigsaw puzzle whiz; monopoly champ.

9. Begin your poem by verbalizing different ways of wording your stanzas. Model the process of choosing the best word combinations and style tools. Self-edit to help a strong voice come through. When you are done, display the final version.

10. Allow students to begin their poems and offer guidance. Encourage constant editing.

11. Students should TCUPSS their rough drafts and write final, polished copies.

12. Allow volunteers to read their poems aloud.

13. Poems can be graded effectively with the traditional rubric.

Contrasting Lists Poem

Objective: Students will write poems contrasting their world to another.

Materials: My World Is Not a Perfect World.

Note: Before class, write the poem you will model and make a display of the sample.

My World Is Not a Perfect World

So loud, who can sleep?

With police sirens and babies screaming?

Glass breaks, a car alarm shrieks,

A shopping cart creaks by on squeaky wheels.

I wake up to Gnnnah! Gnnnah! Gnnnah! Gnnnah!

Smash the clock to shut it up.

No pancakes, no sausage, no eggs, no toast,

Kitchen smells just like a cigarette butt.

Just juice: glug, glug, glug.

Run downstairs to catch the bus.

Rumble, screech, rumble, stop,

The bus weaves through noisy trucks

Honking cars and suffocating fumes.

And the kids up front they never shut up.

They shriek and laugh and actually play

As if they live in a different world than me.

Maybe lullabies put them to sleep,

And all through the night they don't hear a peep.

Bird songs and flapping butterfly wings,

They must wake up to those kinds of things

Along with the smell of coffee and waffles—

For breakfast I bet they get whipped cream and apples.

Sniff perfume and roses before they head to school

And, at the end of the day, dive into peaceful swimming pools.

---

1. Display and read My World Is Not a Perfect World. It describes the world the way the poet sees it and the way he wishes it could be. Students should be able to visualize the city the poet lives in even though he didn't name the place; they should also see the contrasting suburb.

2. Ask students to name the main thing the poet wants: quiet. Contrast the two stanzas: the first is "noisier," less rhythmic, and does not rhyme. The second, describing the perfect world, rhymes, flows rhythmically, and is quieter than the first. Its images are not jarring. Discuss why the poet did this.

3. Work backward to plan the poem. List the concrete images the poet used to symbolize each world. His world: police car, screaming baby, breaking glass, squeaky shopping cart, blaring alarm clock, cigarette butts, noisy trucks, cars, and bus, fumes. The perfect world: lullabies, bird songs, butterfly wings, coffee, waffles, whipped cream, apples, perfume, roses, swimming pool.

4. Draw your plan sheet—only two pickles are needed—and begin planning your model. Brainstorm as many concrete images as you can for the worlds you contrast.

5. Write your poem, emphasizing how concrete details and imagery evoke the worlds.

6. Ask students to plan two contrasting lists using concrete nouns and evocative adjectives. Encourage them to be unique. Tell them we all see the world a little differently and the "perfect world" is different for each of us. Also, their current world might be perfect. In that case, they may write about their perfect world and contrast it to the world of children living in imperfect situations. They may even write humorous poems to spoof the world or from an animal's perspective. Discuss how the real and perfect world might look for the following.
   a. A rich, but lonely child. His world: pretty, but sad; the perfect world: full of friends and family.
   b. A frog. His world: muddy and dirty; the perfect world: a clean aquarium.
   c. Homeless person. His world: cold and hungry; the perfect world: full cupboards.
   d. Scrooge. His world: cheerful, with Christmas; the perfect world: no Christmas.
   e. A princess. Her world: too frilly and pink. The perfect world: black and white.
   f. A child star. Her world: too much attention. The perfect world: some privacy.

7. Monitor student progress and provide help. Allow students to share completed poems.

Object List Poem

Objective: Students will write list poems about objects.

Materials: My Favorite Book.

Note: Before class, write the poem you will model and make a display of the sample. You may bring in the object you write about and encourage students to bring their objects, too.

My Favorite Book

Dog-eared, yellowed,

Stained with buttery cookies,

Its pages constantly threaten

To fall out and crumble.

Taped, re-taped, and re-taped,

But it still calls to me.

The voices inside break out,

The horses, the tree house, the prairie

They spring to life in my head.

That soft paper,

That sugary smell,

That warmth in my hands,

No movie can replace it.

I find it tucked in a corner,

Safe in its private space,

I hug it to my chest,

And get ready to unleash

The adventure inside.

1. Display and read My Favorite Book. Discuss the images, including physical descriptions, emotional reactions, and story elements that the poet uses to bring the book to life.

2. Discuss that the poet probably brainstormed many images before selecting the ones he used. Draw a plan sheet with one extra large pickle and make a list of the included images. Then, outside the pickle, list things the poet might have brainstormed but left out of the final poem.
   a. Included: pages are old, yellow, soft, sweet smelling with oily stains, taped, adventure story about horses on prairie; hidden behind couch for when I want to read it.
   b. Left out: Read ten times; a boy's struggle; takes one day to read; got it for my birthday.

3. Discuss how the images are arranged. Even though the poem is short, it has a beginning, middle, and end. Also, the object is named in the title, but is not directly mentioned again.

4. Display your object (if desired) and begin planning. Draw an extra large pickle under a small bun. Name your item in the bun and brainstorm concrete images you associate with the object in the pickle. Then choose what you consider to be the best images for the final poem.

5. As you model the poem, discuss different ways of organizing the items in the list to best tell about your inanimate object. Discuss syntax and why you choose to write your poem the way you do. Your poem need not be eighteen lines long.

6. Unless your students have already chosen objects and brought them into class, encourage them to brainstorm objects that hold special meaning to them. They should choose items that evoke multiple memories or images.

7. In one extra large pickle, have students brainstorm physical characteristics and emotions attached to their objects. Encourage them to use sensory details, Awe-Inspiring Adjectives, and crisp nouns to convey the feelings and facts related to their objects. Then ask students to choose the best items on their brainstormed list. There is no limit to the length of the poem, but discuss how less is often more.

8. Allow students to read poems aloud when they have been TCUPSSed and redrafted.

10 Beyond Tests and Stories: Applying Narrative Writing Knowledge

Your students can write expository and narrative essays effortlessly, and now many have added journalism, research reports, and poetry to their repertoire. However, they are also likely giving you bored "end of year" stares. Reenergize them with the following narrative-related projects.

NARRATIVE-RELATED PROJECTS

Narrative writing projects include autobiographies, chapter books, plays, and poetry. Be prepared to introduce the projects with published examples. Allow students to read a short autobiographical sketch written from a child's point of view before writing autobiographies. Read and discuss short serial chapter stories before they write theirs. Review plays and act them out before you introduce playwriting. And immerse your students in poetry while teaching them to write it.

Project 1: Autobiographies

Autobiographies are fun narratives that allow your students to tell the interesting things that have happened to them since they were born.

In writing autobiographies, your students will be given five headings: my first few years; my family; my home and home life; school life and friends; and my future. You may add topics to extend this project. Also, this is an ideal project to allow your students to publish and bind. As such, you may teach word processing skills during this lesson by allowing students to type and print out final drafts on computers. If you do this, provide disks for students to save their work as they proceed. Students can illustrate printed pages with icons, personal photos, uploaded digital pictures, or magazine photos.

My First Few Years

Objectives: Students will learn how to begin their autobiographies; they will write about their childhood, from birth to kindergarten.

Materials: Figure 10.1; your written model.

Note: Before class, write your model based on Figure 10.1. You will work backward to plan this. Make a display of the sample.

Figure 10.1   My First Few Years

> The day I was born, my older sister, Jeannie, had her fifth birthday party. I was supposed to come two weeks later, but my mom thinks I heard the commotion and wanted to join the party. I was born after the party was over, so I didn't get to eat cake, play with clowns, or watch the magician. But my little brown eyes were probably too scrunched up anyway; I wouldn't have seen a thing.
>
> From the day I was born, I was a party animal, though. By the time I was two, I sang and danced whenever I could. If we had guests, I'd put on my shiny purple leotard, pink tutu, and Burger King crown, and I'd perform Little Orphan Annie songs. I've seen videos of me doing this. I wasn't very good and my black hair always looked like a gigantic bird's nest. But people clapped anyway. My mom says I was a ham, but I wasn't fat. My brown, skinny body looked more like a vibrating, shriveled up piece of bacon whenever I performed.
>
> As I grew up, I started enjoying playing pretend newscaster. I'd play pretend by myself all the time because Jeannie thought the game was stupid. I'd walk around interviewing things in the house because everyone in my family was sick of me interviewing them. As a pretend news announcer, I talked to all sorts of famous people. Of course, they were pretend famous people.
>
> My first day of kindergarten, I was so excited I even let my mom comb my hair. As soon as I met the other kids, I started playing pretend. I pretended the kids were famous movie stars I was interviewing. No one understood the game, and the teacher didn't like me bossing kids around because that was her job. I got along okay, though, because for most of kindergarten, I pretended to be the world's best kindergartner.

Copyright © 2006 by Karen Donohue and Nanda N. Reddy. All rights reserved. Reprinted from *180 Days to Successful Writers: Lessons to Prepare Your Students for Standardized Assessments and for Life* by Karen Donohue and Nanda N. Reddy. Thousand Oaks, CA: Corwin Press, www.corwinpress.com. Reproduction authorized only for the local school site or nonprofit organization that has purchased this book.

1. Discuss the meaning of autobiography: written by the person whose life story is described, comprehensive to the point they've lived. Most are written by famous people, describing life achievements. Discuss that even though you are calling this an "autobiography" project, it will be considered a memoir when students are older, covering a short period of their lives.

2. Display and read Figure 10.1, My First Few Years. Ask students if this is narrative or expository writing. They should see that it is more like a narrative—story-like, using a time continuum. However, they should notice that it has no central conflict and some expository elements. Tell students autobiographies are mainly narratives with some expository lists and explanations.

3. Work backward to plan the sample. Draw a tier cake without the lines that create the setting, character, and conflict boxes in the top tier. Tell students you don't need these because there isn't a main conflict or main setting. Instead, you will write a description of the author there. Discuss that the description is woven throughout the piece. In the topic sentence area, write "My First Few Years."

4. In the remaining tiers, sketch the author's story. As you do this, point out time progression, minor conflicts, interesting details, and reasons the piece feels like it has a beginning, middle, and end even though it's not a traditional story.

5. Tell students they will plan their own autobiographies as you plan yours. Like the example, you will all start from birth and work up to kindergarten. You will describe your general personality and preschool experience. Emphasize that students should only include interesting details. They should relate funny, weird, or unique anecdotes, focusing on minor conflicts.

6. Draw your plan, write the description of yourself, and start with the earliest stories you've heard about yourself. As you plan, think of boring anecdotes that will not be in your final piece; decide verbally that they are not interesting enough and leave them out of your plan. This shows students how to filter out mundane information.

7. In boxes two and three of the tier cake, move on to your toddler and preschool years. Box four and the "conclusion" box should be used to tell your kindergarten story. Tell students that it would be boring to say: "I was five when I started kindergarten." Everyone starts kindergarten around that age. A more interesting story might start like this: "The first day of kindergarten, I insisted on wearing my old cowboy boots." Relate your interesting story to complete the plan.

8. Observe and help students as they complete their plans.

9. Display your modeled example. Discuss how you turned your plan into an interesting narrative. Point out anecdotes and discuss how you wove in your physical description. In the event you were unable to write the model in advance, model the process of organizing information about your childhood into a narrative.

10. Post your completed copy or the sample for reference.

11. Guide students as they write their first autobiography page.

Family, Home, School, and the Future

Objective: Students will complete their autobiographies.

Materials: Figures 10.2 to 10.5; your complete autobiography.

Note: Before class each day, make a display of the sample and use it to write your model page.

Figure 10.2 My Family

Some days I think my family is the best in the world, and some days I want to trade them in for a new one. But overall, I guess they're okay. Jeannie, my older sister, is fifteen years old, and Davie is my four-year-old baby brother. Jeannie's really cool unless she's being grumpy and acting like a know-it-all. Davie is a brat twenty-four/seven. I only like him when he's watching videos and staying out of my hair. And my parents—well, I guess they're normal parents.

My dad works at home, so I see him the most. He makes my breakfast and lunch, and he picks me up from school every day before he picks Davie up from day care. Our special thing is singing in the car. He runs a computer company, so he's always on the computer. But he'll leave the computer to play basketball with Jeannie and me any time, and I like playing with him because he doesn't cheat the way Jeannie does.

My mom works at a bank and she's always rushing me out the door to school in the morning. Then when she gets home, she forces Jeannie and me to do our homework at the kitchen table while she makes dinner and tries to keep Davie from banging pots and pans. My mom is the strict one, always yelling at me about my messy room and tangled hair. But she can be okay, too, like when she bakes chocolate chip cookies or reads the Narnia books (with voices) to me at night.

My family's best times are on weekends. Every Saturday morning, we hit ten garage sales. Later, we'll picnic or barbeque at the park, or we'll clean the house while dancing to loud radio music. Saturday nights we play games like Monopoly (my mother always wins), Scrabble (Jeannie's favorite), or charades (what I'm good at). I love weekends with my family.

The only time I don't like my family is when they gang up on me, like the time I got a mean note from my teacher saying I talk too much. But overall they don't gang up on me too much, and I'm glad they're my family. I'll keep them.

Copyright © 2006 by Karen Donohue and Nanda N. Reddy. All rights reserved. Reprinted from *180 Days to Successful Writers: Lessons to Prepare Your Students for Standardized Assessments and for Life* by Karen Donohue and Nanda N. Reddy. Thousand Oaks, CA: Corwin Press, www.corwinpress.com. Reproduction authorized only for the local school site or nonprofit organization that has purchased this book.

Figure 10.3 Home and Home Life

The first place I ever lived was Atlanta, Georgia. That's where I was born and where my family lived until I was two. We lived in a little blue house with huge trees, but I don't remember any of it. I only know that house from pictures.

When I was two, we moved to North Carolina for my father's computer job. We lived in an apartment then. I shared a room with Jeannie, and I had my own twin bed. We lived there until I was six, when Davie was born. I didn't want to move at first because I liked the elevators at the apartment. But when I heard we were moving to Florida and that I'd get my own room, I was the first one to start packing the apartment.

However, I didn't get my own room right away. My parents wanted to build our house from scratch, and while we waited for the house to get done, we lived in a huge trailer in the backyard of our unbuilt house. I shared a room with Jeannie again, but I didn't mind because there was a curtain in the middle of the room that separated me from Jeannie. I made my mom hang curtains all around the room on the walls so I could pretend I was a princess. My mom hung the most beautiful white curtains all around my room. Well, they were really white sheets, but they were beautiful.

After our house was built, we didn't get rid of the trailer. It sat in our yard, and it's still one of my favorite things about our new house. Anytime I want to get away, I can go and sit in my old curtained room in the trailer. I pretend I live on my own and I'll even make my own grilled cheese sandwiches in the old kitchen. But even though I love the trailer, I love my new house. It's a two-storied house with a ton of stairs to run up and down on. I hope we live in it forever and keep the trailer in the back of course.

Copyright © 2006 by Karen Donohue and Nanda N. Reddy. All rights reserved. Reprinted from *180 Days to Successful Writers: Lessons to Prepare Your Students for Standardized Assessments and for Life* by Karen Donohue and Nanda N. Reddy. Thousand Oaks, CA: Corwin Press, www.corwinpress.com. Reproduction authorized only for the local school site or nonprofit organization that has purchased this book.

Figure 10.4   School Life and Friends

What can I say about school—I'm stuck there till I'm 18! Actually, it's not that bad unless I'm getting in trouble for talking. I like my classmates and I have two best friends in my class. I do kind of miss school when we're on vacation. Sometimes, during really long breaks, I even miss Mrs. Dietrich, my fourth-grade teacher.

I'm not the best student (not like Leo Perry), but I'm not the worst either (I won't name names). I make As and Bs, and my best subjects are reading, writing, and spelling. One of my favorite projects ever was our class play. I plan on becoming an actor when I'm older, so I know a thing or two about plays. That's why I made myself honorary director. But some kids can't take criticism, so Mrs. Dietrich told me to stop bossing people around. The play would have been better if everyone took my advice; when I'm famous, they'll regret it. The subject I can do without is math, but Mrs. Dietrich says actors need math skills to manage their money. I plan on being a really rich actor, so I'm letting Dad get me a math tutor. Pretty soon, I'll be ready for Broadway!

I hang out with my best friends Cameron (a girl) and Taylor (a boy) a lot during school. Some teachers call us the three stooges because we're always doing silly things. One day at recess, we tricked Mrs. Dietrich into doing a chicken dance. Kids still talk about that. Cameron, Taylor, and I are always thinking up pranks to pull on teachers and other kids. But we have to be careful with the kid pranks because once we accidentally hurt someone's feelings and got in trouble. Lately, we've been making up silly sketches to act out for our class during lunch and recess. Taylor's very good at voices and Cameron is a pro at writing little songs. So since I'm a natural actress, we make a great team. Even though school isn't always fun (like during math time every day), I don't mind it much. I have a good teacher and great friends, so I'm in no hurry for 18 to get here.

Copyright © 2006 by Karen Donohue and Nanda N. Reddy. All rights reserved. Reprinted from *180 Days to Successful Writers: Lessons to Prepare Your Students for Standardized Assessments and for Life* by Karen Donohue and Nanda N. Reddy. Thousand Oaks, CA: Corwin Press, www.corwinpress.com. Reproduction authorized only for the local school site or nonprofit organization that has purchased this book.

Figure 10.5   My Future

In front of a camera is where I belong! That's what everyone says, from Jeannie to Mrs. Dietrich to Cameron, and how is it possible for so many people to be wrong? It's not, because that is exactly where I'll be when I'm older. I just know it.

I used to want to be a reporter because I really liked the lady on the six o'clock news. She wore the best little suits, had great hair, and asked people all kinds of great questions. But my hair isn't something that's easy to tame, so I gave up that plan pretty quickly.

Figure 10.5 (Continued)

To prepare for my life as an actress, I practice plenty. I often "get into character" at home and play different roles. My mom really hates my "bratty Princess" character, but it's one of my favorite roles. Kids at school love it when I get into that character. I plan to sign up for any play or talent show that's being put on in middle and high school and to take every acting class. I also want to try out for talent shows on TV, but mom says I have to wait till I'm thirteen.

My dream is to go to a big university in New York and study drama after high school. I'll try out for parts on Broadway, in commercials, and on TV shows. Those will help me land a big movie role one day. I know my family will support me the whole time and they'll be rewarded for it. I plan to buy my family whatever they want when I'm rich and famous. I just want everyone in my family to be happy and for my mom to be able to quit her stressful bank job. I also plan to use my fame and money to help feed the starving kids around the world when I can afford to do that.

I know I'll be a successful actress when I grow up, so I don't understand why my mom insists that I have a backup plan. But since I have to have one, I guess I could study writing and reading so that I could write plays and movies even if I'm not in them. But I know that won't happen because I plan to work hard to make my dream come true.

Copyright © 2006 by Karen Donohue and Nanda N. Reddy. All rights reserved. Reprinted from *180 Days to Successful Writers: Lessons to Prepare Your Students for Standardized Assessments and for Life* by Karen Donohue and Nanda N. Reddy. Thousand Oaks, CA: Corwin Press, www.corwinpress.com. Reproduction authorized only for the local school site or nonprofit organization that has purchased this book.

1. Follow the format given for My First Few Years. Read the sample, plan it backward, plan yours as students plan theirs, read and discuss your model, and guide students through their own work. Use the following to help students plan and write each remaining section.

2. In the Family section, a more expository-like section, include poignant or touching anecdotes if possible. Write brief descriptions of family members, including quirky habits and jobs. Discuss favorite activities and family traditions. Focus on minor family conflicts, including sibling rivalry and problems with parental rules.

3. In the Home and Home Life section, write descriptions of your home including favorite rooms and smells. How did you decorate your room? Do you share a room? Discuss different places you've lived and what you miss or hated about them. Describe hobbies and typical, but interesting facts about life in your home. What is your yard like, and what do you do there?

4. In School Life and Friends, discuss what makes you stand out in school. What makes you unique, different, etc.? It might be that you are a troublemaker, a ham, a class clown, smart, observant, etc. Discuss school friends, including good and bad times. Highlight any conflicts with friends and teachers, or minor internal conflicts.

5. In My Future, write about what you see for your future. What will you become when you're older? Imagine life in middle and high school.

What will you do that's different and meaningful to the world? What will your family be like? What are your dreams?

6. Allow students to TCUPSS and polish their rough drafts. They may turn drafts in for grading as they complete each section, allowing you to provide valuable feedback as they complete the project. Allow students to publish final drafts as desired.

Project 2: Chapter Books

Chapter books, as presented here, adapt easily to the narrative structure you have been using. However, instead of writing separate narratives, students will write five related narratives.

Students will write serial narrative stories about a single animal character. Each narrative will feature a different, but related conflict. You can remind students of the Peter Rabbit and Pooh stories, which are serial stories about animal characters. Resource H is an easy template that can help students publish their books; however, you may choose any method of publishing.

One way to extend this project is by turning your class into a publishing house to simulate the real process of book publishing. You may "hire" students to act as editors, illustrators, or publishers. Editors and editorial teams will spend time poring over the stories, fixing mistakes, and suggesting changes or improvements to the authors. Illustrators can draw pictures and cover art for the books. Publishers can type up the stories, paste art in appropriate places, and bind the book according to preference.

If another classroom is writing chapter stories, you can also collaborate to act as each other's publishing house; or you may split your class into two publishing houses that swap stories. Students may even start a "professional" rapport with their peers to discuss editorial needs. To further extend, you could turn your project into a fundraiser and teach invaluable lessons about business and finance. However, such a project will take intense planning as students will have to act as marketers and advertisers, and each publishing house would have to choose their best works for publication. Further, you will need to gather resources in order to produce numerous copies of chosen books.

Character Sketches

Objectives: Students will plan serial stories and sketch main characters for their chapter books.

Materials: Sample books; Figure 10.6.

Note: Before class, collect books that feature stories about animals, especially serial stories. Make a display and student copies of Figure 10.6. Also, if desired, be prepared to provide research time for students to study their animals in Step 5.

Figure 10.6 Character Sketch One

Name: _____ Animal: _____

Portrait:

Description

Age: _____

Hair/skin: _____

Face: _____

Clothes: _____

Height/Weight: _____

Habits: _____

Defining characteristics: _____

Home/Family:

Home: _____

Family: _____

Friends: _____

Likes and dislikes:

Food and drink: _____

Activities/hobbies: _____

Hopes and Dreams

Wishes for: _____

Wants to be when grown up: _____

Copyright © 2006 by Karen Donohue and Nanda N. Reddy. All rights reserved. Reprinted from *180 Days to Successful Writers: Lessons to Prepare Your Students for Standardized Assessments and for Life* by Karen Donohue and Nanda N. Reddy. Thousand Oaks, CA: Corwin Press, www.corwinpress.com. Reproduction authorized only for the local school site or nonprofit organization that has purchased this book.

1. Tell students they will be writing chapter stories. Introduce the concept by showing them familiar chapter stories and reading sample chapters or excerpts. Discuss realistic and fantastical stories, such as *Charlotte's Web* and *Trumpet of the Swan* by E. B. White, *Runaway Ralph* and *Socks* by Beverly Cleary, *Bunnicula* by Deborah Howe, *Sounder* by William Armstrong, *Black Beauty* by Anna Sewell, *Incredible Journey* by Sheila Burnford, and *Just So Stories* by Rudyard Kipling.

2. Tell students that they will plan each of five chapters like separate narratives with different conflicts. However, the conflicts are related and sequential, and the characters, which will be animals, stay the same. Conflicts for the five chapters follow.
   - In Chapter 1, the character will run away from home for some reason.
   - In Chapter 2, the character will be hungry, homeless, and get lost.
   - In Chapter 3, the character will devise a plan to get home, but the plan fails.
   - In Chapter 4, a new friend tricks the animal and gets the character in trouble.
   - In Chapter 5, the animal gets out of trouble and goes home.

3. The details of the plot are up to the students and depend on the animals and circumstances.

4. Allow students to brainstorm animal characters. Suggest unusual choices such as armadillos, hippos, platypuses, parrots, and koalas.

5. When students select their animals, display and pass out copies of Figure 10.6, Character Sketch One. Tell them that they need to know their characters before writing about them. If desired, students may research their animals to find interesting facts.

6. Model the character sketch for students with an animal character you make up, and then observe student work. You may follow this example.
   - Dylan, aka "Aristotle," is an Armadillo. Age: one (ten in human years). No hair, pink skin, pink nose, pointy ears, and tiny purple spots on his shell (an exoskeleton).
   - Wears glasses (he invented those), weighs five pounds, is very clean, and is smart.
   - Home: hollow of a tree with parents and nineteen siblings; has one friend, Tim the turtle.
   - Enjoys inventing things, strawberry plants, green beetles, and clean water (no mud).
   - Hates cold weather, the smell of pine, and peppers (which can look like strawberries).
   - Dreams that one day people won't think armadillos are dumb, blind pointless animals.
   - Wants to be the Armadillo Leader when he grows up and invent great things.

7. Allow students to complete their character sketches. Use the following questions to help.

- What does the animal look like? Is it strangely colored, dirty, or eight feet tall? Does it fit in with its type or is it different from other animals? Is it well dressed? What are the defining traits for the character, its good and bad habits, and ways of speaking (proper, slang, etc.)? Does the animal stutter? Does it often chew its nails?

- Does the character live with humans or other animals? Does it live in a house, zoo, or an animal-like dwelling in the wild? Does it wear clothes? Is it rich or poor? Is it nice or mean? Does it usually get in trouble or help people get out of trouble?

- What are his favorite foods—human food or animal food? And does it enjoy human activities or animal activities like digging, chewing wood, etc.? What are his goals—human related or animal related?

From Outline to Story Draft

Objective: Students will finish planning their chapter books.

Materials: Previously written character sketches; Aristotle Leaves Home.

Note: Before class, decide on a method of publication; you may use Resource H. Also, make a display of the sample chapter, Aristotle Leaves Home.

1. Display and read the sample Chapter 1. Discuss style, characterization, and original aspects of the story. Note that the story starts with dialogue, while introducing the setting, characters, and a conflict. Many of Aristotle's character traits show up as the plot moves along so that readers can form a strong image of him. Also, the story blends human traits with animal traits. Discuss his motivation for running away and his goals. Ask students what they think would happen to him and if he'd reach his goals.

Aristotle Leaves Home

"My name is Aristotle!" the spunky little armadillo shouted, jumping up and down on his hind legs. Aristotle hardly ever shouted or jumped, but he was sensitive about his name.

"Well the last time I checked your birth certificate, it said your name was Dylan. So get used to it, *Dylan*." Maddie, Aristotle's little sister, wasn't his only sibling who still called him Dylan. Most of his nineteen siblings did it when they wanted to get on his nerves. The sun had set and the two armadillos were out gathering the family's dinner. Maddie was mad at Aristotle because he refused to collect grubs. Instead, Aristotle insisted on going after hard-to-catch shiny green beetles, his favorite food, with a new invention he made.

"That dumb thing won't work," Maddie complained. "And because of you, Dylan, we'll be out hunting food all night. Or we'll starve!"

Aristotle grumbled and adjusted his glasses, another one of his inventions. He hated his siblings, always making fun of his name change and treating him like another blind, bumbling rodent. Couldn't they see

---

that he was smarter than the average armadillo and needed a name to live up to that? He refused to talk to Maddie and continued shaking his beetle catcher (a tin can with a leaf funnel on top) under the bushes. He had caught quite a few beetles, eleven to be exact, and on a normal night, an armadillo is lucky to get two or three. His invention was working. The two worked for another hour, Maddie jabbering away, and Aristotle caught fifteen more beetles.

"Is this it?" their father growled when they got back to the hollow under the tree. "Look at Maddie, with three cans full of grubs. And all you show up with is this mouthful of beetles?"

"But they're a delicacy," Aristotle insisted. "I mean, we always eat those filthy gritty grubs for dinner. But how often do we have beetles?"

"We don't need delicacies. We've got twenty mouths to feed, and this won't do it." His father shook Aristotle's can of beetles, then passed it around to the kids. "Next time, you do as you're told, Aristotle. And take that shiny toy off your face. It's distracting me and you look silly."

You're the silly ones, and you'll regret treating me this way, Aristotle thought as he stormed off to bed, his stomach growling. He decided right then and there that he had had enough of his family. They were only holding him back, keeping him from working on his inventions. He'd never make the armadillo world better if he continued living with them, and he'd never become the armadillo's first leader like he dreamed.

He was glad to be alone in the room he shared with his ten brothers. He quickly packed his things: an inventor's kit that his turtle friend Tim gave him for his birthday, and the encyclopedia (volume A) he found one day. He wrapped everything in his cleaning rag and tied it with some string from his inventor's kit before strapping it to his back. Then he started digging a hole to go under the tree's trunk. Even though he normally hated digging (it was such a dirty job), it was the only way to leave the hollow unnoticed. Plus, when his brothers saw the hole, they'd know he ran away, and he didn't feel like leaving a note because only Armand could read.

On the other side of the trunk, Aristotle cleaned his glasses and breathed in deeply. He felt free and excited for the first time in a long time. "Look out world, here I come," he whispered, and shuffled off into the night.

2. Ask students to take out five sheets of paper, one for each chapter, and draw narrative plans on each sheet. They should label the sheets Chapters 1 through 5, and write in the conflict for each chapter as presented in the previous lesson.

3. Tell them you will model plans as they write their own. Begin modeling Chapter 1. You may use the example chapter as a guide. Discuss why your character wants to run away and how the character will do it. The chapter should begin with characters at home and end with them

successfully running away. After you plan, observe and guide student work. Model the plans for the other chapters similarly; note that other sample chapters are not provided.

4. Chapter 2 should begin with the character finding a place to stay after running away. The character will experience trials and tribulations of being alone. The character will wander, possibly looking for food or company, and should end up lost at the end of the chapter.

5. In Chapter 3, the character will get fed up with being alone, want to go home, and devise plans to do so. Along the way, the character meets a stranger who acts like a friend. The friend distracts the character, and they have some fun together. But the character's plan to get home fails.

6. During Chapter 4, the main character finds out that the new friend is not really a friend. The friend tricks or uses the character, causing the character to get into trouble.

7. In Chapter 5, when all seems lost, the character is saved or finds a way home. The character is thankful to be home and decides never to run away again.

8. Guide your students to work on one chapter at a time using their plan sheets. If desired, you may write out your story pages as a model or continue the story started by the sample. However, this is not necessary as this lesson closely mimics the traditional narrative short story. Remind students to include their characters' odd traits as they write to make the stories interesting, and remind them to use the writing tools they've learned, such as metaphors, similes, Awe-Inspiring Adjectives, and Vivacious Verbs.

9. As students complete chapters, remind them to TCUPSS. Grade the chapters with a standard rubric as students complete them and offer advice accordingly.

10. When students have completed a full first draft of their chapter stories, they may move on to publication. Students may write polished drafts on copies of Resource H. This template can be copied two sided, folded over, and stapled to create a lined blank book. The template has boxes for illustrations. Students should create separate illustrated covers.

11. Allow students to share their books. You may instruct students to summarize their stories orally for the class and then read excerpts or favorite passages.

Project 3: Plays

Playwriting allows students to format narratives in a unique fashion. Students need to become familiar with special terms related to scripts and technical aspects of writing a play. To thoroughly familiarize students with these special aspects, preface this lesson by having your students read and act out plays.

Extend this project by allowing your students to produce their plays completely, including props and costumes. If you choose to do this and a stage is available, you may allow your students to write their plays on stage to help them visualize the play. Students will need to memorize their lines, practice on stage, and then put on the plays. Production time will vary, depending on the scale of your project and size of your audience. Students will need time and materials to produce props and costumes, to practice with these props and stage directions, and to learn to set up and dismantle props efficiently. Additionally, they may need help and lessons focusing on enunciation, acting, and dealing with a large audience.

Introducing Plays and Sketches (Pair Lesson)

Objectives: Students will learn special terms associated with plays and write short sketches.

Materials: Playwriting terms; playwriting rules; sketch summaries.

1. Tell students that they will begin writing plays today. Discuss the following playwriting terms. Students should have learned some of these when they read and acted out plays.

Playwriting Terms

Act: A major section of a play. Most modern plays have three acts—the beginning, middle, and end. Each act may be divided into scenes.

Cast: The actors who play the characters. One actor may portray more than one character so the cast does not have to be as large as the list of characters.

Characters: A list of different people who show up in the play, including those whose voices are heard. The same actor may play several characters.

Costume: The clothing worn by characters. Certain characters wear distinct clothing to distinguish them or help define their jobs and personalities.

Dialogue: The conversation between characters, not written with quotes.

Mime: To act out something and show objects without words or props.

Narrator: A speaker who is not part of the play but who tells the audience important information. He may or may not be seen.

Prop: An object that an actor touches or uses during the play.

Set: The stage where the play occurs. It may include props, background decoration, and items to suggest a setting. Example: couch = living room.

Sketch: A short, light-hearted play, often funny.

Sound effect: Written in parentheses, a sound made by an actor on- or off-stage.

Stage direction: Written in parentheses, a direction to an actor giving him an action to do as he says his lines.

Suggested props and costumes: Props and costumes that actors pretend are present (e.g., an actor miming eating a banana or fixing his clothes).

2. Tell students they will write short sketches today to practice using these terms and the playwriting rules.

3. Model the following sketch, "The Power of the Dark," for students. Discuss that since this is a sketch, there are no acts, only one scene.

The Power of the Dark

Characters: Chris, Sam, Narrator

Scene: A bedroom during a blackout.

Narrator: Eight-year-old twin brothers, Chris and Sam, have been sent to their room by their parents for fighting. But the power just went out.

   (Chris enters the bedroom tentatively with a flashlight; Sam pushes past him.)

Chris: (Angrily) Hey, you better watch it.

Sam: Yeah? Or else what?

Chris: Or else . . . or else . . . I'm gonna hit you with this flashlight.

Sam: (Throwing himself onto the bed) I'd like to see you try. And I'd like to see you get out of a whipping when dad finds out.

   (Sam tosses a pillow at Chris just as a soft hiss comes from the closet.)

Chris: (Nervously) Did you hear that?

Sam: I heard you whimper like a baby, that's what I heard.

Chris: It came from the closet.

Sam: Well if you're so sure, go see what it is.

   (A minute later, a loud hiss comes from under Sam's bed as he jumps on it to get settled.)

   Wait a minute. Wh . . . what was that? Did you hear that?

   (Chris scrambles under his sheets and nods vigorously.)

   Hand me that flashlight.

   (Chris throws the flashlight too hard and it rolls under the bed. The hiss repeats and then the light goes out. Both boys shriek.)

Chris: (Whispering) Sam? What do you think it is?

Sam: (Whispering even lower) I don't know.

Chris: Are you scared? Do you want to come over there?

Sam: Yeah, sure, if you want me to.

(Sam creeps over to Chris's bed and the boys fall asleep nervously.)

Narrator: In the morning, their parents are surprised to find them huddled together. And the boys are embarrassed when they find the cause of the hisses. A ball in the closet hissed as it deflated, and a toy snake wedged under the bed hissed whenever Sam's bed moved vigorously. The flashlight hit the toy snake causing a second hiss, and the flashlight went out because the batteries became dislodged when it fell.

4. After modeling the sketch, point out the following playwriting rules and how you used them.

Seven Golden Rules of Playwriting

1. Identify characters. All characters that appear or speak should be listed at the beginning of the script. Use the fewest number of characters possible.

2. Tell the settings. The setting is described to identify each scene.

3. Do not use quotation marks. Write the name of the character followed by a colon, and then write the character's words.

4. Begin a new line for each speech. Start each character's words on a new line, no matter how short, and keep all speech indented at the same place for easy reading.

5. If not spoken, parenthesize. Write all stage directions (e.g. dance, walk away, etc.) and sound effects (e.g., cough, birds chirping, etc.) in parentheses, using present tense, when the actor should perform or hear them.

6. Narrate briefly. The narrator should have the fewest lines. Do not allow the narrator to tell the story; the characters should.

7. Tell the actors how to feel. Use directions (annoyed, sweetly, hurried, etc.) and punctuation (ellipses, exclamation points, etc.) to help actors portray emotions.

---

5. Display and review the following list of sketch summaries.
   a. A magician loses his rabbit in a classroom while performing a trick.
   b. A fairy is discovered by a human and tries to disguise herself.
   c. A forgetful teacher picks up the wrong students from lunch.
   d. A veterinarian examines a squirmy puppy.
   e. A shopper knocks over a display in a grocery store.
   f. A farmer discovers someone has turned his cornfield into a maze.

6. Choose one summary to write a whole class two-character sketch. Tell students that they are in charge and allow them to volunteer all of the information to write and format the sketch. After completing the sketch, read and discuss.

7. Pair up students to write two-character sketches based on one of the remaining summaries. You may assign summaries or allow students to choose.

8. Students should TCUPSS and edit sketches. Allow students to share their sketches.

9. If desired, extend this lesson by allowing students or pairs to write longer sketches based on all of the above ideas or their own ideas.

Three-Act Plays (Group Lesson)

Objectives: Students will plan and write scenes in a three-act play.

Materials: Play outlines.

Note: Before class, organize your students into four groups.

1. Discuss the difference between a sketch (only one short scene) and a three-act play (three or more scenes since some acts include several scenes).

2. Display and read the following outline for a play about friendship.

A Play About Friendship—6 scenes

Act One: (Trouble begins)
Scene One: A person and best friend (BF) are fishing. Something occurs, they argue, separate.
Scene Two: The person meets another friend and vents about BF. The second friend suggests the person not invite BF to a birthday party.

Act Two: (Trouble intensifies)
Scene One: The person and second friend plan the birthday party; BF overhears.
Scene Two: BF confronts the person, wishes to make up. But the person says he has a new best friend.

Act Three: (Trouble ends)
Scene One: During party, the person gets annoyed by friend two and misses BF.
Scene Two: The person works to regain BF's friendship.

---

3. Discuss that the outline is generic—the details are up to the playwrights. Relate this outline to the list of conflicts given for the chapter books. Tell students they will use the outline to write a complete play with five scenes in three acts and that you will write the first scene together.

4. Draw a narrative plan sheet and use the outline to plan the first scene as a class. Choose characters, a setting, and a conflict; then use student suggestions to sketch the plot.

5. Use the plan to write the scene following the "Seven Golden Rules of Playwriting."

6. Group students. Explain that each group will complete one of the remaining scenes. Assign scenes or allow groups to choose scenes they will write.

7. Instruct students to plan their scenes. They should continue the story and use characters introduced in scene one. However, they may introduce new characters. Their settings and conflicts will be different from Scene one.

8. After planning, groups should write their scenes. Observe student work and collaboration.

9. Students should TCUPSS scenes, then share their scenes even if the scenes do not come together to create a seamless play.

Three-Act Plays (Independent Practice)

Objective: Students will work in groups to write three-act plays.

Materials: Figure 10.7.

Note: Before class, photocopy and cut apart the play outlines on Figure 10.7. Plan to group students so that each member can write one scene (i.e., three groups of six, two groups of five). If necessary, create another set of outlines.

Figure 10.7   Play Outlines

Play One: A Twisted Fairy Tale—6 scenes

Act One: (Stumbling onto trouble)
  Scene One: A princess and her favorite maid sneak off into the forbidden woods to play.
  Scene Two: The princess dresses up as Robin Hood and her maid dresses as Merry Man. As they play, they hear a cry for help.

Act Two: (Messing with trouble)
  Scene One: A famous prince (whom no one likes) and his horse are trapped in a bog. The prince thinks the princess is a woodsman and pleads for the woodsman to save him.
  Scene Two: The princess and the maid conspire. They tease the prince. They pretend they won't save him until he agrees to marry the person of the princess's choice.

Act Three: (A twisted end)
  Scene One: The prince agrees and the girls pull him out with rope, then they all work on the horse. The princess and the maid reveal themselves.
  Scene Two: The prince thinks he'll be marrying the princess or her beautiful maid, but the princess chooses an old, hardworking scullery maid to be the prince's bride.

Play Two: An Accident—5 scenes

Act One: (Oops)
  Scene One: Two friends are sledding. The first friend convinces the second to build an obstacle course through the trees even though the second friend doesn't think it's a good idea.
  Scene Two: The obstacle course is dangerous, but fun. The friends invite a third friend to join them and the first friend dares the third one to do a careless stunt. He smashes into a tree.

(Continued)

Figure 10.7 (Continued)

Act Two: (What now?)
  Scene One: The friends are afraid and the first one runs away, not wanting to get in trouble. The second stays and discovers the third friend has broken a leg.
  Scene Two: The second friend puts the third onto the sled and carefully drags him down. He takes him home and calls for help.

Act Three: (Problem solved)
  Scene One: Neither the second or third friend gets in trouble, and the third friend's leg heals. But when the first friend invites them camping, they both decline.

Play Three: Switcharoo—5 scenes

Act One: (A troubling idea)
  Scene One: Two identical twins are studying for tests. One has trouble with math, the other with English. They try helping each other.
  Scene Two: They continue to have trouble, but decide they'll pull an old stunt; they plan to switch places and take each other's tests the following day.

Act Two: (The idea in action)
  Scene One: At school the next day, they meet in the bathroom and switch for math and English class. Their teachers suspect the switch and come up with a plan.
  Scene Two: Everything goes well until one twin gets called by the PE teacher to demonstrate something and the other twin gets called by the office to review some documents.

Act Three: (The idea fails)
  Scene One: The twins can't do the tasks they're called to do and their crimes are discovered. They both earn a punishment and fail their tests.

Play Four: The Shipwreck—6 scenes

Act One: (A troubled sea)
  Scene One: Friends are kayaking near the ocean. They accidentally go out farther than they intended.
  Scene Two: A storm brews and tosses them around. They lose sight of land as night falls.

Act Two: (A more troubling island)
  Scene One: The storm rages and they crash. They wake up that morning on a rocky island.
  Scene Two: They hear things crashing inland on the island, strange moans, and squeals. They make a fire and write HELP in the sand, but they are starving.
  Scene Three: They enter the wooded island in search of food and get chased by wild pigs.

Act Three: (A soothing cut)
  Scene One: After they make it to a cave, they see someone running after the wild pigs with a camera and microphone. They hear, "Cut!" as the cameraman spots them. A crew is using the island to make a film and saves the friends.

Play Five: Haunted—6 scenes

Act One: (A disturbing phenomenon)
  Scene One: Three friends decide to play ball on in an abandoned lot. The lot is near a deserted house that people say is haunted, but the friends don't believe that.
  Scene Two: One of them accidentally hits a ball into the second story window. Seconds later, the ball comes flying out of the window back at them and the friends run away.

Act Two: (The investigation)
  Scene One: The friends discuss the phenomenon and discuss that the ball could have just bounced against something. They decide to try an experiment. They'd throw balls into different windows to see if the balls continue to fly back at them.
  Scene Two: They throw the balls in, but nothing happens. They feel better and decide to go into the house to retrieve the balls.
  Scene Three: They enter the house through a broken front door and joke as they walk around looking for their balls. Strangely, they can't find any of them and they don't see anyone in the house. After coming together and wondering where the balls could have gone, they hear, "Get out!"

Act Three: (A disturbing end)
  Scene One: They run out of the house and in the abandoned lot, they find their balls, lined up neatly on the ground. They grab their balls, head home, and decide never to mention the incident again.

Copyright © 2006 by Karen Donohue and Nanda N. Reddy. All rights reserved. Reprinted from *180 Days to Successful Writers: Lessons to Prepare Your Students for Standardized Assessments and for Life* by Karen Donohue and Nanda N. Reddy. Thousand Oaks, CA: Corwin Press, www.corwinpress.com. Reproduction authorized only for the local school site or nonprofit organization that has purchased this book.

1. Group students and explain that each group will write a complete play in three acts.

2. Pass out outlines for each group and discuss that each set of outlines includes a scene for each group member. As such, each group member will be in charge of one scene.

3. Have each student take out one sheet of paper and draw tier cakes. Remind students that a scene often represents a change in setting and usually has a different conflict. However, this is a collaborative effort, so the person writing the scene is not the only person planning. All group members should make suggestions for each scene.

4. Indicate that the cast cannot surpass the number of group members. However, cast members can play more than one non-conflicting character, or characters who are never on the stage at the same time. Also, discuss the way the play will be produced (in class, on stage, etc.) as this may limit or control the complexity of props, costumes, and cast assignments.

5. Allow time for students to brainstorm the details of their plays. They should also assign group members to different scenes.

6. Instruct students to begin writing using the "Seven Golden Rules of Playwriting."

7. Provide hints as students work. It sometimes helps to "act out" certain things to make sure they are necessary. Remind students to picture the whole thing on stage even if they will not be producing plays on a real stage. Encourage students to include stage directions and to keep actors moving while talking.

8. Monitor students' progress as they write and offer assistance when necessary.

9. As students complete scenes, the group should TCUPSS together.

10. Grade scenes as they are completed according to a modified rubric. You may use Resource I.

11. When all scenes are complete and have been polished, make copies so that each group member has a complete copy. Students should practice performing their plays. Group members may highlight individual lines to help them memorize their parts.

12. Allow students to put on their plays.

Project 4: Narrative Poetry

Narrative poetry is slightly more difficult to teach than list poetry. Students are used to using complete sentences to tell a story, so the transition to using phrases and key words might be bumpy. The best way to approach this is to do what you've been doing all year: model and provide examples. For ideas on how to extend this project, consult the list poetry section in Chapter 9.

One-Sentence Narrative Poems

Objectives: Students will read and write one-sentence narrative poems.

Materials: The Laughing Boy.

Note: Before class, make a display of The Laughing Boy.

The Laughing Boy

The laughing boy rolled on the grass,
Clutching his belly
With his eyes closed,
So he didn't notice
The ant pile nearby,
And when he landed on it,
His laughs turned into cries
But no one could tell
If he was laughing or crying
Until he looked up with tears in his eyes
Showing that he had learned how easy
Laughter can turn into cries.

---

1. Tell students you will be writing poems, this time using the tier cake.

2. Display and read The Laughing Boy. Point out that it is essentially one sentence broken apart into twelve lines. Students might notice it's a run-on sentence. Tell them that this is the one time a run-on is appropriate.

3. Discuss the story of the poem: the characters are a boy and ants; the conflict is that ants bite him; the lesson is that happiness can quickly turn to sadness.

4. Draw a tier cake with small boxes on the overhead and "work backward" with the students to plan the story in the narrative poem. Emphasize that this is a modified plan because the story is so short. Only a few words should be written in each box.

5. Draw a tier cake, and tell students that you will plan and write a similar poem together.

6. Brainstorm, think aloud, and plan your poem with a small tier cake. Remember to have a character, a problem, and a solution. If possible, include a lesson that the character will learn.

7. Then write the story in one long sentence without breaks. You may write several versions of the sentence until you decide on the "best" one. Your final sentence should use many sensory details, include the entire plot, and demonstrate good word choices.

8. Use student suggestions to break your sentence apart into ten to twelve short lines. Each time you consider a breaking point, ask students if it "sounds right." Tell students that where you choose to break the line is important because line breaks affect the overall sound of the poem, and sound is important since poetry is usually read out loud.

9. Instruct students to draw small tier cakes and plan brief stories. Monitor their progress. Remind them not to make their stories too complex, or it won't fit in a small poem.

10. Instruct students to convert their plans into one-sentence stories. Tell them to try out as many sentences as needed to find the best way to tell the story.

11. Afterwards, students should break their sentences apart to create ten-line poems. They should then TCUPSS the poems and redraft.

12. Allow student volunteers to recite their poems aloud. Students may turn them in for grading. Grade all narrative poems according to a standard rubric (i.e., Resource B).

Humorous Story Poems

Objectives: Students will read and write narrative poems.

Materials: Mr. Toiler.

Note: If desired, work on your model before class. This poem might take longer to model than the previous since it compresses a "full length" narrative into a poem. Also, make a display of Mr. Toiler before class.

Mr. Toiler

Mr. Toiler, meanest teacher in town,
Proudly assigned more work than the others.
But on his birthday night, he sat at his desk
Wondering if he'd ever get his grading done.
For upon his desk was the largest pile
Of grading there ever was to do.

Mr. Toiler decided that once in a while,
On birthdays for example,
Cheating wasn't such a terrible sin.
So he picked up a paper and without looking,
He wrote whatever his pen decided.
An A or a B, a D or a C, it didn't matter to him.

Mr. Toiler got done so quickly,
He had time for a fancy dinner with his wife.
He roasted a roast
While she baked a birthday cheesecake,
And afterwards they headed to the theater.

But the very next day
After he gave the papers back
And thought, "I need to cheat more often."
His students, they all shouted at him.
"This is wrong," "This isn't right,"
"Wait till I show my parents this."

So Mr. Toiler stayed up all that night
Grading the papers again.
He didn't eat, he even didn't shower,
And he certainly didn't catch a movie.
But he learned a valuable lesson:
Assigning work means you have to grade it,
And he never assigned too much again,
At least not around his birthday.

1. Display and read Mr. Toiler. It is humorous with a somewhat unrealistic conflict. Discuss why this poem is funny and ask students if there's anything "real" about it. Tell students that humor sometimes comes from exaggeration. Mr. Toiler's pile of grading and his frustration are very real, and sometimes teachers wish they hadn't assigned so much work to grade. These realistic conflicts make the poem funny because others can relate.

2. Draw a mini tier cake (one with smaller boxes) and work backward to plan the poem. Discuss that because it's a funny poem, the narrative plan does not necessarily follow the "story arc" of traditional narratives.

3. Brainstorm humorous subjects and conflicts with your students prior to modeling your poem. Imaginary or non-human characters are sometimes easier to use for such humorous poems.
   - Human examples: forgetful professor with an important project; bossy child who puts on a show; and a neat freak who visits a sloppy person or vice versa.
   - Non-human examples: lost Martian; dog who can't find a bone; squirrels arguing over nuts; and a monkey who steals hairclips.

4. Choose a subject and conflict. Plan your poem using a mini tier cake and minimal words. Then model the writing, making it silly or funny on purpose. Be sure you have a setting and a resolution to your conflict.

5. Guide and observe students as they plan and write their poems. Allow students to redraft poems after TCUPSSing and provide time for volunteers to read their poems aloud.

Real Life Ballads

Objectives: Students will read and write narrative poems

Materials: Harriet Tubman's Escape.

Note: If desired, work on your model before class; you may choose to include a refrain. You may also allow students time to research topics before writing poems. Also, make a display of Harriet Tubman's Escape.

Harriet Tubman's Escape

The sun had set
And the master snored in his bed.
It was now, or she'd never be free, so Harriet fled.
Sweating, moving as fast as a jet,
Yet quieter than the dead,
Northward, Harriet Tubman's body receded.

Bloodhounds sniffed her trail
And she limped with blisters and sores.
But with secret knocks on station doors,
Helpful folks determined to see slavery fail,
And stars leading her as if giving a tour,
Harriet Tubman found freedom.

Deciding all slaves should feel freedom's elation
She went back to show them the way.
She helped three hundred slaves hide during the day
Using the Underground Railroad as protection.
It was a kindness no slave could repay
But to Harriet Tubman their freedom was compensation.

---

1. Display and read Harriet Tubman's Escape. Discuss that it's similar to previous poems in that it has a conflict and resolution, but it differs because it's based on a true event. It's also different because it has a rhyme scheme and some repetitive elements (e.g., Harriet Tubman's name).

2. Analyze the rhyme scheme. Then discuss that this poem loosely fits the definition of a ballad, a traditional story that tells a story with a beginning, middle, and end in a few short stanzas; the only thing it's missing is a refrain.

3. Discuss that students will write ballads based on a real life event. The event can be historical, something that is in the news, something that happened at school, something that occurred in their personal life, or an event from their family history.

4. Ballads can rhyme and have refrains, but it's not necessary. Students simply need to have three stanzas with five to seven lines each. The first stanza should represent the beginning of the story and describe a setting; the second stanza is the middle of the story; the final stanza is the end of the story and the resolution. All stanzas should feature some conflict.

5. Brainstorm historical figures and topics. Some examples include Martin Luther King Jr., Elizabeth Cady Stanton, Lewis and Clark, Sitting Bull, the American Revolution, George Washington, Paul Revere, and Albert Einstein. Also discuss current events that might be applicable and allow students to discuss personal and school events that they could write about. Encourage students to think about significant family history like emigration, a birth, a death, or a serious family conflict. Students may need to research their topics for facts.

6. Choose a topic and model the plan on a tier cake. Model the writing, focusing on word choice, rhyme scheme, and repetition.

7. Monitor and provide close guidance as students plan and write their poems. Allow students to redraft after TCUPSSing and conferring with you.

8. Allow volunteers to read their poems out loud.

11 Writing Outside the Lines: Advanced Lessons

In every classroom, there are students who master new skills and concepts faster than everyone else and quickly become bored with the repetition other students require. These students might treat writing fundamentals as "common sense," rarely making grammatical mistakes and applying new skills correctly the first time. Often, they are voracious readers (at or above their grade level) with active imaginations. Students that fit this profile in this curriculum are probably accelerated writing students. To promote their talent, they require advanced instruction, or instruction that goes "outside the lines." The lessons in this chapter aim to fulfill that need.

USING THIS CHAPTER

The lessons in this chapter are meant to supplement the rest of the book and are best woven in throughout the school year as needed for accelerated students. However, they may also be isolated as a unit for a pullout group. It is important to note that the lessons are organized according to subject; some may take days to complete while others can be accomplished as mini lessons.

If you teach a supplemental gifted class, you may use these lessons exclusively. However, for the lessons to be successful, homeroom teachers should continue providing instruction geared toward fundamentals.

Homeroom teachers should keep in mind that students need not be identified as "gifted" or excel at every subject to qualify as accelerated writing students. If the majority of your regular classroom students fit the accelerated profile, replace repetitive lessons with these more advanced lessons at your discretion. However, be sure students are ready for advanced instruction and do not skip fundamental lessons from preceding chapters. Writing rules can only be broken when effectively mastered, and all students need to learn the fundamentals first.

If you need to prepare for a state test, be aware that teaching advanced techniques might thwart some students' application of test-taking skills. Students need to be sophisticated enough to understand that the accelerated stylistic strategies usually require more thought and time than is given for state tests.

ADVANCED NARRATIVE WRITING

In previous chapters, you directly or indirectly introduced the following fundamentals of narrative writing: point of view, voice, hooks, setting, characters, transitions, and plot organization. You also provided tools to help your students improve word choice, dialogue, and imagery in their stories. You will build on those fundamentals in this section, as well as bend some of the rules you taught.

Point of View: Who Is Telling the Story?

Objectives: Students will learn the difference between first-, second-, and third-person narration. They will read examples of each, learn through modeling, and write stories in each point of view (POV).

Materials: Popular books to highlight points of view in Step 6.

Note: Before class, collect popular books of varying points of view.

1. Write the phrase "point of view" and its abbreviation "POV" on the board. Ask two students to face each other and act/mime out the following scene. One student (Mark) is walking down a road, when the other (Leah) approaches him and asks for her money back. They argue.

2. Explain to the class that if you wanted to write a story about the disagreement, the story would be from your viewpoint, as a teacher witnessing it. You would be the narrator, but the story wouldn't be about you. You would talk about the students who are fighting and use the terms "he" and "she." You might begin, "Mark was walking down the road when Leah came up to him. Mark said hello, but Leah immediately started yelling at him, accusing him of owing her money." This is third-person POV, written from an outside perspective.

3. If one of the students told the story, it would change because the student would tell the story about him- or herself, using the word "I." Leah might begin the story as such: "I was so glad when I spotted Mark walking home. I knew it was my only chance to get that cheapskate to

pay up." Mark might write this: "I was minding my own business, heading home, when Leah came up to me like a raving lunatic." This is first-person POV.

> Remind students that a story told in first person is not necessarily autobiographical; the use of "I" does not mean the writer is speaking about personal experiences. As such, the word "writer" or "author" isn't an accurate term to use when referring to first-person perspective. Rather, the term "narrator" should be used to signify the speaker's voice.

4. Discuss that there is another, somewhat complicated POV. In the example being used, assume one of the students or the teacher wants the other students to feel as if they were involved in the argument. They would use the word "you" as they tell the story. They may begin, "You're walking down the road when an old friend approaches you. You haven't seen her in a while, so you say hello, but she immediately starts shouting at you, claiming you owe her money." This is second-person POV, slanted toward Mark's experience. The story may also open like this: "You're not rich and there're some things you've been needing to buy. But someone out there owes you some dough and hasn't been paying up. So what do you do when all of a sudden you spot this person? It's simple. You walk up to him and demand your money immediately." This second-person POV is slanted toward Leah's experience to try to put the reader in Leah's head.

5. Explain that the POV of the story indicates who is telling the story and what that person's relationship is to the story.
   - In first person, the story is narrated by someone who is directly involved. It's a personal story with personal opinions. Students should be familiar with this POV as they've been writing their stories this way until now.
   - In second person, the story tries to put the reader into the shoes of the character. The story is told using "you" instead of "I" and the reader is the main character. The narrator can be an outsider (more objective) or a person intimately involved in the story (more personal), but the narrator is not identified. This is a difficult POV to write and even professional writers hardly ever employ it. Discuss that you will only ask students to write in this perspective so they can understand the technique; you will not expect them to perfect this POV.
   - In third person, an outsider tells the story; this narrator acts as a third party to the story but usually does not show up in the narrative. The narrator can express opinions, but mainly tries to tell the story objectively, explaining what the main character thinks and feels. Students should imagine that this narrator reads the main

character's mind and follows the character around without being noticed. There are a couple of different kinds of third-person narration, but you will only focus on this basic version.

6. Show examples of each kind of narration using popular books, and read opening paragraphs if time permits. If you are lucky enough to find books written in second person, explain how scarce they are. Some examples of books in each POV follow.
   - First person: Amber Brown stories by Paula Danziger. If you want to emphasize that first person does not mean autobiographical, ask students if they think Paula Danziger, the author, is Amber Brown. They should see that Amber is fictional and is telling the story of her fictional life.
   - Second person: Few popular examples as of date of publication. *Freewill* (ages 14+) by Chris Lynch and *Moondial* (ages 10+) by Helen Cresswell.
   - Third person: Most books are written in this format. Read the first few lines to emphasize that an invisible narrator tells the story. The narrator doesn't come first in these stories.

7. Discuss that the narrative writing prompts students have received thus far encouraged them to write only in first person. Furthermore, test prompts often require autobiographical first-person narration because they ask students to tell their opinions and experiences first-hand. Show students an example of this type of prompt and summarize an example answer.
   - The prompt: Imagine that you fall asleep on your school bus and the bus driver leaves you in the bus parking lot. Think about what you would do. Now write a story about a time you were left behind on a school bus in a parking lot.
   - Such a story might begin, "It was cold and dark when I woke up."
   - The narrator is the main character; the story is told from the narrator's POV and may or may not include autobiographical elements.

8. Reword the prompt so that it does not specify first-person narration as follows.
   - What would it be like to fall asleep and get left on a school bus in the bus parking lot? Think about the things a person in this position might experience. Now write a story about being abandoned on a school bus in a parking lot.

9. Display and read the following three paragraphs that begin to answer this prompt.
   - First person: The sun was setting when I awoke. But for some reason, I thought I was seeing a sunrise and that I was late for school. I scrambled up, or tried to, only to hit my head on a seat cushion and find myself on a cold metal floor. I looked around, confused. Then I saw my book bag and it dawned on me. I fell asleep on my school bus and they left me there.

- Second person: You're in the middle of a beautiful dream about swimming when a loud noise suddenly awakens you. Thump! You open your eyes slowly, annoyed about being awoken, expecting to find your little brother Timmy making the ruckus. But it's dark, there's no Timmy, and you're suddenly cold. Very cold. You realize you're lying on metal instead of your cozy bed, and your head is on a hard book, not your pillow. Where are you? You sit up, and the empty seats around you announce that you're on your school bus. Only it's empty. Thump! The sound is coming from above. You look up in time to see two raccoons jump from the roof of the bus.
- Third person: "Let me out!" Shelley knocked against the windows and shook the door of the bus, but nothing worked. She had been abandoned and locked in her school bus. She closed and rubbed her burning eyes one more time, hoping to wake up from this bad dream. How could it have happened? How could she have fallen asleep on the bus and gotten left behind? It wasn't the sort of thing that ever happened to her. Shelley opened her eyes; she was still on the bus. She sat down in the driver's seat and began to cry.

10. Ask students to identify the POV each paragraph is written in and which POV seems to provide the best answer. If students can't choose, explain that there is no right answer. No one POV is inherently better than another, although sometimes there is a best POV for a story.

11. Read the following prompt. Then follow the examples given to model a generic plan and the first paragraph of the story in third person, second person, and first person.
    - Prompt: Everyone has met a "new kid in town" before. Think about what it's like for most new kids. Now write a story about being a new kid in town.
    - Example plan: setting—classroom; character—new kid; conflict—can't get along right away. Paragraph 1—new student enters class, other students stare at her, she senses trouble. Paragraph 2—others pick on the new kid at lunch and recess, new kid defends herself. Paragraph 3—new kid almost gets in trouble for defending herself, but someone stands up for her. Paragraph 4—new kid has a friend and things improve at school. Paragraph 5—new kid distinguishes herself at school and begins to enjoy it. This plan is vague since the story will develop in three different points of view.
    - Example third person: She is wearing overalls and carrying a Sponge Bob book bag when she walks into the classroom. The kids look at her like she's an alien, and she stares back. A couple of girls in the class giggle, but Maria refuses to let them scare her. "I'm Maria Vicente. I'm new," she says in her loudest don't-mess-with-me voice. But one girl is smirking. Maria already knows being the new girl won't be easy.
    - Example second person: Your heart is racing. You're sweating. You feel like you'll just faint. It doesn't matter how many times you've

done this—being the new kid is never easy. You stand at the door of your new classroom and wonder, what'll they say? What'll they think? Will they like me? You take a deep breath and enter. They stare at you, so you stare back. You can sense it already. There's going to be trouble.

- Example first person: I've lived almost everywhere—Florida, Texas, California, and now New York. I'm sick of being the new kid. But here I am, sitting in the back of the classroom at an empty desk, with kids staring at me like I'm a freak show. One freckly kid looks at me, whispers to his friend, and they both giggle. This is not a good start.

12. Students may notice that the examples are in present tense. Tell them you will discuss tense in another lesson. Save these examples for use in the next lesson.

13. For guided practice, collaboratively write the second paragraph for each of the above example paragraphs. Allow students to volunteer sentences and encourage them to use the stylistic devices they've learned all year.

14. Allow students to complete the stories (Paragraphs 3, 4, and 5 for each POV) independently. You may allow students to complete part or all of this assignment in pairs.

15. Monitor students and provide help. Remind students to TCUPSS.

16. Generally discuss POV choices. Which ones do students like or dislike; which ones seem easy or hard; what are the pros and cons of each; is the freedom of choice appealing?

17. For additional POV work, ask students to write stories for the following prompts. You may require a specific POV, allow students to choose, or ask students to complete all three prompts in different points of view.
- Imagine taking a train ride through an enchanted place. Think about what could happen during a train ride through a popular or make-believe enchanted place. Write a story to tell about a train ride through an enchanted place.
- Families are important, but they can get annoying. Think about family traits that might be annoying. Now write a story about getting annoyed with family.
- Learning to do something new can be scary. Think about something that might be terrifying to learn at first. Write a story about a terrifying experience while learning to do something new.

18. To further challenge students, present the following prompt and ask students to write the stories (or opening paragraphs) from three perspectives: the parent, the child, and the friend. They may write all of the perspectives in the first-person voice or third-person voice, or they may use a combination of both. They should probably not attempt second person since the assignment is challenging enough.

- Everyone has arguments with loved ones. Think about an argument between a parent and child, involving the child's friend. Write a story about this argument.

Tense: Once Upon a Time in the Future

Objectives: Students will learn to tell stories in present and past tense; they will read examples, learn through modeling, and practice writing in both tenses independently.

Materials: Example paragraphs used in Step 11 of the POV lesson.

Note: If desired, collect popular books to demonstrate stories written in present and past tenses.

1. Display and read the three example paragraphs from the POV lesson. Ask students if they see a grammatical similarity among them. Help students identify that they are all in present tense.

2. Discuss the meaning of present tense (occurring now) and past tense (has occurred). If desired, emphasize this point by showing students examples of popular books written in present (Amber Brown series by Paula Danziger) and past (*Holes* by Louis Sacher and the Narnia series by C. S. Lewis).

3. Rewrite the example paragraphs in past tense as follows. Students may participate if desired.
   - Third person: She wore overalls and carried a Sponge Bob book bag as she walked into the classroom. The kids looked at her like she was an alien, and she stared back. A couple of girls in the class giggled, but Maria refused to let them scare her. "I'm Maria Vicente. I'm new," she said in her loudest don't-mess-with-me voice. But one girl smirked. Maria knew being the new girl wouldn't be easy.
   - Second person: Your heart raced, and you sweated bullets. You felt faint. It didn't matter how many times you had done this—being the new kid was never easy. You stood at the door of your new classroom and wondered, what'll they say? What'll they think? Will they like me? You took a deep breath and entered. They stared at you, so you stared back. But you could sense it already. There was going to be trouble.
   - First person: Growing up, I lived almost everywhere—Florida, Texas, California. By the time we moved to New York, I was sick of being the new kid. But there I was, sitting in the back of the classroom at an empty desk, with kids staring at me like I was a freak show. I remember one freckly kid looking at me, whispering to his friend. Then they both giggled. That's when I knew I wasn't going to have a good start.

4. Discuss that in the second and third person paragraphs, changing the verbs didn't affect the meaning much. However, the first-person voice

needed more changes in addition to the verb tense. The meaning of the story changed with simple verb changes.

5. Read the present and past tense versions aloud, and then discuss which version sounds better and why. Discuss if the students have preferences and what they feel the major differences are in the two ways of writing. Also discuss which tense they feel is easier to write.

6. Tell students that when writers tell stories, they have to decide two big things before starting: what POV will be used, and then what tense it will be in. Tense is important for the following reasons.
   - A story that is written in past tense indicates that the writer already knows what has happened and is retelling the story. The reader already knows that the main character will be okay in the end.
   - A story that is told in present tense indicates that the character has no clue what will happen. The character tells the story as it happens, right here, right now. This helps readers feel like they are right there with the character, and they aren't sure what will happen to the character. This is often a more difficult tense to write in because kids write about things that happened to them and most books are written in past tense.

7. Provide students with the two following writing opportunities and ask which tense they think might be better for each. Note, these prompts are not written in the traditional manner. You may reformat them to fit that form if desired.
   - A spoiled child goes off on an unexpected and dangerous adventure where he learns to depend on himself.
   - Two siblings live opposite lives at school. Everything goes wrong for the shy one, while the popular one gets everything she wants. All evens out when the shy one publicly rescues her sibling.

8. After students choose tenses for the prompts, tell them there is no right answer. The writer simply needs to have a reason for his choice. Discuss further that in adventure stories, it's almost always a "given" that the hero survives. It's common to tell these stories in past tense because the reader expects survival and usually only cares about the "journey." However, a story involving relationships and emotions related to a specific narrator usually works well in present tense because the reader enjoys experiencing the story intimately with the narrator.

9. Tell students that you will plan stories for each prompt. Decide that you will tell the first story (adventure) in third-person past tense and the second story (relationship) in first-person present tense. Discuss that first person is the POV that often works best with present tense.

10. Begin your modeling using the following examples. Plan, then write the opening paragraphs.
    - Prompt one—plan. Setting: mansion; Character: spoiled child, Aaron; Conflict: kidnapped; Plot: whines about going to school;

sneaked back into house and plays video games after mother leaves; hears noise; burglars; burglars are surprised and take him; he struggles and is tied up; burglars want to ask for ransom, but he escapes when he goes to the bathroom; he hides, lives in woods, eats berries, figures out how to survive while trying to find his way home; he is found by a hunter, but he is no longer spoiled.

- Prompt one—Paragraph 1. "Aw, Mom, school's stupid. That dumb teacher doesn't teach me anything useful," Aaron whined. His mom gave him a stern look before continuing to jam papers into her briefcase. She rushed Aaron out of the house, sent him on his way with his bike, and sped off in her car. Aaron grumbled as he slowly pedaled to school. He'd rather be playing his video game—he was almost at the platinum level! He looked toward his house at his bedroom, where the video game waited for him. His window was open! His mom, in her rush, forgot to set the house alarm. Aaron smiled. It looked like he didn't have to go to school after all. NOTE: Despite being in past tense, dialogue is always written in present tense, or exactly as the character said the words.

- Prompt two—Plan. Setting: school; Character: twins Elsie and Emma; Conflict: don't get along. Elsie complains about Emma to best friend Kelly; they make fun of Emma; Kelly decides to pull a prank on Emma; Elsie doesn't want to, but doesn't want to lose her friend; they snatch Emma's book bag and trash her books; they find plans for science project; Kelly decides to use the plan; Emma gets in trouble for not having her homework (project plan) and losing library books; Emma cries and complains at home; Elsie feels guilt, doesn't confess; Emma does extra chores to pay library fines and rewrites her plan; at science fair, Emma's project is the same as Kelly's; Kelly accuses Emma of copying, cheating; Elsie finally defends Emma.

- Prompt two—Paragraph 1. "Oh my God, Elsie. Emma's wearing the same outfit as us!" my best friend Kelly says to me. I roll my eyes. "Don't you think I know?" Emma, my twin, is on the playground swing, her nose buried in a book. And she's wearing the same plaid skirt and white shirt that Kelly and I decided to wear today. When Emma put on the same outfit this morning, I went ballistic. But that only got me in trouble with Mom. I hate Emma for always copying me, and right now, I'm glad she has no friends and has to sit alone. I link arms with Kelly and saunter past Emma. She doesn't show it, but I know she's jealous I'm more popular than she is. NOTE: Point out that the narrator is not necessarily the character that readers identify with. The readers might actually not like the narrator and prefer her sister, Emma. This is a method writers sometimes use.

11. Lead a guided writing to complete Paragraphs 2 and 3 for the stories started above. Allow your students to volunteer the words and encourage use of style devices.

12. Instruct students to plan their own stories for the prompts. They must write one in present tense and the other in past tense, but they do not have to make the same choices you did. Brainstorm plots and discuss combinations of POV and tense.

13. Monitor students as they plan and write. Remind students to TCUPSS.

14. Students should be given the opportunity to share their writing orally.

> If desired, discuss "future tense," a seldom-used device. It is just as rare, if not more, than second-person POV. An interesting class project would be to write a story in second person, future tense. The finished product would read a lot like an astrologer's prediction.

Characterization, Part I: Nose Pickers and Football Quarterbacks (Pair Lesson)

Objective: Students will learn to emphasize characters' personalities through particular traits.

Materials: Figures 11.1 and 11.2.

Note: Before class, make a display of Figure 11.1 and student copies of Figure 11.2. If desired, collect fairy tales for use during Step 7.

1. Ask students to think of the weirdest person they know, identifying one trait that makes the person weird. The only rule is they may not offend classmates.

2. Draw a two-columned chart to list the persons and characteristics. Before getting student ideas, provide the following examples: little sister—has funerals for dead insects she finds; aunt—blows her nose 100 times an hour; neighbor—hangs underwear out on a clothesline in front of the house; best friend—has a collection of broken pieces of glass in a box.

3. Have students volunteer their ideas, refraining from names if possible.

4. Tell students everyone has quirks or behaviors that are unique to them. Not all characteristics are strange, but they often define a person. Offer a "defining characteristic" of yourself and one of a teacher very different from you; add them to the list. Tell students that if they were to write a story that includes a teacher, they have to decide what the teacher is like. It's not enough to say "teacher." You might want to emphasize that the Magic School Bus books would be different without Mrs. Frizzle.

5. Tell students the more different their characters are, the more interesting their stories will be. Use a book to exemplify this. For example, point

out that part of the fun with the Harry Potter books is that Hermione loves to study while Ron hates school; the Weasley twins spice up the story with pranks and jokes. If the characters were different, the story would change.

6. If desired, make another chart to briefly brainstorm famous characters from stories or movies along with their defining characteristics.

7. List popular fairy tales or stories on the board. Examples include Three Little Pigs, Cinderella, Snow White, Little Red Riding Hood, Little Mermaid, Jack and the Beanstalk, Bambi, etc. Tell students they are going to change the main characters in these stories by altering their defining characteristics. Then, they'll list all of the things that would have to change in the story because of the "new character."

8. Display Figure 11.1, The True Goldilocks. It changes Goldilocks into an obsessive-compulsive person, or "neat freak," causing the story to change. She washes spoons before tasting food, replaces all of the sheets on the beds before trying them, and scrubs the floor after she spots spilt honey. Ask students to add two more story points to the list with changes.

9. Pair students and pass out copies of Figure 11.2, the fairy tale re-do form. Ask the pairs to choose fairy tales, identify characters they wish to alter and their defining traits, and then decide on different or opposing traits. Then, students need to list at least ten things that would change in the story based on the new character. They may add more if desired.

10. Since this is an exercise, encourage students to emphasize their characters' quirks, even if they end up with slightly bizarre results. However, the characters' traits should be consistent and there should not be too many new defining characteristics. If students make their characters too quirky, they will never get to fully develop each characteristic. For example, if Goldilocks also had asthma/allergies, ate everything with her toes, corrected all misspellings she saw, walked on her head, and told jokes constantly along with being obsessively clean, the story would be chaotic and impossibly long.

11. Allow students to share their work.

12. Afterwards, warn students that although "quirks" are necessary for characterization, unrealistic or bizarre quirks can make a character seem too cartoonish, and subsequently annoy or put off readers. In their "real writing," they must focus on strong, realistic characteristics to define their characters. You should emphasize that the exercise they completed was to prove the point that characters' traits help to dictate how a story is told.

Figure 11.1   The True Goldilocks

Title of Story: *Goldilocks and the Three Bears*

Character: Goldilocks

Defining Characteristic: She uses others' personal belongings without care to get comfortable.

New characteristic: She is obsessive-compulsive about cleanliness and is grossed out easily.

Old Story Points	
Enters quickly	
Walks immediately to food	
Looks around, notes furniture	
Tries out chairs	
Gets out of soft cushy chair easily	
Finds baby's chair just right	
Tries out beds without thinking	
Falls asleep on baby's bed quickly	
Wakes up and runs away when bears return	
Bears chase Goldilocks away	
Goldilocks learns never to go into strange homes again	

Copyright © 2006 by Karen Donohue and Nanda N. Reddy. All rights reserved. Reprinted from *180 Days to Successful Writers: Lessons to Prepare Your Students for Standardized Assessments and for Life* by Karen Donohue and Nanda N. Reddy. Thousand Oaks, CA: Corwin Press, www.corwinpress.com. Reproduction authorized only for the local school site or nonprofit organization that has purchased this book.

Figure 11.2 Fairy Tale Re-Do

Title of Story: Character:

Defining characteristic: _____

_____

New characteristic: _____

_____

Old Story Points	New Story Points

Copyright © 2006 by Corwin Press. All rights reserved. Reprinted from *180 Days to Successful Writers* by Karen Donohue and Nanda N. Reddy. Thousand Oaks, CA: Corwin Press, www.corwinpress.com. Reproduction authorized only for the local school site or nonprofit organization that has purchased this book.

Characterization, Part II: What Color Are Your Socks?

Objectives: Students will complete character studies and flesh out characters from old stories.

Materials: Figures 11.3 and 11.4; previously used display model; students' old writing samples.

Note: Before class, make a display of an old narrative to use during Step 8. Also, make student copies and a display of Figure 11.3 and make a display of Figure 11.4.

1. Ask students what they know about characterization. They will likely remind you of the previous lesson, which discussed that characters' defining traits should influence the story.

2. Tell students that authors who write long stories and novels often go one step further. They do not only create defining characteristics, they usually write full sketches of their characters. A character sketch outlines the full history and personality of a character.

3. Remind students that for short or timed lessons, character sketches are not a good idea. But for longer works, like chapter books, they should know their characters well.

4. Pass out copies of Figure 11.3, the blank Character Sketch Two. Review the boxes and questions and discuss how these can help to "flesh out" characters.

5. Display Figure 11.4, a completed sketch on Hansel and Gretel's Witch. Read and discuss.

6. Tell students you will model a character sketch using an old narrative. Display and read the old narrative. Discuss that you want to fully characterize a minor character, not the main "I" character, as that is you. Choose a minor character.

7. Display your copy of Figure 11.3, the blank sketch, and complete it with student input. Ask students to help you answer the questions at the bottom.

8. Now, reread the story to add, delete, or rewrite lines in order to reflect the character's full personality. This can be mostly verbal modeling, as you will be providing the students with many verbal alternatives, and choosing a few. An example follows.
   - Original story might say this: Gene walked behind me. He was holding the stick to hit the monster. When we saw the monster, Gene ran and hit the monster on the leg.

9. Changes to indicate that Gene is a clutzy and slow follow.
   - Gene huffed and puffed behind me. He dragged the stick he was going to hit the monster with. When we saw the monster, Gene grunted and yelled, "Geronimo!" Gene tried to run, but got tangled up and tripped. He flung the stick and hit the monster in the eye.

Figure 11.3   Character Sketch Two

Name: _____

Description:

Age	Race	Eyes	Hair	Height/Size	Skin

Clothes: _____

_____

Defining Characteristics: _____

_____

History:

Birth (where/when)	Important events in life

Environment:

Room/Home description	Family	Friends

Loves and Hates:

	Food/Drink	Color	TV show/ Book	Person	Object	Hobby/ Sport
Favorite						
Dislikes						

1. What does the character dream about? What are his goals?
2. What makes him happy? What was his happiest moment?
3. What makes him sad? What was his saddest moment?
4. What would he do if someone stole something of his?
5. If he had three wishes, what would he wish for?
• *Write your answers on back.*

Copyright © 2006 by Karen Donohue and Nanda N. Reddy. All rights reserved. Reprinted from *180 Days to Successful Writers: Lessons to Prepare Your Students for Standardized Assessments and for Life* by Karen Donohue and Nanda N. Reddy. Thousand Oaks, CA: Corwin Press, www.corwinpress.com. Reproduction authorized only for the local school site or nonprofit organization that has purchased this book.

Figure 11.4 Hansel and Gretel's Witch

Name: Beany, Witch of Hansel and Gretel

Description:

Age	Race	Eyes	Hair	Height	Size
16	Pygmy witch	Green with purple flecks	Red with gray stripes	4'3"	Small

Clothes: Too large for her, drag on the floor; long purple witch's gown with foot-long pointy hat to make her seem taller; high-heeled shoes that are hard to walk in

Defining Characteristics: Has always been too small, is made fun of by other witches, wants to eat as much as she can so that she might grow; making a growth potion

History:

Birth (date/place)	Important events in life
Orphaned at birth in a forest; was found by an old warlock	1. Witches pulled pranks on her in school, stuffed her in cubby hole 2. Warlock (adopted father) died when she was thirteen 3. She dropped out of school and decided to live alone 4. Began work on her growth potion in the forest, needed humans 5. Built a gingerbread house to attract children

Environment:

Room/Home description	Family	Friends
Outside: Gingerbread house covered in fake candy, but smells sweet . Inside: Old wood floors/dark/bubbling cauldron/snakes, toads, odd scents	Warlock father who found her; he was always a little crazy, and was 7 feet tall. He has died. She doesn't know her real parents were pygmies.	None. Occasionally, old "friends" from school drop by to make fun of the gingerbread house.

Loves and Hates:

	Food/Drink	Color	TV show/Book	Person	Object	Hobby/ Sport
Favorite	Marrow	Purple	Book;-black magic potions	Warlock; - adopted father	Old cane of her father	Black magic
Dislikes	Candy	White	Happily ever after fairy tales	Everyone else	Dolls	Games

1. What do you dream about? What are your goals? *To grow.*
2. What makes you happy? Remember your happiest moment. *Father showing me magic, showing me how to use the wand to turn a frog into a rock.*
3. What makes you sad? Remember your saddest moment. *Father's death.*
4. What would you do if someone stole something of yours? *Kill them, curse them.*
5. If you had three wishes, what would you wish for? *Taller, taller, taller.*

Copyright © 2006 by Karen Donohue and Nanda N. Reddy. All rights reserved. Reprinted from *180 Days to Successful Writers: Lessons to Prepare Your Students for Standardized Assessments and for Life* by Karen Donohue and Nanda N. Reddy. Thousand Oaks, CA: Corwin Press, www.corwinpress.com. Reproduction authorized only for the local school site or nonprofit organization that has purchased this book.

10. After your modeling, instruct students to select old narratives from their binders. Students should aim for stories with vague characters so the characters can be easily altered.

11. Students should reread their stories and choose a minor character to sketch. Instruct students to fill out their blank character sketches for their characters.

12. Then students should rewrite their stories, changing them to appropriately show the new character traits. Remind students to TCUPSS.

13. Allow volunteers to discuss what specifics they had changed in their stories to reflect new personalities. Have students read important aspects of their character sketches along with changes that reflect those characteristics.

14. To extend this lesson, students may create a list of "personality profile" questions and compile them. Creating such questions helps students to think deeply about personality traits and to make their characters more concrete and realistic. Trigger their imaginations with this question: What color are your socks?

Setting: It Was a Dark and Stormy Night

Objective: Students will create complex settings for their stories with vivid descriptions.

Materials: Magazine photos.

Note: Before class, prepare a display of the scenarios in Step 1. Also, find photos for use in Steps 5 and 6, and provide magazines and travel brochures for Step 7.

1. Ask students to close their eyes and imagine the following scenarios as you read them.

   • A light breeze brushed against my back like a cool feather, making it easy to remain as I was, baking in the sun. I know I should have turned a half hour before, but I couldn't. I was drugged by the salty air, the lap-lap-lap of the waves and screeching song of the gulls, the smell of fresh fish, and the old 80s music sounding distant though it blared to compete with my chattering friends. Then someone shouted, "Look!" and I slowly eased up, just in time to see a tail of a giant splash beside me and feel my back blaze as if on fire.

   • Krizan tiptoed barefoot down the cold, stone stairs, his back against the brick wall. Dim lamplight flickered, deepening shadows and making him see things. He blew out his candle a minute before thinking he saw someone's back. But it was only dents in the wall resembling a toga. The candle's phosphorescent smell lingered, mingling with the aromas of dank earth and pungent chemicals emanating from below. Glass tinkled, and Krizan pressed himself even tighter to the wall. His uncle was there, possibly conducting one of his grizzly experiments, and Krizan might be lucky enough to see the whole thing.

- The only thing that disturbs the pristine white walls are blocks of paint, some neat, some splashed on their canvases as if in a rage. A hush lives here, and I think, "This might be what it sounds like in a vacuum," until the click, click of heels on the glossy marble floors interrupt my thoughts. "Looks like a kid did it, huh?" I say to her as she studies a rectangle of paint, but she ignores me and the guard near the door finally cracks a smile. I've been hogging the only seat in the room, a wooden bench, and I don't even give it up when a gang of school kids pass through, loud as a circus and saying things like, "I could do that myself." They look at me as if I'm on display too, and I give them my widest toothless grin. They squeal—the highlight of my day.

2. Display the scenarios, and ask students to tell you where (location as exact as possible) and when (approximate date, day, and time of day) the scenario takes place. Answers follow.
   - On a boat in the ocean, fishing and tanning. Current date (since 80s is "old"), possibly a weekend day (friends are all there), and definitely in the middle of the day (11 a.m.–3 p.m).
   - A dungeon in an old stone/brick building. Sometime in the past (candles, lamplight), possibly a hundred years ago (chemicals), at night, near Rome (toga).
   - Modern art museum in a big city (bum inside). Middle of a school day (kids on a tour), current date.

3. After reading and identifying each setting, ask students how they were able to discern the settings although none is explicitly stated. Students should point out how the language, dialogue, smells, sounds, tastes, and other sensations in the paragraphs reveal the settings.

4. Discuss that students used sensory descriptions to improve their stories before. But now they will rely on those descriptions to give their readers an accurate sense of their stories' settings without explicitly stating where the story takes place.

5. Display the magazine photo for the following example; if you are unable to find a close match, model a different photo using this example as a guide. Study the photo with students and brainstorm a list of concrete details and sensations to create a sensory map. Then write the paragraph, weaving in as many of the details that you can.
   - Sensory map: smell—backed-up drain, car exhaust, wet garbage; taste—coffee; touch—slick door handle; hear—honking, tires splashing, shout; see—puddle, umbrellas, taxis, buses, people with heads down.
   - Paragraph: The air reeked of wet garbage and car exhaust. Ana jumped over a puddle in her high heels and nearly tumbled onto a man. He jerked his black umbrella up and yelled, "Hey, watch it," but he didn't look up. No one was looking up. The sidewalk was crawling with people in gray suits; they matched the gray day. Taxis honked, buses braked, and tires splashed through the flooded streets. Ana

hailed a cab. But as she reached for the slick door handle, a heavenly smell tickled her nose. Coffee. She could taste it. She waved the cab away and followed her nose.

6. Display another picture and tell students you are going to brainstorm sensory details together, focusing on the vivid images from the photo. Then you will write a paragraph together. Use student input to brainstorm concrete images that you weave into a paragraph.

7. For independent practice, allow students to choose two photos from magazines. Students should find photos with a sense of setting as opposed to photos of models, actors, and merchandise. Travel magazines, brochures, and *National Geographic* often work well.

8. Students should brainstorm sensory maps and write paragraphs for each of their photos. Monitor students and remind them to TCUPSS.

9. After students have written their paragraphs, collect and display the photos. Read the paragraphs one at a time, and allow the rest of the class to guess which photos the paragraphs refer to. You may spread this activity out over a few days, reading some each day.

10. If your class has experience critiquing each other's work, you may extend this activity by instructing partners to improve each other's work.

Hooks: Beyond "Bang!"

Objective: Students will learn varied ways to begin a narrative.

Materials: List of first lines from favorite/popular books; magazine photos.

Note: Before class, compile first lines for Step 4 and photos for Steps 7 through 9.

1. Review the five hook rules previously taught: start with a bang; write a famous quote; reword the prompt; state the setting; state the problem. Tell students these are mostly fine ways to start stories, especially if they are done well. But these methods can be used poorly, too.

2. Make a t-chart on the board. Write SO-SO on one side and YES on the other. Tell students you will show them some good and not-so-good ways of hooking readers using the five hook tactics. Tell students this will be based on a prompt asking students to write about their most embarrassing day. You'll list the ho-hum examples first, identify the problems with them, rewrite them, and explain why they work better.
   - Bang: Splash! I walked into a puddle.
     a. Problem—gimmicky, sound does not seem authentic.
     b. Improvement—Squeak, squeak, squeak—my wet shoes practically announced to the class that I had stepped into a huge puddle.
     c. Reason—more realistic sound, brings the embarrassment factor out without having to say "I'm embarrassed," readers can relate.
   - Quote: "When it rains, it pours."
     a. Problem—it's a cliché, something most writers try to avoid.
     b. Improvement—"Arg! I'm never going to live this down."

    c. Reason—author's personality is showcased; not cliché; readers wonder what she's not going to live down.
- Reword the prompt: Let me tell you about my most embarrassing day.
    a. Problem—sounds like you're writing to a prompt, not that you're writing a story you want to tell.
    b. Improvement—I try to forget it, but the day I suffered pure embarrassment is stuck in my memory forever.
    c. Reason—lets readers know it must be a good story if she can't forget it.
- Setting: It was a Thursday morning when I got to school.
    a. Problem—boring, doesn't grab reader enough.
    b. Improvement—The rain had grown wild by the time I got to school that Thursday morning.
    c. Reason—provides more vivid setting images and gets across same information.
- Conflict: I was embarrassed.
    a. Problem—boring.
    b. Improvement—And so there I was, standing in front of the class, my cheeks burning, my clothes dripping wet.
    c. Reason—more vivid, and conflict is introduced in a way readers can relate.

Note: "And" can be an effective first word for a sentence. "And" immediately draws readers into stories, making them feel as if they entered the story right in the middle. However, "and" should always be used wisely and never overused.

---

3. Discuss that the key is to start with a statement that will intrigue readers. You want the reader to be interested in the story's action, characters, or plot. But whatever you choose to write, it can't be gimmicky and false, the way "bang" seems. It has to really pertain to the story and feel authentic.

4. Read the story starters you compiled from famous stories and discuss how the first lines grab the readers' attention. Analyze the first lines to determine if any start with bangs, quotes, settings, conflict, or something that sounds like a reworded prompt. Identify those.

5. Some of your first lines might fit the previous five tactics of starting a story, while others might conform to the five methods listed below.
   - Conversational tone. This first line is written to the reader, full of author's personality and attitude. It also makes assumptions about the reader.
   - Curious or charged dialogue. It does double duty—makes the reader wonder what's going on and immediately tells the reader about the character.
   - In the middle of the action. This involves starting a story as something crucial is happening or has happened to bring the reader right into the thick of things. Sometimes this also involves dialogue.

- Intriguing character description, especially a quirk. This is used when the character's personality is the main drive for the story. It makes the reader automatically aware of whom they are dealing with.
- Fascinating or unusual setting aspects. This type of opening is often best used when the setting is not something readers are used to.

6. Published examples of the above five methods follow.
   - Conversational—Roald Dahl often does this. For example, in *Matilda*, he begins: It's a funny thing about mothers and fathers. Even when their own child is the most disgusting little blister . . .
   - Curious dialogue—From *Strawberry Girl* by Lois Lenski, "Thar goes our cow, Pa!" said the little girl. From *Charlotte's Web* by E. B. White, "Where's Papa going with that ax?" From *Number the Stars* by Lois Lowry, "I'll race you to the corner, Ellen!"
   - In the middle of the action—From *The Trumpet of the Swan* by E. B. White: Walking back to camp through the swamp, Sam wondered whether to tell his father what he had seen. From *Triplet Trouble* by Dadey and Jones: "Watch out!" I yelled. A paper airplane flew past Ashley Tucker's head.
   - Intriguing character description—*Peter Pan*, by Sir J. M. Barrie: All children, except one, grow up.
   - Fascinating or unusual settings: From *Eragon* by Christopher Paolini: Wind howled through the night, carrying a scent that would change the world. And from *Holes* by Louis Sachar: There is no lake at Camp Green Lake.

7. Display one of the photos you collected for the lesson and begin to write a total of five first lines for the picture. Model each of the starters: conversational, dialogue, middle of the action, intriguing character description, and unusual setting trait. As you write the sentences, try to vary them further by making some humorous, suspenseful, and emotional.

8. Display another photo. Work together as a class to come up with another set of first lines.

9. Display five to ten photos so that everyone can see them. Number the photos. Tell students that the photos are for inspiration so that they can create a total of five outstanding first lines. They can write all five lines based on one photo, or they may rely on five different photos. However, they need to indicate which photo inspired each first line using the photo's number. Of their five sentences, one should start with dialogue, one with action, one with a character trait, one with a conversational tone, and one with a unique setting element.

10. Monitor students and provide help.

11. When students are done, allow them to share their work. Go through the photos and ask for the first lines each photo prompted.

12. To follow up this lesson, you can start a contest: Best First Lines. Post a picture every week to prompt first lines. Collect the students' entries and vote on them (alone or as a class). Paste the winning first lines along with students' names below the pictures and display.

Plot and Pace: And Then What? (Pair Lesson)

Objectives: Students will learn the general arc of a story, then plot and write stories using an arc.

Materials: Figure 11.5.

Note: Before class, make a display of Figure 11.5.

Figure 11.5 Story Arc

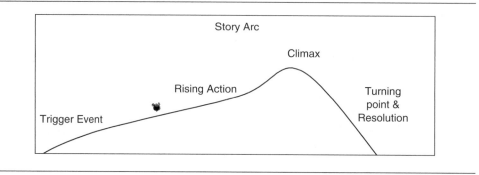

1. Display Figure 11.5, Story Arc. Discuss that most stories can be plotted on such an arc.

2. Review the main aspects of a story's plot—trigger event, rising action, climax, turning point and resolution. Discuss the definition of these terms and why they appear where they do on the arc.
   - Trigger event: The action, event, or situation that starts the story.
   - Rising action: The events that occur in the story to increase the suspense.
   - Climax: The crucial, most intense or suspenseful part of the story.
   - Turning point and resolution: The solution to the conflict and release of suspense.

3. Tell students that professional writers often outline their basic story plots in this manner. This keeps them from writing stories where nothing happens. As they write stories, they think about the arc and ask themselves, "Are things getting more and more exciting for the reader?" Using a plot arc helps to keep stories exciting and readers in a state of suspense.

4. Tell students you will plot the story of Beauty and the Beast. Draw an arc and write the plot points in the appropriate places.
   - Trigger event: Beauty is captured by Beast.
   - Rising action: Beauty discovers Beast isn't so bad; villagers plan to kill Beast to rescue Beauty; Beauty and Beast fall in love.
   - Climax: Villagers raid Beast's home and get ready to kill him.
   - Turning point and resolution: Beauty protects the Beast; Beauty and Beast marry and live happily ever after.

5. Plot another story together, for example, Cinderella. Allow students to offer suggestions.

- Trigger event: Cinderella's mother dies; father remarries.
- Rising action: Cinderella is abused; isn't allowed to go to the ball; decides to go to the ball; gets a fairy godmother; meets Prince; they fall in love.
- Climax: She has to leave at midnight, almost exposing herself.
- Turning point: Prince uses shoe to search for her; shoe fits.
- Resolution: Cinderella leaves her stepmother, marries Prince.

6. Pair students. Ask pairs to choose a favorite childhood story to plot. Discuss that some stories do not fit perfectly on the arc. If the stories don't have climaxes, they should write "no climax" near that plot point. Monitor student work.

7. Now tell students you will plan a story using the story arc, not the tier cake.

8. Use a story starter of your own or the following: Write a story about telling a little lie that turns into a much bigger lie. Model an example first; one follows.
   - Trigger event: In an essay, Jim says his dad is a movie director, not a truck driver, to impress his class.
   - Rising action: Teacher wants to invite Jim's dad for career day; Jim say he's out of town on a job; but Dad shows up to pick Jim up; Jim rushes away, says Dad's too busy; teacher runs into Jim and his dad at grocery store; teacher and Dad misunderstand each other as they discuss his exciting job that keeps him away from home and lets him meet a lot of exciting people; dad agrees to go to career night.
   - Climax: Dad shows up at career night to talk about being a truck driver.
   - Turning point and resolution: Jim introduces his dad and explains what he does. No one mentions Jim's lie; and his dad is a big hit. Jim appreciates his dad and regrets the lie.

9. Ask students to individually plot stories along an arc, using the story starter. You may also allow students with original ideas to use their own story starters.

10. Monitor students as they plan their stories with the arc.

11. If desired and necessary, write your sample story as a model. Otherwise, monitor students as they flesh out their plots into stories. Allow students to compare the tier cake tool to the arc: what do they prefer or feel is easier? Which tool helps to create more tension in stories?

12. For publication, point student toward websites and contests for young writers.

Dialogue: Well, um, She Was Like All That!

Objectives: Students will use dialogue to show characterization and setting; they will also learn varied ways of writing dialogue and tags.

Materials (optional): Paper bags; list of settings and stock characters.

Note: Before class, make a display copy of the dialogue in Step 8.

1. Tell students that dialogue in stories does more than show what people are saying. Dialogue helps the plot, characterizes, shows setting, and provides variety in story structure.

2. The first job of dialogue is to move the plot along, or to tell the story to the readers. As characters speak to each other, they discuss their motives, plans, and reactions to situations, and they provide information for the reader to understand the plot.

3. The second job of dialogue is characterization. To demonstrate this, list the following "stock" characters on the board. For example: country girl, city boy, very rich heiress, poor homeless person, and foreign visitor. Ask, will all of these characters speak the same? Why do people speak differently? Students should surmise that speech often reflects a person's background, including culture and education.

> Note: Be sure to not foster inappropriate stereotyping. Emphasize that while there are "stereotypical" or "stock" aspects to speech, no two people are identical no matter what they sound like. Tell students that developing "an ear" for different speech patterns is just one step in building characters. Characters also need thorough histories, as described in the lessons on characterization, to become complete.

4. For each of the characters listed, have students volunteer how such a person might greet a waitress and order something to eat. Discuss that if they were to hear the different quotes without context, they should begin to figure out the characters' personalities/situations. Write their suggestions. Some examples follow.
   - The rich heiress might say: "I'll start with the seared scallops appetizer, follow with a Waldorf salad, then the encrusted salmon entrée (special sauce on the side please). I'll finish with a crème brûlée."
   - The homeless person might say: "You got anything good I can buy for a dollar seventy-five? I'll take what you got for a dollar seventy-five."

5. Another role of dialogue is to reflect the setting. Reread the quotes of your stock characters ordering their meals. If you cannot tell where the characters are, rewrite their quotes to indicate setting. In the examples, you can tell the heiress is in a fancy restaurant. In an extended dialogue, she can comment on the view from the restaurant or the live music to further indicate setting. The homeless person might be at a cafeteria counter, a fast food place, or a roadside stand. To reflect a hotdog stand, you could write: Over the roar of traffic, Ellis yelled, "Pardon me mister. How many hotdogs can I get for a dollar seventy-five?"

6. To further emphasize the relationship between dialogue and setting, take four of your stock characters and put them in odd settings. For

example, the country girl in a fancy restaurant; the heiress at a meat market; the city boy at McDonald's; and the homeless person in someone's home. How would they order or discuss their food? What might they say to indicate their settings as well as their personalities/situations? Write the answers together.

7. A final job of dialogue is to make stories interesting to read by breaking up sentence structure. However, if dialogue is written as "he said-she said" it can become boring quickly. There are many different ways of writing dialogue other than using the he-said-she-said tags.
   - Action, followed by dialogue: Gus choked and stood up. "What? You cannot be serious!"
   - Tag and action in the middle: "What?" Gus choked. He stood up. "You cannot be serious!"
   - Skipping tags and using names (review "implied speaker" grammar rules):
     "What? Sheila, you cannot be serious!"

   "Gus, please. Just hear me out."

   "I refuse to listen to this."

8. Display the following dialogue. It employs the above techniques, as well as these other dialogue techniques: answering questions with questions, evading topics, interruptions, unheard words, and silence.

Mom inched away from the schoolyard at fifteen miles per hour. "Artie, where is your report card? Gail said Robbie got his yesterday."

"Hey Ma, did you know chimps are related to us?" Artie tossed his bag in the backseat pretending not to hear the question. "Monkeys even." *(Answering a question with a question)*

"Artie, I asked you a question."

"Ma, when we make our ice cream stop, I want—" *(Evading)*

"The report card, Artie!" *(Interruption)*

Artie played with his seatbelt. *(Silence)*

"Artie?"

He mumbled under his breath. "Artie, Artie, Artie. That's my name, don't wear it out." *(Unheard words)*

"I can't hear you."

"That's 'cause I didn't say anything."

Outside of the school zone, she sped up and the tires squealed. "That's it. I'm calling your father as soon as we get home."

"Sure Ma, whatever. But, hey, can we still get ice cream?"

---

9. In the example, you find out the setting (car, after school), a plot point (report card trouble), and characters' personalities (mom has a temper, but is weak and backs down to call Dad; Artie is energetic, sarcastic, and seems accustomed to getting what he wants). Point out that there isn't a lot of he-said-she-said and you can tell who is speaking

because of the characters' personalities. Discuss how the techniques create tense and break up the story structure.

10. Ask students to write a dialogue scene between a parent and child on their way home from school, using the following guidelines. If desired, complete a guided lesson first.

- Speakers should interrupt each other once, answer questions with questions, evade topics, and remain silent between one of the interactions. Limit use of he-said-she-said.
- The speakers could be walking home, driving in cars, taking the bus, or using unique vehicles (electric car, moped, skateboards, etc.).
- The child could be the one questioning the parent about something.
- The personalities should emerge and drive the conversation.

11. Share students' dialogues.

12. Follow up this lesson periodically with the following exercise. Make and print a list of generic settings and stock characters; cut them apart and place in separate brown paper bags. Ask students to blindly select two characters and one setting, and then write a one-page dialogue between the characters employing the techniques they learned.

Symbols and Themes: What's Your Drift?

Objective: Students will learn to enrich their stories with symbols and themes.

Materials: *Charlotte's Web*, by E. B. White; *Charlie and the Chocolate Factory*, by Roald Dahl; *The Little Princess*, by Frances Burnett; *The Wizard of Oz*, by Frank Baum.

Note: Because theme is a difficult concept, only select students will benefit from this lesson.

1. Tell your students to imagine the following plot as a story. A young boy, who is nice but a little geeky, has trouble fitting in because he doesn't think much of himself. He is depressed a lot and buries himself in computer work. One day, his school's computers break down. He bravely comes forward and fixes them, aware that the kids might call him a computer nerd. However, he becomes the school hero and no longer has trouble fitting in. Because he accepts himself, people appreciate him for who he is. And he begins to find himself beautiful.

2. Remind students of the plot of The Ugly Duckling. Ask if they see any similarities between the stories. Students should see that they have somewhat parallel plots. Tell students that you did this on purpose.

3. Ask students to identify the "moral" of the ugly duckling's story. They should say something similar to any of the following: beauty is only skin deep; when you accept yourself, the world will accept you; we grow into ourselves. The same moral applies to your adapted story.

4. Indicate that if you were to make the moral show up continuously throughout the story, it would become the theme of the story. You

could accomplish this several ways: by symbolizing, by repeating the moral in different, subtle ways, or by weaving a metaphor throughout the story.

5. You can instill the story with theme as follows.
    *   Using symbols—in the story, your main character can watch his pet hamsters grow from wet, naked babies into cute, fuzzy creatures. Don't use swans, as it's too obvious of an example. The hamsters are symbols because they are not human. They are a nice touch because they hint at the moral of the story in a very subtle manner.
    *   Repetition of the moral—at some point, the character can find childhood pictures of his beautiful mother that are not flattering. He might laugh at them, and she can comment on them, hinting at the moral. Also, he can meet someone who is vain or obsessed about being popular, but who doesn't accept herself either. These examples are similar to symbols, but they aren't since they reflect the moral of the story through other people's stories. You would need to be sure the characters are developed enough so that their appearance doesn't seem like "thematic ploys," put there on purpose to tell the theme.
    *   Metaphor weaving—the main character can be compared to a computer chip throughout. In the beginning, you can say he's as boring, invisible, etc., as a computer chip. As the story progresses, it becomes obvious that your main character is quite analytical and hard-working, much like a computer chip. In the end, your readers will realize that he is like the computer chip in his importance and intrinsic beauty.

6. Reiterate to your students that a theme is an idea that is woven throughout a story. Even if a story has a moral or lesson, the moral is not a theme if it shows up just once. The moral can only be called a theme if it is alluded to throughout the story.

7. The purpose of imbuing a story with theme is to create richness. A "rich" story is more satisfying to readers because in the end, everything seems to come together and make sense. A theme makes the writing seem connected and purposeful.

8. Warn students that if the theme becomes too blatant in a story, it becomes annoying. Readers will feel like the writer is preaching, and readers often don't like to be told what to think. As such, writers should not go overboard with symbols, metaphors, and moralizing. They should choose a few subtle tools and work them in so that the readers "get it" in the end.

9. Applying theme to stories is difficult, and writers do it differently. Some writers naturally instill their theme in their stories in first drafts. These writers often know exactly what they want to say and what they want readers to get out of their stories. But many writers have to rework first drafts intensely to achieve this richness. Those writers figure out the overall meaning of their stories after they have written, then they return to the stories to make sure that they hint at the meaning throughout.

10. Common themes in stories are often clichés. However, unless the cliché is blatantly stated, the theme usually works nicely. Some examples follow: don't judge a book by its cover; eye for an eye; can't teach old dogs new tricks; all is fair in love and war; can't see the forest for the trees. Clichés are often good themes for beginning writers to use. As writers improve and begin to find their individual voices, personal themes will come to them naturally.

11. There are endless themes in literature, and the best way to learn about theme is by reading books and analyzing them for thematic content. Provide your students with the books suggested in the materials list or provide your own. Ask students to choose one, read the story, and look for the theme. They are not looking for a moral or lesson at the end of the story, but a repeated "meaning" that the author hints at throughout the story. This is a long-term lesson, which can be completed outside of class. As students complete this aspect of the lesson, you may skip ahead to Step 13. Return to Step 12 to discuss the themes of their chosen books.

12. When students identify the themes, they should list reasons why they came to their conclusions, citing specific parts of the stories. Students might point out symbols, metaphors, or "repeated morals" in the stories. And students might discover different themes than you expect. As long as they provide reasonable support, their answers should be accepted. Possible themes for the four suggested books follow.
    - *Charlotte's Web*: Selflessness is a virtue; life is circular; life is a wheel of fortune; anything is possible if you work hard enough.
    - *Charlie and the Chocolate Factory*: Resist temptation; cheaters (or the greedy) never prosper; kindness and generosity will be rewarded.
    - *The Little Princess*: Your goodness comes back to you tenfold; you reap what you sow; be true to yourself no matter how hard.
    - *The Wizard of Oz*: Everything we need is within us; look inside yourself for support; appreciate yourself and you'll be happy.

13. Ask students if there is a theme, idea, or concept that they would like to write a story about. This is not at all like writing from a prompt. Instead, they will think of a story that will best convey the message they want to tell. Brainstorm possible themes; examples follow.
    - Envy of others means you'll never learn to appreciate yourself.
    - The thing that is hardest to do is often the right thing to do.
    - With true friends, you can survive anything.
    - The older you get, the more confusing and complicated life becomes.
    - Blind eyes always see.
    - The early bird gets the worm.
    - Fools rush in.
    - Following others can lead you astray.

14. Ask students to think of stories to tell their themes. You may allow students to brainstorm with partners, or you may assign this as a paired writing.

15. Students may plan out the skeleton of their stories using the tier cake or story arc.

16. After planning their stories, they should brainstorm secondary characters, symbols, and metaphors that they'll use to weave their themes throughout their stories. Offer the following example to symbolize envy. Students may work in the image of hermit crabs chasing shells or hyenas salivating over then scavenging a lion's catch. Also, an envious character can have posters of her idols all over her walls, but no mirrors. Metaphors can allude to being blind or blinded. The character actions can be compared to those of a deer in headlights, always forgetting herself when seeing the bright, shiny things in front of her. Or, she can be entranced by material things the way cobras are attracted to flute music.

17. Students should begin their rewriting only after they have a complete idea of what they want to tell their readers and how they plan to do it throughout the story. You could tell students that most writers don't approach writing this way and that the lesson approaches theme in a somewhat "backward" fashion because it's an exercise in theme.

18. After students rewrite and are satisfied with their stories, have volunteers share their stories as the rest of the class guesses the theme.

19. Follow up this lesson by simply reminding students of theme every time they rework first drafts. Another way to reinforce the concept of theme is to have students figure out the themes of books they read for the rest of the year.

Putting It All Together: The Complete Package!

Objective: Students will write stories that incorporate all of the accelerated skills they've learned.

Materials: Story starters—magazine pictures, family photos, stock characters and settings, etc.

> Discuss that another rule students may break is the "four to five sentences per paragraph" rule. There is no such hard and fast rule; their objective is simply to tell the story well.

1. Tell students they will be combining the advanced techniques they learned to write a story. Warn them that the planning process for the story might take longer than they are accustomed to. Also, tell them that the story will be completely their creation, with no rules regarding content (of course, explicit, profane, or disparaging works should not be accepted).

2. Provide students with a variety of story starters including photographs, prompts, first lines, subject ideas, and themes. Allow students to peruse the ideas until they get an idea for a story. Students

should jot down key words and phrases so that they won't forget their story ideas.

3. Next, students are to figure out if they want to write the story in first person or third person. Second person might be too experimental for this.

4. Students should also decide if they want to write the story in present tense or past tense. How "immediate" do they want the stories to seem to the readers?

5. After securing POV and tense, students should begin working on character sketches. They should fill out personality profiles for their main characters.

6. Next, they should write sample dialogue lines to identify their characters' speech patterns. They may place the character in random settings such as graveyards, kitchens, and bus stops.

7. Students should then brainstorm a sensory map of their proposed settings. What would someone see, hear, feel, smell, or taste at each location? They might want to close their eyes and picture themselves in their settings before brainstorming. They should write down as much detail as they can. If applicable, they can even make small sketches of their locales, especially for fantasy or futuristic stories.

8. After students have a good idea of their settings and characters, they should draw story arcs and plan their stories along arcs.

9. Finally, students who are capable should begin to think about the themes of their stories and how they'll weave the theme in throughout the story. Remind students that this step can be accomplished after the first draft of the story.

10. After planning, students should begin to brainstorm great first lines for their stories. You can review their options with them, referring to the "hooks" lesson.

11. Students should begin to write their stories. Remind them that they are writing first drafts and that the published stories they read often go through four to five drafts before publication, if not more. Now that they are thinking of many things as they write, tell them that they should not focus on getting everything "perfect" but rather to get the story on paper as a complete draft. Tell them to try not get bogged down by the skills they learned and to just write. They can employ their advanced skills during critiquing and revision.

12. After students complete their writings, explain that you will put them in groups and allow them to critique each other's work. Real writers often rely on their critique groups to help them get everything right, which is why you are doing this with them. For long stories, create a page limit for the critique—five pages is an acceptable maximum at this level.

13. Tell students they will read each other's work to identify a consistent POV, a consistent tense, good character development, vivid setting details, an interesting and "arced" plot, a catchy hook, crisp dialogue, and possibly a theme. You may provide a checklist of these items to students and model the process of critiquing a story.

14. Tell students that when they read another person's work, they should read it without marking anything, not even grammar mistakes. Then they should re-read it to edit. They should identify which of the advanced skills the person executed well with notes in the margins. They should also indicate the problems they find in the margins, including grammar but focusing more on the advanced skills. Finally, they should make one positive and one negative general comment regarding the person's story. They should also offer solutions to give the writer ideas on how to improve the story. It is best to model this technique. You could use an old sample story or use a student volunteer's story.

15. Emphasize that critiquers shouldn't feel like they are picking on their friends by listing the story's problems. Instead, they need to feel that they are helping someone improve their writing, possibly helping that person become a published writer.

16. In turn, tell students that when their critique partners give them criticism, they should think about the criticism objectively and honestly. They should say, "How can I improve on those skills? Do I understand those skills or need more of my teacher's help?" Tell students that no one will have written perfectly and that even famous writers have lots of problems in their first drafts. It is when they get feedback and really analyze their stories that they begin to know what parts of the stories need to be fixed.

17. If your group is small enough (no more than eight or nine), provide copies of each member's story to everyone. Ask students to read the works and critique as directed. If your group is large, create small critique groups of three to four students.

18. Depending on your group, follow up by having students face each other in a circle and give the critiques orally after writing them, or pass the critiqued papers back to their owners. You should have also read and critiqued your students' writings. Return these.

19. Students should use the critiques to formulate second drafts. They may draft the stories even further if time permits.

20. Encourage students to publish their stories on websites or in magazines or to enter them in contests. Tell students that it's okay if their works are not accepted or do not win awards; the process of submission is rewarding and educational in itself.

21. Follow up this lesson by repeating it and encouraging students to use the process independently.

ADVANCED EXPOSITORY WRITING

While your students might not mind writing expository essays, they probably find the writing too formulaic, even boring. In this section, students will find out that expository writing goes beyond making glamorized lists, the five Ws, and research reports. As students express their opinions on the state of the world, describe life experiences, and share ideas on humorous philosophical matters (like belching), they will realize that essays are powerful vehicles for their voices.

Essay Topics: My Own Prompts

Objective: Students will generate lists of topics that interest them.

Materials: Student binders.

1. Discuss that an expository essay can be written on any topic that the writer has an opinion about. The writer can write about love, world peace, the best hamburger recipe in the world, or how to keep cats from tearing up furniture—it doesn't matter. The writer can even write on humorous or unrealistic topics: why teachers should all be sent to Mars, why his sister should be in an asylum, or the tricks to winning a belching contest. All that matters is that the writer has a thesis (an opinion that readers can agree or disagree with) and provides sufficient proof to back up the thesis, even if the proof is funny or very questionable in humorous pieces.

2. Tell students that you will no longer present prompts to them (during these advanced sessions), as they will write only on topics they care about. As long as they apply the fundamental rule about expository essays—a thesis statement followed by proof—they can write about any interest, care, and idea that they have.

3. Allow students to brainstorm topics they are interested in, topics they have opinions on, and popular ideas with which they honestly disagree. You may brainstorm along with them or before they do to give them ideas. Encourage them to list topics they know a lot about, want to learn about, find funny, and get sad or angry about.

4. Here are some examples of general categories for topics: war, cliques at school, bullying, allowance, sibling rivalry, curfews, love and crushes, girls vs. boys, sports techniques, hobbies, drugs and alcohol, music, grandparents, sports, memories, things they get yelled at about, things that embarrass them, things that they like to do in private.

5. Ask students to keep their personal lists of ideas handy in their binders.

A Non-Prompted Essay: Organized Free Writing

Objective: Students will write an essay on a subject of their choice.

Materials: From Chubbsie to Cheerleader.

1. Ask students to refer to the lists of topics they brainstormed during the last lesson.

2. Ask students to choose a topic, one related to their strongest opinion or deepest passion. Tell students they won't have to share their essays and that all opinions will be confidential.

3. Examples of topics that students often have strong opinions about include cliques, bullies, parental authority, privileges, getting in trouble, being ignored, and success in school/sports.

4. Instruct students to work as you model an essay. You may choose a topic of your own or use the following example, From Chubbsie to Cheerleader—My Middle School Metamorphosis. If using the example, do not share this title with students yet and discuss that you are not writing from a personal point of view, but assuming someone else's identity.

From Chubbsie to Cheerleader: My Middle School Metamorphosis

"Chubbsie" was the nickname I got in third grade, and it almost stuck. No one calls me that anymore, but it stings every time I see a kid laugh off a fat name or joke. I know the shame, guilt, embarrassment, and anger they're actually hiding. The truth is no kid needs to feel that way. I'm living proof that it's possible for very overweight kids to turn their lives around.

"Just go on a diet," people say, but the toughest thing about losing weight is getting started. When you've got nearly a hundred pounds to lose at age thirteen, you think, "Why bother?" When I used to say that, I was really just scared. I knew it would be tons of work to lose the weight and I was afraid I'd fail. But one day the scale hit 175 pounds; I knew then I didn't have a choice. If I didn't change my life, I could become lost in fat. I cried the day I announced to my family that I'd finally get healthy. Mom says she knew I would succeed, that there was something in my voice. That something was determination. If you want to lose weight, you can't lie to yourself. You must mentally prepare for a whole new lifestyle and announce it to the world.

After deciding to lose weight, everything was easy. Yeah, right! Creating a new life meant I needed a serious plan and tons of support. It was tough. My family literally emptied our pantry into trash bags and we began to eat boiled food. I missed Oreos most, but kept telling myself Oreos weren't worth my health. Exercise was another hurdle because I was a kid who had nightmares about PE. But my mom woke me at five every morning, and we walked for half an hour. I huffed and puffed and didn't get far those first few months, but I worked up to walking two miles daily. Now I even take dance classes and gymnastics. But that didn't happen overnight. I kept a record of everything I did and ate in a daily diary, and it shows progress was slow.

According to my diary, I lost forty pounds that first year, three to four a month. Four a month was my goal, and every time I reached it, I wrote an uplifting note to myself. My parents also rewarded me with a movie or clothes. But there wasn't always progress. My diary includes gory details of many "Oreo days," days when I binged because I was depressed. Those days made my monthly goals harder to reach and started cycles of depression, binging, and not working out. If it weren't for my parents' encouragement and the positive notes in my diary, I might have completely given up several times. Luckily, I didn't, and two years later, I'm eighty pounds lighter. Now people know my name, Chelsea, and no one wonders why I made the cheerleading squad.

When you've been overweight, your work is never completely over. I try to eat healthy and exercise every day, and if I'm ever depressed, I have to work hard not to binge. I still have some "Oreo days" I'm not proud of, but the changed person I see in the mirror is usually enough to keep me on the right track. I look at myself and laugh: "From Chubbsie to Cheerleader," and I think, anything is possible.

5. Tell students to write their general topics on the top of blank pieces of paper. If you're following the above example, write: Topic = Being fat and losing weight as a kid.

6. Next, they should write their intended audiences down. You write: Target Audience = Overweight children.

7. Now, they should brainstorm their top three opinions on the topic. Remind students that opinions, by definition, can be disagreed with. Write the following three opinions for your example.
   • Being fat as a kid is hard.
   • Losing weight takes a lot of work.
   • It's possible for kids to lose weight and change their lives.

8. Tell students that of the three opinions, you'd like to focus on the third one. It is the one you have the most support for, and in thinking about your core audience, you believe it's the article they'd be most interested in. Explain that in the essay you will model, you are writing from the point-of-view of an author who wants to encourage overweight kids to lose weight because she lost weight as a kid.

9. Students should now decide which opinion is most important to them, most "supportable," and would be the most interesting to their intended audience. That opinion is their thesis.

10. Now, students need to generate a list of supporting information for their theses. Tell them to brainstorm freely on the same piece of blank paper and not to worry about the expository plan sheet as yet. Your modeled brainstorm might look as follows.

- Hard to start losing weight and exercising, but important
- It's a tough decision involving junk food, family, friends, and activities
- Think about making a lifetime change, not part-time change
- Support from family and friends; a buddy
- Self-talk to ward off peer pressure, ads, and temptations
- Make clear goals that are realistic and cut into small steps
- Have an exercise routine
- Get their parents to restock the fridge and pantry
- Keep a diary of positives and negatives
- Don't get bogged down by negatives
- Don't give up; start over if you have to
- Focus on non-food rewards

11. Draw a pickle sandwich. Tell students that you will keep your core audience in mind as you organize the model essay; you will write in a way that will make sense to overweight children. Instruct students to watch your demonstration before planning their essays.

12. Write your topic, "Being fat and losing weight as a kid," in the topic sentence area of the plan sheet. Then write your thesis statement in the bubble. Do not list three supporting ideas. Tell students that now that they understand how to organize expository essays, they can stop repeating themselves in essays. Indicate that your thesis sentence will be the last sentence of your introduction paragraph and that you will write other information.

13. Before writing in the first pickle, say something like this: "If overweight kids are reading this article, they probably need to be told how to get started on losing weight. As the author, I need to discuss the difficulty of being overweight, list some reasons why students should lose weight, and then tell them how 'I' got started, as if speaking from experience."

14. In the first pickle's topic area, write "getting started" and follow with these details: hard but important; need family and friends; tough decision, but lifetime change. Cross off the items on your brainstorm sheet as you write in the details.

15. Discuss that the audience will need the nitty-gritty details of how to lose weight.

16. As the topic of the second pickle, write "the hard work." Follow with these details: need plan and goals; clean out pantry; fun exercise plan; diary. Cross off brainstormed items.

17. The audience now needs to know that the work is never completely over. Once they reach their goals, they have to set new goals; and if they have difficulty reaching their goals, they should keep trying.

18. In the third pickle, write "setbacks and rewards" in the topic area. Follow with these details: nonfood rewards; don't give up; self-talk;

new goals. Cross off brainstormed items. Indicate to students that it is okay if you didn't use all of your brainstormed ideas.

19. Finally, the essay needs a catchy title that also tells what it is about. Read the title and discuss how this title reflects the topic and thesis statement, while remaining interesting.

20. Read the completed example.

21. Discuss how the introductory paragraph is organized. It is full of opinions and personal anecdotes to grab the targeted reader's attention; it is clearly about the topic, but the information is general. Then the last sentence becomes specific, stating exactly what the writer wants to talk about. This is called the "funnel" approach: starting general to grab readers' attention, and becoming specific when stating the thesis statement.

22. Ask students to discuss other interesting aspects of the essay, including its conclusion.

23. Students should now organize their essays. Remind them to think about their audiences as they organize. Also, they should try to plan introduction paragraphs that "funnel" from a general discussion of their topics to their thesis statements.

24. Monitor students and provide feedback.

25. Students should write their essays using their plan sheets and the sample as a guide. Monitor students and encourage them to edit their work as if they are members of their core audiences. Further, as they write, they should feel free to change the direction of their essays as new ideas occur to them; the plan sheet is merely a guide and is not meant to stifle the essay.

26. Follow up this assignment by encouraging students to write on topics of their choices and submit their essays to their core audiences. There are many specialty magazines geared toward children (paper and online), and they are always looking for great non-fiction pieces. Help your students follow the guidelines (including word limits) posted by the magazines, newspapers, or websites.

Knowledge-Based Writing:
I Am the Expert—Listen to Me

Objective: Students will write essays on subjects about which they know a lot.

Materials: Expert articles; Picture Perfect Model Railroad Scenes for Free (Almost!).

Note: Before class, compile a few "expert articles" for Step 2 from online and paper resources.

1. Ask students to name some experts. They will probably say doctors, lawyers, teachers, policemen, etc. Some might even mention experts such as video game players, snowboarders, artists, and athletes. Ask if students think any of these experts write about their professions. They should probably acknowledge that they might.

2. Discuss what makes someone "expert" enough to write an article—experience and success in a field or subject matter; accomplishing a rare goal; having a unique approach that works. Show students the articles you've clipped and discuss the experts and their topics.

3. Tell students that experts write to explain concepts to their peers in an expository format. Many freelance writers (writers who write for magazines and newspapers for a living) often write on topics they know well, such as their hobbies or their lives. Some examples follow: How to Plan a Party; Build the Right Birdhouse for Birds in Your Area; Learning to Skydive; Sandcastle-building Secrets; Writing a Picture Book That Sells.

4. Tell students that most people are good enough at something to be an expert at it. Ask students to brainstorm a list of at least three things they are good at in order of their experience with the subject; they may use their list of generated topics for ideas. They may be creative in coming up with topics and no reasonable topic is off limit. To trigger ideas, suggest games (board, video, playground), sports, cooking, hobbies, and activities like tutoring, being a big sister, having fun with grandparents, and planning sleepover parties.

5. Tell students that you will outline an expert topic, building a model railroad scene. Draw a pickle sandwich with four pickles and indicate your topic and core audience.
   - Topic—decorating a model railroad scene.
   - Core audience—model railroad hobbyists.

6. Write your thesis inside the introductory paragraph bubble: Free and inexpensive materials found around your home can be used to build a professional looking model railroad scene. Remind students that you will write your introductory paragraph with the "funnel" method in order to eliminate repetition. Model the plan.
   - Paragraph 1: Preparation. Details: rummage; decide on a scene/make a plan; lay track.
   - Paragraph 2: Materials. Details: Items in the house; twigs and materials in nature; packaging materials; glues and other necessities.
   - Paragraph 3: Putting it together. Details: the base; the structures; paper mache.
   - Paragraph 4: Decorating. Details: paint; the ground; figurines

7. Read the essay, Picture Perfect Model Railroad Scenes for Free (Almost!). Discuss how the introduction paragraph is funneled and ask students to point out the humor and personal comments that make the essay interesting to read.

Picture Perfect Model
Railroad Scenes for Free (Almost!)

I am cheap, don't get much of an allowance, and love model railroads, three things that don't mesh well together, especially when a true-to-life N-scaled birch tree costs almost twenty bucks. But I manage, well enough in fact to win seventh place in the model railroad scenes competition last year. You might laugh at that, but it's a darn good accomplishment considering I made my scene practically for free. And I'm going to tell you exactly how you can use junk around your house and other cheap or free things to build a pretty good-looking model railroad scene.

To begin, you've got to get some details out of the way, stuff like what kind of scene you want, the scale, and where you're going to put it. I don't suggest putting it near your dog's bed or it ain't gonna last long! Before deciding on a scene, rummage around in junk drawers, attics, garages, your sister's toy chest—wherever you might find materials. I did just that, found a bunch of old zoo animals (don't know which brother they belonged to) and decided to make an amusement park scene with animals. After deciding on the scene (popular ones are mountain, holiday, and city), draw a layout and all the things you want in it. I included a Ferris wheel in my plan, but of course never found one. Finally, lay your tracks out as desired. Now the fun starts.

After you lay the tracks, go rummaging for junk again. This time, focus on foam, cardboard, Styrofoam, wood, newspaper, sand, egg cartons, cereal and other boxes, packaging supplies, sand, and dirt. These things will make the base. Then walk the dog, and while you're doing that, pick up the best looking twigs, dead branches (evergreens are great!), pieces of moss, lichen, and small rocks you can find. I'd steer clear of stuff the dog peed near though. After you get back, raid your family albums and go online to get photos of clouds, mountains, and other things that can make a background for your scene. Print and cut out road signs if you need those, and collect all sorts of toys (dump trucks, figurines, etc.) that fit the scale of your train. Finally, get the glue! Collect spray paint, tempera paint, any adhesive you can find, tape, flour and water (or wallpaper paste if your parents have any lying around), and a hot glue gun (I'd bet your mother has one in her craft box).

When you get your junk together, I wouldn't spread it out in the living room. Parents don't take well to that. Go where you've already set up your track, put newspaper on the floor, and dump your treasures there. Make sure you really like the spot though because you'll be spending the next few months there. First, you'll make the base with wood or cardboard. Wood is better, unless you have to cut it; otherwise use cardboard, which is easier to move anyway. Transfer your track layout onto the base, and use boxes, egg cartons, glue, and tape to make the basic layout for the buildings in your plan. Add decorative details (like window boxes and shutters) to your buildings with strips of cardboard. It doesn't matter if these look ugly now because you'll paint them. Decide where you want features like tunnels and mountains. Use newspapers and tape to make papier-mâché armatures, and then use the flour and water (or wallpaper paste) to papier-mâché right onto the set. If you don't know how, check online. I made animal homes, a tunnel, and a water ride out of papier-mâché. Before the papier-mâché dries, it'll look pretty bad; in fact, you might be tempted to let your dog play with it. But don't do that until you decorate.

Decorate by painting the houses and papier-mâché structures. Mix sand into your paint for texture. Then, cut a cardboard border to place around your whole scene. Paste the pictures you swiped here for a background; panoramic clouds work best. Use green spray paint, "tree dust" (something you'll have to buy), and glue to make your branches and twigs look like trees. Glue sand, dirt, and moss on the ground and make roads with cardboard and black paint. Arrange toys, railroad signs, and realistic touches like thimbles of flowers at places. And you're done!

On your first try, you won't be winning any awards. Not even seventh place. But if you work at this for a couple of years like I've been doing, you'll be placing tenth before you know it, and since practice makes picture perfect, you'll be winning first soon. But not before me, I hope.

8. Now ask students to plan their topics. They should outline topics, audiences, and thesis statements. Then they should organize their supporting details. Students may need time and materials to research their topics fully.

9. Students should write their essays focusing on their audiences. Tell them they should picture the essays in magazines that cater to their audiences. Encourage students to TCUPSS and redraft their essays, then share them with the class. If desired, students may bring in props when they make their presentations.

Contemplations: What's Your Theory?

Objective: Students will write essays on eccentric, unsubstantiated theories.

Materials: Student-generated list of topics; Rich and Famous, No Way!

1. Ask students to peruse their lists of generated topics for funny ideas or something they have a funny opinion about.

2. Discuss how statements that contradict conventional thinking or that are obviously warped are often funny. Examples follow. Fish is poisonous and should be an illegal food; if more adults played freeze-tag, the world would be a better place; beware—veggies make you stink; Britney Spears should have married me.

3. Students may volunteer their ideas and you may brainstorm ideas out loud.

4. Read Rich and Famous? No Way—I'd Rather Be Poor and Unknown.

Rich and Famous?
No Way. I'd Rather Be Poor and Unknown

What's with everyone wanting to be famous these days? Do you like people gawking at you while you eat? You'd never eat spinach or sloppy joes again! And you'd never be allowed to have an ugly day again. I personally like being able to dash outside with gnarly hair, still in PJs to grab the newspaper. And I don't think I could give up spying on people, my favorite hobby. That's why it doesn't matter how much money I could make. I'd rather be an unknown any day.

I'm speaking from experience folks! Or sort of. I know a gal who knows a guy whose sister's best friend got famous on a reality show. Anyway, things were great for a while for this famous person—fans sent letters, people asked for her autograph, and she got the royal treatment. Plus, she was raking in the dough! But one day, she walked by an open window of her house before she put on any makeup. Big mistake! That ugly picture of her became more popular than she was. Then, she went grocery shopping in disguise, but someone recognized her as she was putting away groceries. At that point, people mobbed her car like monkeys, swiping all her groceries. People just wanted to touch something she touched. I could do without all that.

I don't mind the being rich part (I hear she takes some pretty swanky vacations!), but fame's not worth it. I like living—you know, skateboarding at the mall, going to dinky thrift stores, and eating at hot dog stands my mom says are gross. I couldn't do that if I were famous. Plus, I'd have to get rid of my binoculars and people-watching paraphernalia and forget ever being an undercover detective, my dream. You can't watch people if they're constantly watching you.

You probably think I'm nuts, and maybe I am. Who knows, if someone lets me be rich and famous for a day or so, I might try it just to make sure. But the last thing you'll catch me doing is one of those TV reality shows. Unless it's about being a spy, but only then.

5. First, identify the items that make this essay funny. Do the students agree or disagree with the author? Is the author being serious? Did they enjoy the essay? Who is the author's audience?

6. Next, analyze the essay's thesis statement, introductory paragraph, and supporting ideas.

7. Ask students to plan their essays on conventional pickle sandwiches. They should list possible theses on their subjects; then choose the best one. Remind them of the "funnel" model. They should also identify their core audiences.

8. Students should brainstorm opinions on the thesis. They should then categorize their opinions, keeping their audiences in mind.

9. Monitor students as they write their essays and TCUPSS their first drafts.

10. Pair students and allow them to critique each other's work. Students should help each other refine ideas and add humor.

11. Allow students to rewrite final drafts and read them aloud.

12 Going Schoolwide: Ideas to Create a Spiraling Curriculum

Effective instruction is built on prior knowledge. Reading and math instruction are commonly implemented as spiraling curricula, each year reaching toward higher order skills. Writing instruction also should be implemented this way. In order to achieve a spiraled curriculum, schools must have clear missions and decide their basic method of writing instruction.

SPECIFIC WRITING GOALS

To adapt this book's curriculum for your school, definite writing goals must be set for each grade level. Teachers will need to follow the book's basic framework: teach through modeling, guide, foster independence, assess and diagnose problems, and reteach. Teachers will also need to adapt the pickle sandwich and tier cake to fit their grade levels. Goals for specific grades follow.

- Kindergarten: Students will work toward writing one- to three-sentence expository essays. They should begin to use capital letters at the beginning of sentences and punctuation marks.
- First Grade: Students will work toward writing one-paragraph expository essays. These will be five to six sentences in length and should

include a main idea, three details, and a closing sentence. During the last quarter they may be capable of writing a simple narrative of up to eight sentences. They should form complete sentences and spell words phonetically. They will use the TCUPSS process and edit their work for capital letters, proper nouns, and punctuation marks.

- Second Grade: Students will work toward writing expository essays and narrative stories that are three paragraphs in length. They should spell words correctly, use capital letters, punctuation marks, and begin using descriptive language. They should learn to correct their own errors through the TCUPSS process.

Lessons in the previous chapters were written for third- through sixth-grade students. Goals for those grades can be found in Chapter 1. If multiple grade levels simultaneously use the lessons, all grades may use them as presented the first year. In subsequent years, teachers in Grades 4 through 6 will need to amend the sample writings and prompts to avoid overexposure.

ADAPTING THE CURRICULUM

In this section, you will learn exactly how to adapt the curriculum to fit the primary grades. Each subsection describes how to adapt the graphic organizer, provides sample lessons, and suggests writing topics.

Kindergarten

Consistent writing instruction is important to include from the beginning of the year. Introduce writing as a whole group activity using words and pictures. Toward the middle of the year begin modeling and guiding. By the end of the year your students will be ready to draw their own graphic organizers and write independently.

The Graphic Organizer

These young students are just beginning to understand that text is read from left to right. Therefore the graphic organizer should be very simple and used from left to right also. We suggest drawing a caterpillar made out of adjoining circles. You will use the caterpillar's body parts, from left to right as you make your plan. This will also allow you to differentiate instruction because as students become ready for additional details, they may add circles to the body.

Sample Lessons

The lesson plans provided are broken up into two categories: whole group modeling and guided writing. Reuse them throughout the year with different topics.

Whole Group Modeling. For these lessons, gather the students at the front of the room or wherever you normally read stories to them.

Day 1

Objective: Students will listen to stories about friends.

Materials: Books about friends.
1. Read fiction and non-fiction texts about friends to the class. Discuss how the two types of books are different.
   - Fiction stories are made up and will most likely have cartoon pictures drawn by an illustrator. Explain that the stories could be realistic or fantasy.
   - Non-fiction stories are real, sometimes have real photographs, and are about real people or animals.

2. After reading about friends, ask the students to raise their hand if they have made a new friend at school. Then ask them to think about the things they do with friends at school. You may ask a few students to share.

Day 2

Objectives: Students will learn the Mr. Caterpillar plan and participate in whole group planning.

Materials: Chart paper; markers.
1. Fasten chart paper to the board horizontally.

2. Tell students you are going to write together about the things they do with friends at school. You might say, "When we write we will ask Mr. Caterpillar to help us think and plan about what we want to write. This way we will not get stuck or forget what we want to write about." Tell them that the authors of the books you just read also planned what they were going to write about before they wrote their books.

3. Draw Mr. Caterpillar on the chart paper. Be sure to make him big enough so you may write and draw inside of each circle.

4. Tell the students that on his head you want to write down the main idea so you won't forget what you are writing about. Ask a student for help, then write "things I do with friends" or "my friends at school" inside the first circle, the caterpillar's head. You may also want to draw pictures of friends and a schoolhouse.

5. Ask one or two volunteers to tell you things they do with friends at school. Write or draw each activity inside its own circular body part.

6. Tell the students that they will continue writing using Mr. Caterpillar tomorrow.

Day 3

Objective: Students will participate in a whole group writing activity using the plan created yesterday.

Materials: Plan; chart paper; markers.

1. Fasten a sheet of chart paper on the board vertically next to the one with Mr. Caterpillar that you created yesterday.

2. Ask students what they did yesterday during writing. Call on one or two students to "help" you remember that you drew Mr. Caterpillar to make a plan, wrote the main idea on his head, and listed things you do with friends at school on his body.

3. Inform the students that the next step in writing is to use Mr. Caterpillar to write.

4. Demonstrate how to take the main idea from Mr. Caterpillar's head and make a complete sentence out of it. Your sentence could be: "There are lots of things to do with friends at school." Write this or the sentence you create on your second sheet of chart paper. As you write you might ask the students what letter they think each new word will start with. Make the sound and have them tell you the letter to write. Let them know that at the beginning of each sentence you will use a capital letter and at the end of each sentence you will use a period or other ending mark.

5. Model continuously using Mr. Caterpillar to guide your story.

6. When you are finished, read it over with the students. Display this story and Mr. Caterpillar for a few days.

Day 4

Objective: Students will use a sentence starter to write about what they like to do with friends at school.

Materials: Sentence starter papers; crayons; pencils; three-prong folders; yarn; hole puncher; markers.

Note: This activity is best done with the students in their own seats or during a time when you have a teacher's aide or parent volunteer to help. Before class, type the following sentence starter at the bottom of a piece of paper. "I like to _____ with my friends at school." Allow plenty of room at the top for the student's illustration. Then copy this sheet for all of the students.

1. Explain that today students will get to do a little writing on their own. They will work to make a class book. Remind them that the topic is "things to do with friends at school."

2. Read the story you wrote together aloud. This may give them some ideas. Be sure, however, to tell them that your class book would be very boring if everyone wrote about the same thing. Suggest that they come up with their own activity that is different from the ones you wrote about together.

3. Allow students time to draw at the top of the page what they like to do with friends at school. While they are drawing, circulate the room and have the students dictate to you what they are drawing. Write what they say in the blank of their sentence starter. Be sure students write their names on their papers.

4. Collect the finished papers and tell the students that you will put the book together and will read it tomorrow.

5. Bind the students' papers together into a class book. There are many ways to do this. One idea is to punch holes in each sheet and place them inside a three-prong folder. Another idea is to laminate the pages, punch holes in each sheet, and tie together with yarn. However you choose, be sure to write the title and the authors' names on the cover page.

Day 5

Objective: Students will listen to a read-aloud of their first class book.

Materials: Class book.

1. Review the process of creating a class book. Ask students to remind you of each step.

2. Share the class book.

3. Display the book in the room so that students may read it anytime.

Guided Writing. Begin guided writing when students show some mastery of phonemes.

Day 1

Objective: Students will listen to stories about feelings.

Materials: Books about feelings.

1. Gather the students today and read both fiction and non-fiction books about feelings. Discuss the differences between the types of books.

2. When you have completed the stories ask the students some questions about their own feelings. Ask them to tell you about several different feelings they've felt. You may make a list of their answers.

Day 2

Objective: Students will use a graphic organizer to make a writing plan.

Materials: Chart paper; unlined paper; pencils; markers.

1. Fasten chart paper on the board horizontally and pass out unlined paper to the students. Explain that everyone will work at the same time to make their own Mr. Caterpillar.

2. Remind them that Mr. Caterpillar helps them write stories.

3. Draw Mr. Caterpillar on the chart paper using two circles. Be sure to make him big enough to write and draw inside of each circle. Then ask the students to draw Mr. Caterpillar on their papers. (If your students have trouble drawing circles independently at this time, you can always make copies for them to use.) Monitor their work.

4. Tell the students that you will write the main idea on his head. Remind them that yesterday you read stories about different types of feelings. Explain that today they will write about a feeling they experienced and what made them feel that way.

5. Tell them that it is your turn to work first and then it will be their turn to work. Think aloud about what you feel. It is important for the students to hear your thought processes as a writer.

6. Choose a feeling of your own and write it inside of Mr. Caterpillar's head. You might choose to write "silly" inside of your first circle. Then ask the students to think of any feeling they have and write it inside Mr. Caterpillar's head.

7. Circulate the room to help students choose feelings and write them inside their plans. Prompt students to sound out the letters if they will be dictating their feelings to you.

8. Tell the students that they will continue writing using Mr. Caterpillar tomorrow. Collect these plans and save for tomorrow.

Day 3

Objective: Students will continue working on the caterpillar plan they started yesterday.

Materials: Chart paper; students' plans; pencils; markers.

1. Pass out the students' plans from yesterday. Review the plan you made yesterday and remind them that they are working on a story about their feelings.

2. Inform the students that today they will finish their plans. Tell them that they will think about the feelings they chose yesterday. Then they need

to think about what makes them feel that way or the times they have that feeling.

3. Remind them that it is your turn to work first, so they must pay attention to you at this time. Think aloud about the feeling you chose yesterday. If you chose "silly" you could say, " I feel silly when I dress up in a Halloween costume. So I'll write Halloween or I can draw a picture of myself dressed up in a costume." Remember to sound out the word(s) you write to reinforce the students' phonemic awareness. You may also have them help you spell the word.

4. When you finish it will be their turn to work. Ask them to write or draw what prompts their feelings. Monitor the students, helping when necessary.

5. Some students may have more than one thing to write about. Allow those students to draw another circle onto Mr. Caterpillar's body and continue to plan.

6. Collect these plans when the students have completed them.

7. Inform them that tomorrow they will begin using Mr. Caterpillar to write.

Day 4

Objective: Students will use sentence starters to write about their feelings.

Materials: Sentence starters; crayons; pencils.

Note: Before class, type the following sentence starter at the bottom of a piece of paper. "I feel _____ when _____." Remember to leave room at the top for students' illustrations. Make student copies.

1. Begin the lesson by asking the students what they have been working on this week. Review the plan you made and ask them to look over their own plans after you pass them out. Choose a few students to share their plans with the class.

2. Explain that today they will use Mr. Caterpillar to help them write on their own. Tell them that it is your turn to work first.

3. Model how to take the main idea from Mr. Caterpillar's head and make a complete sentence out of it using the sentence starter. If you used "silly" as your feeling then your sentence might look like this: "I feel silly when I am dressed in my Halloween costume." Also point out that you are using a capital letter at the beginning of each sentence and a period at the end.

4. Now tell the students that it is their turn to write. Remind them to use Mr. Caterpillar to help them remember what to write. Monitor students and provide help. As students complete their stories, they can begin illustrating.

Day 5

Objectives: Students will complete and share their work.

Materials: Completed student work.

1. Allow those students who have not finished to complete their work.

2. Gather the students. Tell them that they can share their work with the class if they wish. Model appropriate audience behavior as students share their work.

3. Collect the papers and create a class book.

Suggested Writing Topics

The best writing topics for kindergarten will be based on the science and social studies curriculum. Create one writing topic each week based on your science or social studies lessons. Some suggested sentence starters follow.

- Favorite food: My favorite food is _____ because _____.
- Favorite T.V. show: I like to watch _____ because _____.
- Bears: I learned that bears _____.
- Community Workers: A _____ helps me by _____.
- Seasons: In _____ we can _____ outside.

First Grade

During the first nine weeks of school your students will work on writing complete sentences. At this time your writing instruction will consist of whole group paragraphs and guided independent writing using sentence starters. Students will need a great deal of support and modeling. Stress capital letters and punctuation marks.

In the second quarter of the year you may begin guided writing. Students will be familiar with the pickle sandwich and should be capable of writing complete sentences.

During the second half of the year students can think of main ideas, three details, and conclusion sentences. They should begin using describing words and more interesting vocabulary. They should correctly spell known words and phonetically spell unfamiliar words. By this time they should also use TCUPSS to edit their work for capital letters, proper nouns, and ending punctuation marks.

The Graphic Organizer

The graphic organizer for first grade is a modified pickle sandwich. It has a large horizontal oval on the top and bottom with three vertical ovals in the center. The top oval or "bun" is for the main idea, the three "pickles" are for the three details or reasons, and the bottom "bun" is for the conclusion. Each oval corresponds to one sentence of a paragraph. See Figure 12.1.

Figure 12.1   First-Grade Pickle Sandwich

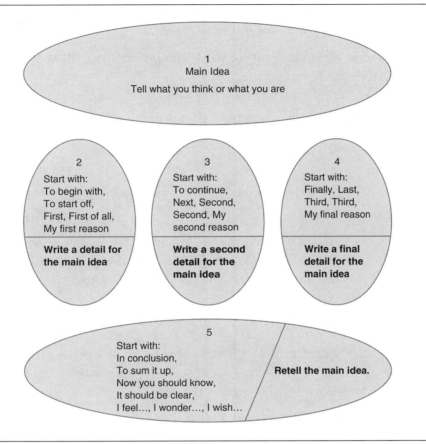

Copyright © 2006 by Karen Donohue and Nanda N. Reddy. All rights reserved. Reprinted from *180 Days to Successful Writers: Lessons to Prepare Your Students for Standardized Assessments and for Life* by Karen Donohue and Nanda N. Reddy. Thousand Oaks, CA: Corwin Press, www.corwinpress.com. Reproduction authorized only for the local school site or nonprofit organization that has purchased this book.

Sample Lessons

Lessons for first grade are broken down into these categories: modeled, guided, semi-independent, and beginning narrative. These lessons may be reused with different topics throughout the year.

Modeled Writing. You will gather students close to the board for these lessons.

Day 1

Objectives: Students will listen to stories about friends and brainstorm a list of things that friends do to help us.

Materials: Library books about friends; chart paper; markers.

Note: Before class, locate fiction and non-fiction books that deal with friends.

1. Read the books about friends. Ask students to listen for how the friends help each other.

2. Discuss the difference between fiction and non-fiction books.

3. Post the chart paper. Write, "How friends help us." Ask the students to help you list how friends helped each other in the stories and how their friends help them. Write their responses.

4. When the list is complete, tell the students that they will use it tomorrow to write a class paper.

Days 2, 3, and 4

Objectives: Students will learn the pickle sandwich graphic organizer and TCUPSS.

Materials: Brainstormed list from yesterday; chart paper; markers; Figures 12.1 and 2.3.

Note: In the beginning it will take you a long time to finish your plan with the class and write the paper. Therefore, this lesson is stretched out over three days. Use Figure 12.1, the First-Grade Pickle Sandwich. Prepare or amend Figure 2.3, the TCUPSS poster. You may find it useful to delete the second S from TCUPSS because first graders may have difficulty grasping the concept of "Support."

1. Post the brainstormed list on the board next to a clean sheet of chart paper. Inform students that today you will start writing as a class about how friends help each other.

2. Discuss that all authors plan before writing. Explain that your plan is called the pickle sandwich because it looks like three pickles standing inside of a bun. Draw the plan on the chart paper for the students.

3. Explain that the top bun of the sandwich is for the main idea. Here is where you make a note of what you are writing about. In this case, the main idea is the ways that friends help each other. In the top bun, write "Friends help each other in many ways."

4. Tell the students that the pickles are where you will plan your details. Let them know that the details help support or tell about the main idea. Explain that you will choose three details that they brainstormed yesterday.

5. Read over your brainstormed list of ways friends help each other. Choose one such as, "Lets you borrow a pencil or eraser." Write that detail in the first pickle.

6. Ask students to give you details for the second and third pickles.

7. Announce it is time to finish the plan by completing the bottom bun. Explain that here you tell something about your main idea in a different way. For example, "Good friends help each other." Sometimes you can add an interesting fact about your topic or make a statement about how you feel. For example if you were writing about spring, the bottom bun might say, "I love spring" or "I can't wait for spring."

8. Tell them that you have now completed the plan and will start writing.

9. Before you write, review the plan and remind the students that you will need their help. Post the plan next to a new sheet of chart paper.

10. Explain that items in their plan need to be in order.

11. Start at your top bun and make a large number 1 next to it. Tell them that the top bun comes first when you write. Continue numbering each part of the plan: first pickle-2, second pickle-3, third pickle-4, bottom bun-5.

12. Now ask the students what you should write first. They should identify the main idea, "Friends help each other many ways."

13. Continue to move through the plan and write complete sentences using student input.

14. After you complete the paper, edit. Display the TCUPSS poster and tell them what each letter stands for. Tell them that at this time you will focus on: Tracking with your finger, Checking capitals, and Putting in periods. Explain that good writers always review their own work before making final or "clean" copies.

15. Model using TCUPSS to edit and create a final draft.

Day 5

Objective: Students will use sentence starters to write complete sentences.

Materials: Sentence starters; "draw and write" paper; pencils.

Note: Before class, write the following sentence starter on the board for students to use. "_____ helps me _____." Also, post the brainstormed list you created on Day 1. Allow the students to use this chart when they are writing today.

1. Reread the story you wrote as a class. Tell them they will have a chance to write independently using what you call a sentence starter.

2. Show them the sentence and demonstrate how to use it. Think aloud as you fill in the blank spaces with a name of your own friend and the way that friend helps you.

3. Tell students to use ideas from the brainstormed list to complete their sentences.

4. Monitor their work and provide help.

5. Allow the students to illustrate their writing after they have TCUPSSed.

Guided Writing. As students gain independence, slowly reduce the amount of guidance. First-grade students will generally not achieve writing independence.

Day 1

Objectives: Students will discuss days of the week and brainstorm reasons why each might be their favorite day of the week.

Materials: Chart paper; markers.

1. Post seven sheets of chart paper on the board and gather students so they can see the charts.

2. Tell students that this week they are going to write about their favorite day of the week. Ask the students to remind you the names of the days as you write them in the center of each sheet. Discuss that the days of the week begin with capital letters.

3. Brainstorm ideas for why they like each day of the week and write these on the charts.

4. Keep the charts for tomorrow's lesson.

Days 2 and 3

Objective: Students will make a plan for their favorite day of the week.

Materials: Brainstormed list; chart paper; markers; "draw and write" paper; pencils.

Note: Post the brainstormed lists around the room so that students can see them.

1. Inform students that today you will work first while they watch. Then they will have a chance to work with your help. Ask them to remind you what the pickle sandwich looks like and then draw it.

2. Ask students to draw pickle sandwiches on the blank part of their paper.

3. Remind them to always start with the top bun and write the main idea.

4. Say to the students, "My favorite day of the week is Friday. So I will write 'Friday' in the top bun." Ask the students to choose their favorite day of the week and write it in their top bun. Monitor their progress.

5. Move on to the first pickle. Tell them that now you have to choose three reasons why this day is your favorite. Think aloud as you choose one from the brainstormed list you created with the class. You might say, "One reason I like Friday is that we have pizza for lunch. So, I will write 'pizza for lunch' in the first pickle."

6. Allow the students to choose one reason and write it in their first pickle. Monitor and offer assistance.

7. Ask the students if they know which pickle you should work on next. They should point out the second pickle or the one in the middle.

Remind them that it is your turn to work. Think aloud as you choose a second reason from the brainstorm list and put it inside of your second pickle.

8. Guide students' turn to write their second reasons.

9. Choose and write your reason for why you like Friday and help students write their reasons.

10. Finish your plan by writing in the bottom bun and guiding students to complete their own.

Days 4 and 5

Objectives: Students will write rough drafts using their plans, TCUPSS their paper, and create final drafts.

Materials: Previously written plans; draw and write paper; pencils; crayons.

1. Post your plan and ask the students to retrieve their plan sheets. Tell them that today they will be using this plan to create a rough draft.

2. Model starting with your top bun to write your main idea sentence. Think aloud, "I wrote 'Friday' in my top bun. So, I will write, 'My favorite day of the week is Friday.'"

3. You might want to ask the students to share different ways of phrasing the main idea. They could use, "Friday is my favorite day" or "The best day of the week is Friday." Monitor as they create sentences from their top buns.

4. Continue working through your plan in this way. You may choose to make a mistake here and there to be corrected during TCUPSS modeling. You might spell a sight word incorrectly, leave out a capital letter, or omit a punctuation mark.

5. After completing your paragraph, begin moving through the TCUPSS process. Ask for a volunteer to tell you what each letter stands for.

6. Model reading your paper out loud while tracking with your finger. Tell them that you are listening for mistakes. Correct mistakes as you find them. Now ask students to do the same.

7. Allow your students to create and publish final copies.

Semi-Independent Writing. After sufficient modeling, students will be capable of working semi-independently. Lead a brainstorm session for each topic, remind students of the writing process, monitor as students plan, and then collect plans to check them. After, students will write from their plans as you provide assistance. Some students will require more assistance than others. Finally, students will TCUPSS, revise, and publish final drafts.

Beginning Narrative Writing. Narrative writing may prove to be difficult for most first graders. For the majority of the year they lack the maturity to create organized stories that make sense. However, toward the end of the year when they are competent writers, they may be ready to attempt simple narratives. You will need to model and closely guide them through this assignment.

You should probably continue using the pickle sandwich since students are comfortable with this tool. However, if you feel your students can handle it, adapt Figure 12.3, the Second-Grade Tier Cake. The narratives students write should include a problem, a character, and an event. Students may write three actions related to the event.

Suggested Writing Topics

First-grade students should write mostly expository paragraphs based on the science, social studies, or literature curriculum. Each week you may choose a topic that is related to another content area. For example, during Fire Safety Week you can have them write a main idea, three rules for fire safety, and then a conclusion sentence. Some other ideas are listed below.

- Favorite person: three special things about this person
- Favorite season: three things you can do during that time of year
- Favorite holiday: three things you like about that holiday
- Favorite food: three reasons why you chose it
- Animal report: three facts about the animal
- What you want to be when you grow up: provide three reasons why
- Class pet: three things you like about the animal or three reasons your class should have a pet
- Tall tales (narrative): a character with a problem, three actions, and a resolution

Second Grade

You should begin the year teaching your students expository writing. Expository writing can be fictional or factual and is written to explain or tell readers about a specific topic. You will help students stretch the one-paragraph expository essays they learned in first grade into three paragraphs.

Student should be experienced with expository writing, but not narrative. You will teach them the rules for narratives and a modified tier cake to create narrative stories with a clear beginning, middle, and end.

The Graphic Organizer

The pickle sandwich should be adapted to include information covering three paragraphs. The top bun will translate to the first, or introductory, paragraph. The three pickles will provide supporting details for the second paragraph. The bottom bun will serve as the conclusion paragraph. See Figure 12.2, the Second-Grade Pickle Sandwich.

The tier cake will be modified as follows. The top tier will include boxes for the setting, character(s), and main story event. The four boxes in the middle are for the events taking place in the story. Finally, a rectangle at the bottom will be

Figure 12.2 Second-Grade Pickle Sandwich

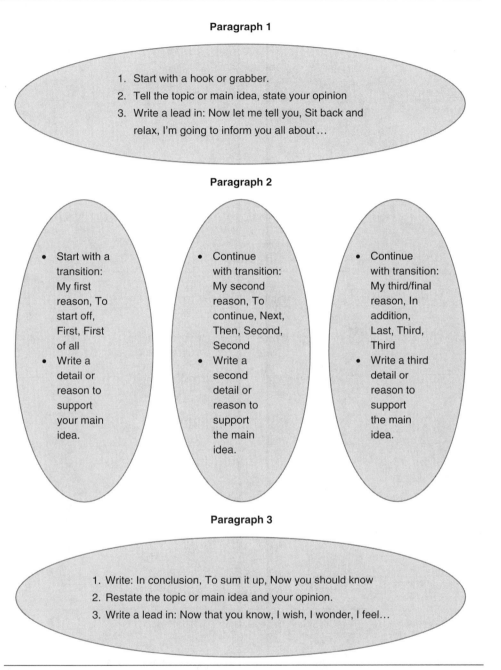

Paragraph 1

1. Start with a hook or grabber.
2. Tell the topic or main idea, state your opinion
3. Write a lead in: Now let me tell you, Sit back and relax, I'm going to inform you all about…

Paragraph 2

- Start with a transition: My first reason, To start off, First, First of all
- Write a detail or reason to support your main idea.

- Continue with transition: My second reason, To continue, Next, Then, Second, Second
- Write a second detail or reason to support the main idea.

- Continue with transition: My third/final reason, In addition, Last, Third, Third
- Write a third detail or reason to support the main idea.

Paragraph 3

1. Write: In conclusion, To sum it up, Now you should know
2. Restate the topic or main idea and your opinion.
3. Write a lead in: Now that you know, I wish, I wonder, I feel…

Copyright © 2006 by Karen Donohue and Nanda N. Reddy. All rights reserved. Reprinted from *180 Days to Successful Writers: Lessons to Prepare Your Students for Standardized Assessments and for Life* by Karen Donohue and Nanda N. Reddy. Thousand Oaks, CA: Corwin Press, www.corwinpress.com. Reproduction authorized only for the local school site or nonprofit organization that has purchased this book.

used for the conclusion and take away. See Figure 12.3, the Second-Grade Tier Cake.

Sample Lessons

The lessons in second grade are divided into four categories: modeled expository, guided expository, modeled narrative, and guided narrative. These lessons can be adapted based on student needs and used repeatedly with other topics.

Figure 12.3   Second-Grade Tier Cake

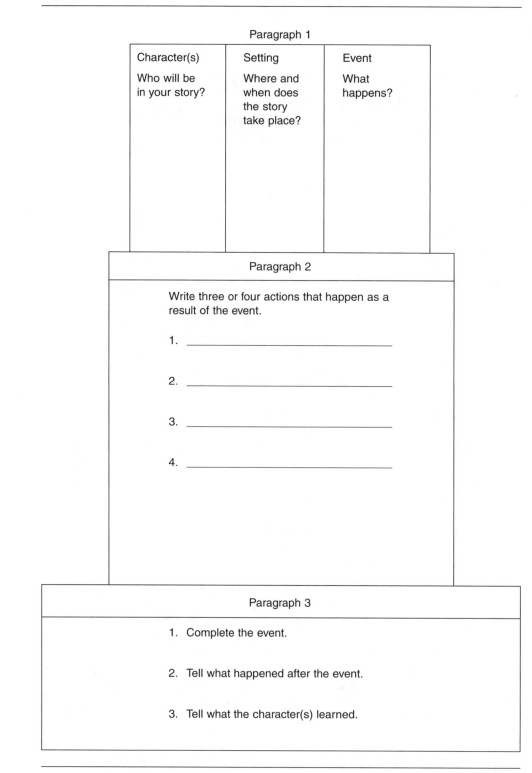

Copyright © 2006 by Karen Donohue and Nanda N. Reddy. All rights reserved. Reprinted from *180 Days to Successful Writers: Lessons to Prepare Your Students for Standardized Assessments and for Life* by Karen Donohue and Nanda N. Reddy. Thousand Oaks, CA: Corwin Press, www.corwinpress.com. Reproduction authorized only for the local school site or nonprofit organization that has purchased this book.

Spend the first two weeks of school modeling expository writing. Then use the guided lesson plan for four weeks. Introduce narrative writing during Week 7 and use the modeled lesson plan format for two weeks. Follow that for six weeks with the guided narrative format.

Switch between the genres every two weeks for the rest of the year, using both the modeled and guided lesson plan formats.

Modeled Expository. Second-grade students are becoming more independent with expository writing. They will generally benefit from some modeling, but too much will constrain growth.

Day 1

Objectives: Students will revisit the pickle sandwich and plan for an expository paper.

Materials: Figure 12.2; chart paper; markers; books written by Dr. Seuss.

Note: Make a display of Figure 12.2, the Second-Grade Pickle Sandwich.

1. Display Figure 12.2, the Second-Grade Pickle Sandwich. Remind students that this is the correct plan sheet to use for an expository paper. Read the hints and discuss the role of each part of the plan. Discuss how this is different from the pickle sandwich in first grade.

2. Read several books by Dr. Seuss.

3. Tell them that this week you'll write about how you like Dr. Seuss. Draw the plan.

4. Refer to Figure 12.2. Read the hint in the top bun. Then think aloud as you plan for the top bun. You might say, "I'm going to be writing about my favorite author, so that will be my topic. And my opinion is that Dr. Seuss is my favorite; that is my main idea."

5. Then explain that a "lead in" is something that you'll write at the end of the first paragraph that tells the reader to keep going and find out more. Some examples of lead ins are: Keep reading to find out _____; To find out about _____ keep reading; and Read on to learn what I think about _____.

6. Explain that when you make a plan, it is not necessary to use complete sentences. Notes are made on the plan sheet so that when you are ready to write, you'll remember what you wanted to say. Write down these notes in the oval with the three dashes.
   • Favorite author
   • Ours is Dr. Seuss, three reasons why
   • Keep reading . . .

7. Ask the students if they know what comes next. Remind them to use the reference poster if they have a hard time remembering that you need to plan your details in the three "pickles" now.

8. Model how you would plan the reasons why you chose Dr. Seuss as your favorite author. Think aloud as you develop each of your ideas. The following is an example.
   - First pickle: many great books; favorite is *One Fish . . .*
   - Second pickle: pictures are great; colors
   - Third pickle: stories make me laugh; hard not to laugh

9. Model how you would rephrase the main idea and three details for the plan's conclusion. Also model how you would include an additional detail about Dr. Seuss. An example follows.
   - One interesting thing about his books is they contain only sight words and nonsense words.

10. Tell the students you will add transition words to the plan tomorrow.

Days 3 and 4

Objectives: Students will learn transition words, insert them into plans, and write a rough draft.

Materials: Previously written plan; rough draft paper; construction paper.

1. Discuss that the plan is finished but that your middle paragraph needs transition words. Let them know that transition means to move. Explain that transition words help readers by allowing them to move smoothly from one reason to the next.

2. List transition words that you could use in each pickle on construction paper. Once you give the first few examples, the students may be able to contribute to the list as well. The following are examples of appropriate second-grade transition words.
   - First, One reason, My first reason, To begin
   - Next, Second, Another reason, The second reason, Also
   - Last, Third, Finally, The last reason, The third reason, Lastly

3. Post the list. With the students' input, choose appropriate transition words and write them at the top of each pickle.

4. Start writing your rough draft from the plan. Demonstrate how to take your notes from the top bun to write your first paragraph. Think aloud as you model. Remember to indent. An example follows.
   - Most people have a favorite author. Our favorite is Dr. Seuss. There are three reasons why we like Dr. Seuss. Keep reading to find out why we like our favorite author.

5. Model taking notes from the pickles to write your second paragraph. You might want to leave a few mistakes in this rough draft so that you can model TCUPSS tomorrow.

6. An example paragraph follows.
   - First, Dr. Seuss wrote a lot of great books. Our favorite one is *One Fish, Two Fish, Red Fish, Blue Fish.* Next, his pictures are great. They have

bright colors. Lastly, all of his stories make us laugh. Sometimes we have a hard time not laughing out loud.

7. Model your conclusion. An example follows.
   - Our class reads a lot so we have a favorite author. Dr. Seuss' books are the best. Do you have a favorite author?

8. Reread your rough draft.

Day 5

Objective: Students will learn TCUPSS.

Materials: Previously written class paper; markers; TCUPSS poster.

Note: Before class, prepare or amend Figure 2.3, the TCUPSS poster.
1. Introduce or review the TCUPSS poster. Then model each step of the process with your rough draft. Track and correct any mistakes that you made on purpose and add adjectives.

2. Now make your final draft and share with the students.

Guided Expository. These types of lessons should constitute the bulk of your writing instruction.

Day 1

Objective: Students will brainstorm ideas for an expository essay about a season.

Materials: Resource posters; chart paper; markers.
1. Post four sheets of chart paper. Ask students to name the four seasons of the year and write them on the charts.

2. Discuss the types of things that are unique to each season. You might include the kind of weather the season brings, the activities you do during that time of year, when that season falls, or the holidays you celebrate within the season.

3. Allow the students to share their ideas. Write them on the chart paper.

Day 2

Objective: Students will create a plan for their expository essay.

Materials: Resource posters; previously written plans; brainstormed list; paper; markers; pencils.
1. Review your brainstormed lists about the seasons.

2. Draw the expository plan on chart paper. Then ask the students to draw their pickle sandwiches while you monitor.

3. Review the pickle sandwich by asking the students how you should start planning for your paper. Model planning for a season you have chosen to write about.
   - Four seasons; all different; my fave is spring; read on to find out. . .

4. Monitor as students write the topic, choose seasons, and write lead ins. Walk around and help students as they work independently.

5. Model planning your first pickle. An example follows.
   - One reason; baby animals born; chicks are fuzzy and yellow

6. Monitor as students plan their first pickles with transition words.

7. Continue modeling and guiding students. Examples for the remainder of the plan follow.
   - Second pickle: Another reason; flowers bloom; air filled with scent
   - Third pickle: Most important; mini-vacation; family to the beach
   - Bottom bun: All seasons are great; special; My mind is made up; spring; What is your fave season?

8. The remainder of class should be spent allowing the students to finish their plans. Collect student plans for tomorrow's lesson.

Days 3 and 4

Objective: Students will write rough drafts from the plans they created.

Materials: Previously written plans; chart paper; paper; markers; pencils.

1. Post your plan and hand out student plans.

2. Model how to turn your notes into Paragraph 1. An example follows.
   - There are four seasons in the year. They are all different. My favorite is spring. Read on to find out why spring is my favorite season.

3. Guide students as they write their first paragraphs.

4. Follow the same procedures with the second and third paragraphs. Examples follow.
   - One reason is that baby animals are born. I like to see baby chicks when they are fuzzy and yellow. Another reason is that flowers bloom. The air is filled with their scent. Most important, I like spring because we have a mini-vacation. During Spring Break, my family goes to the beach.
   - All of the seasons are great. They are all special. My mind is made up about which one is my favorite. It has to be spring. What is your favorite season?

Day 5

Objectives: Students will TCUPSS and publish final drafts.

Materials: TCUPSS poster; *Spring Is Best*; rough drafts; chart paper; paper; markers; pencils.

1. Inform students that it is time to edit and revise their papers. Model TCUPSSing your own rough draft. Add more details where possible and change boring words to more exciting, descriptive words. An example final draft is provided below.

Spring Is Best

There are four seasons in the year. They are summer, fall, winter, and spring. They are all different in their own way. My favorite season is spring. Read on to find out why I like spring the best.

One reason I like spring is that baby animals are born. I like to see baby chicks when they are fuzzy and yellow. Another reason is that flowers bloom in spring. The air is filled with their sweet scents. Most important, I like spring because we have a mini-vacation from school. Spring break is the time my family takes off for the beach.

All of the four seasons are great. Each of them is special. Still, my mind is made up about which one is my favorite. It has to be spring. What is your favorite season?

---

2. Monitor students as they TCUPSS. Encourage them to add details. Allow them to revise and publish. Students may share their work.

Modeled Narrative. Narrative writing is a new concept for second-grade students. As such, they will require extensive modeling.

Days 1, 2, and 3

Objectives: Students will learn the tier cake and narrative transition words.

Materials: Figure 12.3; chart paper; construction paper; markers.

Note: Use Figure 12.3, the Second-Grade Tier Cake, to help you make a poster today.

1. Discuss your previous writings, which were called expository essays. They were written to explain or tell about something. Tell the students that today they will learn a new kind of writing called narrative. Narratives can be true or made up, but they all show the passing of time and have characters, a setting, and an event.

2. Tell them they will learn about a new plan sheet called the tier cake. They will use it to plan narrative stories.

3. Draw the tier cake on chart paper. Explain that you will post this chart for use as a reference tool. It will be placed in a central location where each student can see and use it to help them write terrific narrative stories.

4. Post a clean sheet of chart paper and ask the students to direct you in drawing the tier cake.

5. Tell them you will use the tier cake to write a story that shows the passing of time.

6. Explain that authors often use real facts when they write stories. The story you'll write this week will contain facts about the water cycle. Explain the process of a water drop going through the cycle.

7. Begin planning the setting, character, and event. Refer to the tier cake hints. An example follows.
   - Character: Walter Waterdrop
   - Setting: creek in the forest; last Saturday
   - Event: evaporates

8. Ask the students what you should do next. They should use the tier cake to tell you that it is time to write three or four things that happened to the character as a result of the event.

9. Stop here to ask what they did with expository writing to help readers move through the paper. They should tell you that they used transition words. Explain that transition words are necessary in narrative writing as well, but that not all expository transition words work in narrative writing; you will need to generate a new list.

10. Label the large construction paper, "Narrative Transition Words." Brainstorm transitions that show the passing of time. Example transitions follow:
    - First, Next, Then, Last
    - It all started, After that, Finally, Suddenly
    - In the beginning, Then to my surprise, Immediately afterward, In the end

11. Plan the middle tier with transition words. An example follows.
    - It all started, swirling around rock
    - Then sun warmed me, evaporated
    - Suddenly lifted through air, joined others in a cloud
    - After a few hours, got crowded up there, couldn't move

12. Prompt students to remind you what is included in the last paragraph. Model planning the final paragraph with transition words. An example follows.
    - Thought I'd be squished; heard thunder
    - We fell to ground; was precipitation
    - In the end plop; back in the creek
    - Cool to learn by being part of water cycle

Days 4 and 5

Objectives: The students will learn how to write a narrative rough draft from a previously made plan and TCUPSS.

Materials: Previously written plan; chart paper; markers.

1. Post the plan next to a new sheet of chart paper.

2. Review the plan.

3. Begin writing Paragraph 1, referring to the plan. An example follows.
   - My name is Walter Waterdrop and I've just had an amazing adventure. I am a tiny drop of water and I've always lived in a small creek on the edge of the forest. That is until I experienced the water cycle firsthand last Saturday!

4. Now continue with the middle paragraph. An example follows.
   - It all started last Saturday when I was minding my own business and swirling around a rock. The sun was warming me up and then without warning I started to evaporate! Suddenly, I was lifted through the air and joined other drops in a cloud. After a few hours it got pretty crowded in there. I could hardly move.

5. Use the plan to model the final paragraph with transitions. An example follows.
   - Just when I thought I would be squished, I heard thunder. Then we began to fall as precipitation back to the ground one after another. I landed with a, "Plop!" I was right back in my creek. It was good to be back in my creek, but it was really cool to learn about the water cycle by being part of it! What an adventure!

6. Read the rough draft. Then ask what they do whenever an expository paper is finished. They should remember that it is time to TCUPSS.

7. Review the TCUPSS process. Then model, using it to edit and revise your story.

8. Publish the final draft.

Guided Narrative. While students will likely become capable of writing expository essays independently, they will probably need guidance with narratives all year.

Days 1 and 2

Objective: Students will make plans for their first narrative stories.

Materials: Tier cake; narrative transition words; chart paper; paper; markers; pencils.

1. Tell the students it is their turn to create stories. Explain that they will write a story about a vacation or trip they have taken. Brainstorm a list of trips students have taken.

2. Post chart paper as the students get out their own sheet of paper. Draw the tier cake and review.

3. Plan your character, setting, and event boxes while the students watch you. Tell them that it is your turn to work first. Think aloud as you make the notes inside your plan. An example follows.
   - Setting: summer vacation; Washington State
   - Characters: my family
   - Event: time I visited Mt. St. Helens

4. Guide students as they plan their first paragraphs. Monitor and assist students.

5. Model how to plan for the middle paragraph. An example follows.
   - Early morning; drove from Oregon; few hours
   - After the drive; got out and walked around site; not a lot of trees
   - Later; read about; volcano erupted 1980; blew out side
   - At the end of the day; saw the crater; amazing sight

6. Guide students as they plan their middle paragraphs. Monitor their progress.

7. Model your final paragraph.
   - Learned a lot; was fun with family; great vacation

8. Allow students to complete their paragraphs as you monitor their progress.

9. Tell students they will write a rough draft tomorrow.

Days 3, 4, and 5

Objectives: Students will write a rough draft, TCUPSS, and publish.

Materials: Previously written plans; TCUPSS poster; *My Trip to Mount Saint Helens*; chart paper; paper; markers; pencils.

1. Review the plan. Then model and guide students in writing each paragraph.

2. A completed example follows.

My Trip to Mount Saint Helens

I will always remember the time I visited Mount Saint Helens. It was the best family vacation ever. My entire family traveled to Oregon and Washington State. We had the greatest time.

Early one morning we drove a few hours from Portland, Oregon, to Mount Saint Helens. After a long drive, we got out and walked around a ridge near the site. There weren't a lot of trees. Later in the gift shop, we read about the volcano erupting out of its side in 1980. At the end of the day, we traveled closer to the crater. It was an amazing sight.

I learned a lot about different kinds of volcanoes. My family really had fun being together. I think it was a great vacation that I will always remember.

---

3. Model TCUPSSing and revising your paper.

4. Monitor students as they TCUPSS their papers.

5. Allow students to publish and share.

Suggested Writing Topics

The following are some suggested topics for second-grade writers.

- Solar System: facts about the planets or an imaginative narrative about going to Mars
- Plants: the stages of life or what a plant needs to live
- Matter: three kinds of matter or imaginative narrative on becoming a different form of matter
- Families: different kinds of families, how culture affects family differences, or a story about a family gathering
- How to: make a sandwich, sandcastle, milkshake, or a story about a time you helped someone
- Personal narratives: a vacation, the first day at your new school, a time you were sad

Resource A

EXTRA PROMPTS

The first prompt in each section is formatted for you. The rest of the prompts are "bosses" which you should format before presenting.

Expository

1. Most students know how to succeed in school, but few consider the causes of failure. Think about the things that cause students to perform poorly. Now explain how to do poorly at school.

2. Write to explain how to be a good friend.

3. Explain what your least favorite memory is and why.

4. Explain what your pet peeve is and why.

5. Explain what your least favorite school subject is and why.

6. Write to tell how you get ready for going back to school every year.

7. Write to explain how to make a big family dinner.

8. Explain what you would do if you were in charge of putting on a talent show, haunted house, or fair.

9. If you were a mentor to a young person, explain what your best advice to that person would be.

10. Explain how you would spend a special day with your favorite adult.

Descriptive

1. Everyone has interesting people in their life. Think about an interesting person in your life and this person's personality and traits. Now use sensory details to describe an interesting person.

2. Use sensory details to describe the best (or worst) birthday you've ever had.

3. Use sensory details to describe a loved pet.

4. Use sensory details to describe your favorite (least favorite) board game.

Persuasive

1. Your parents want to sell the house and move, but you do not. Think about the reasons why you should not move. Now write to persuade your parents not to sell the house and move.

2. Write to convince your friends to go on a camping trip.

3. Write to persuade your family to take a vacation to an amusement park.

4. Write to convince your teacher to change a bad grade.

Narrative-Realistic

1. Everyone has hurt someone's feelings before. Think about a person whose feelings you hurt. Now write a story about a time you hurt someone's feelings.

2. Tell a story about a time you visited a hospital or doctor.

3. Tell a story about a time you did something thoughtful or performed a good deed.

4. Tell a story about going to or planning a costume party.

5. Tell a story about a time you went to a circus or zoo.

Narrative-Imaginary

1. Imagine that a talent scout discovers you while you are performing. Think about what could happen if you were discovered. Now write a story about being discovered by a talent scout.

2. Write a story about suddenly finding yourself in a book, movie, or part of a board game.

3. Tell a story about turning into an animal.

4. Tell a story about the day the ground suddenly opened up while you were picnicking.

5. Tell a story about waking up in a different century.

Copyright © 2006 by Karen Donohue and Nanda N. Reddy. All rights reserved. Reprinted from *180 Days to Successful Writers: Lessons to Prepare Your Students for Standardized Assessments and for Life* by Karen Donohue and Nanda N. Reddy. Thousand Oaks, CA: Corwin Press. www.corwinpress.com. Reproduction authorized only for the local school site or nonprofit organization that has purchased this book.

Resource B

GENERIC RUBRIC

Choose a score from 1 to 6 for each category; then find the mean to determine an overall score.

Ideas/Content/Support	0 1 2 3 4 5 6
The writing is enjoyable to read and everything makes sense	0 1 2
The writer provides the right amount of interesting details	0 1 2
The writer has a fresh or unique approach to the topic	0 1 2
Voice/Style	0 1 2 3 4 5 6
The author's personality comes through the writing	0 1 2
The writer is passionate about the topic	0 1 2
The reader feels connected to the writer	0 1 2
Fluency/Flow	0 1 2 3 4 5 6
A variety (long, short, compound) of sentences are used	0 1 2
The writer chooses the best transition words	0 1 2
Sentences are easy to read and in the best order	0 1 2
Word Choice/Vocabulary	0 1 2 3 4 5 6
The writer uses interesting adjectives and strong verbs	0 1 2
The writer provides many sensory details	0 1 2
It is easy to picture details	0 1 2
Organization/Focus	0 1 2 3 4 5 6
The writing starts out with a strong topic sentence or hook	0 1 2
The writer tells relevant information in a logical way	0 1 2

Everything ties together and writing feels finished	0 1 2
Conventions/Grammar/Spelling	0 1 2 3 4 5 6
Periods, capitals, other punctuation are used correctly	0 1 2
Paragraphs are indented and sentences are complete	0 1 2
Few to zero spelling errors	0 1 2
Total	
Divide by 6	
Overall	0 1 2 3 4 5 6

Copyright © 2006 by Karen Donohue and Nanda N. Reddy. All rights reserved. Reprinted from *180 Days to Successful Writers: Lessons to Prepare Your Students for Standardized Assessments and for Life* by Karen Donohue and Nanda N. Reddy. Thousand Oaks, CA: Corwin Press, www.corwinpress.com. Reproduction authorized only for the local school site or nonprofit organization that has purchased this book.

Resource C

Rubric Posters

Score 6
- ☐ Perfect grammar and spelling
- ☐ Author's voice is strong, personable, and inviting
- ☐ Uses complex, interesting sentences and vocabulary
- ☐ Flows easily because of transitions and organization
- ☐ Answers the prompt in a unique way, very logically focused
- ☐ Details and word choice bring the paper to life

Score 5
- ☐ Nearly perfect grammar and spelling
- ☐ Author has a strong voice and personality
- ☐ Many interesting sentences and good vocabulary
- ☐ Uses transitions and paper is organized for easy reading
- ☐ Answers the prompt well
- ☐ Strong details and good word choices make the paper interesting

Score 4
- ☐ Few grammar and spelling mistakes
- ☐ Author's voice and personality comes through often
- ☐ Some interesting sentences and vocabulary
- ☐ Uses transitions and is organized for easy reading
- ☐ Answers the prompt in a predictable manner, focused
- ☐ Overall, good details and word choices

Score 0
- ☐ Does not answer the prompt, off topic
- ☐ Provides an answer that is impossible to read
- ☐ Answers with only a few words or one or two sentences

Score 3
- ☐ Some grammar and spelling mistakes
- ☐ Some of author's voice or personality is present
- ☐ Average vocabulary and simple sentence structures
- ☐ Uses transitions appropriately and is simply organized
- ☐ Answers the prompt, focused
- ☐ Details are present, but not strong, and word choice is average

Score 2
- ☐ Many grammar and spelling mistakes
- ☐ Little of author's voice or personality is present
- ☐ Below average vocabulary and poor sentence structures
- ☐ Uses transitions inappropriately at times or few transitions
- ☐ Somewhat answers the prompt but goes off topic at times
- ☐ Below average word choice and poor details

Score 1
- ☐ Grammar and spelling mistakes make for difficult reading
- ☐ Little or no personality is present
- ☐ Poor vocabulary and sentence structures
- ☐ Poor transition and organization
- ☐ Does not answer the prompt fully or is often off topic
- ☐ Few details and poor word choices

Copyright © 2006 by Karen Donohue and Nanda N. Reddy. All rights reserved. Reprinted from *180 Days to Successful Writers: Lessons to Prepare Your Students for Standardized Assessments and for Life* by Karen Donohue and Nanda N. Reddy. Thousand Oaks, CA: Corwin Press, www.corwinpress.com. Reproduction authorized only for the local school site or nonprofit organization that has purchased this book.

Resource D

Grading Tool

Student	Ideas, Content, & Support	Voice & Style	Fluency & Flow	Word Choice & Vocabulary	Organization & Focus	Conventions, Grammar, & Spelling	Total & Average
Total							
Average							

Copyright © 2006 by Karen Donohue and Nanda N. Reddy. All rights reserved. Reprinted from *180 Days to Successful Writers: Lessons to Prepare Your Students for Standardized Assessments and for Life* by Karen Donohue and Nanda N. Reddy. Thousand Oaks, CA: Corwin Press, www.corwinpress.com. Reproduction authorized only for the local school site or nonprofit organization that has purchased this book.

Resource E

Expository/ Narrative	Ideas, Content, & Support	Voice & Style	Fluency & Flow	Word Choice & Vocabulary	Organization & Focus	Grammar & Spelling	Overall (Average)
Name:	1 2 3 4 5 6	1 2 3 4 5 6	1 2 3 4 5 6	1 2 3 4 5 6	1 2 3 4 5 6	1 2 3 4 5 6	1 2 3 4 5 6

Expository/ Narrative	Ideas, Content, & Support	Voice & Style	Fluency & Flow	Word Choice & Vocabulary	Organization & Focus	Grammar & Spelling	Overall (Average)
Name:	1 2 3 4 5 6	1 2 3 4 5 6	1 2 3 4 5 6	1 2 3 4 5 6	1 2 3 4 5 6	1 2 3 4 5 6	1 2 3 4 5 6

Expository/ Narrative	Ideas, Content, & Support	Voice & Style	Fluency & Flow	Word Choice & Vocabulary	Organization & Focus	Grammar & Spelling	Overall (Average)
Name:	1 2 3 4 5 6	1 2 3 4 5 6	1 2 3 4 5 6	1 2 3 4 5 6	1 2 3 4 5 6	1 2 3 4 5 6	1 2 3 4 5 6

Expository/ Narrative	Ideas, Content, & Support	Voice & Style	Fluency & Flow	Word Choice & Vocabulary	Organization & Focus	Grammar & Spelling	Overall (Average)
Name:	1 2 3 4 5 6	1 2 3 4 5 6	1 2 3 4 5 6	1 2 3 4 5 6	1 2 3 4 5 6	1 2 3 4 5 6	1 2 3 4 5 6

Expository/ Narrative	Ideas, Content, & Support	Voice & Style	Fluency & Flow	Word Choice & Vocabulary	Organization & Focus	Grammar & Spelling	Overall (Average)
Name:	1 2 3 4 5 6	1 2 3 4 5 6	1 2 3 4 5 6	1 2 3 4 5 6	1 2 3 4 5 6	1 2 3 4 5 6	1 2 3 4 5 6

Copyright © 2006 by Karen Donohue and Nanda N. Reddy. All rights reserved. Reprinted from *180 Days to Successful Writers: Lessons to Prepare Your Students for Standardized Assessments and for Life* by Karen Donohue and Nanda N. Reddy. Thousand Oaks, CA: Corwin Press, www.corwinpress.com. Reproduction authorized only for the local school site or nonprofit organization that has purchased this book.

Resource F

EXPOSITORY STUDY GUIDE

- ☐ Key Words: explain, tell why, tell how

- ☐ Planning: five paragraphs, pickle sandwich, introduction, three detail paragraphs, conclusion

- ☐ Example: Everyone has a favorite time of year. Think about your favorite time of year. Now explain what your favorite time of the year is and why.

- ☐ Hooks: Everyone has a favorite time of year. Do you have a favorite time of year?

- ☐ First Paragraph: Listen as I tell you about . . . , Lend me your ears as I tell you about . . .

- ☐ Second Paragraph: My first reason . . . , To begin with . . . , To start off . . .

- ☐ Third Paragraph: My next reason . . . , Another reason . . . , Next . . .

- ☐ Fourth Paragraph: My final reason . . . , Most important . . . , Last but not least . . .

- ☐ Final Paragraph: Now you know . . . , As you can see . . . , In conclusion . . . , In summary . . . , It should be clear . . . (Did you answer the Boss?)

- ☐ Final Sentence: I wish . . . , I feel . . . , I hope . . . , I wonder . . . , Now that you know . . . , Tell me your favorite . . . , Do you have a favorite . . .

- ☐ Ways to Elaborate: Anecdotes, Mind-Bending Metaphors, Sensory Details, Awe-Inspiring Adjectives, Vivacious Verbs

- ☐ TCUPSS: Track with your finger, Check Capitals, Umph, Punctuation, Spelling and Sound, Support

Copyright © 2006 by Karen Donohue and Nanda N. Reddy. All rights reserved. Reprinted from *180 Days to Successful Writers: Lessons to Prepare Your Students for Standardized Assessments and for Life* by Karen Donohue and Nanda N. Reddy. Thousand Oaks, CA: Corwin Press, www.corwinpress.com. Reproduction authorized only for the local school site or nonprofit organization that has purchased this book.

Resource G

NARRATIVE STUDY GUIDE

☐ Key Words: tell a story, imagine, tell events in order

☐ Planning: six paragraphs, tier cake, characters, setting, and problem in first paragraph

☐ Example: Imagine seeing a door appear out of thin air. What could happen if you walk through a strange door? Tell about a time that you walked through a mysterious door.

☐ Hooks: Make a noise—pow, bang, swish, zoom, ker-plunk; Ask a question—Have you ever been to ____; Tell where you are and what you are doing—In a land far away, there was . . . ; Hint at the conflict—I'll never live down that horrible moment

☐ Transition Words: It all started when . . . , Later on . . . , Just hours later . . . , Finally . . . , At last . . . , After a short time . . . , Afterward . . . , Later . . . , Soon . . .

☐ Final Paragraph: The thing I learned . . . , I promise never again to . . . , I wish . . . , I hope . . . , I believe . . . , Have you ever had an adventure like this? (Did you answer the Boss?)

☐ Vivacious Verbs: screamed, scurried, dashed, high-tailed, shrieked, exclaimed, devoured, noticed, observed

☐ Awe-Inspiring Adjectives, Rainbow Words, Sensory Details: slippery, fuzzy, metallic, bumpy, velvety, scratchy, crashing, banging, screeching, whispering, delicious, ivory, scrumptious, mouth-watering, ancient, wrinkled, multicolored, baby blue, burnt

☐ TCUPSS: Track with your finger, Check Capitals, Umph, Punctuation, Spelling and Sound, Support

Copyright © 2006 by Karen Donohue and Nanda N. Reddy. All rights reserved. Reprinted from *180 Days to Successful Writers: Lessons to Prepare Your Students for Standardized Assessments and for Life* by Karen Donohue and Nanda N. Reddy. Thousand Oaks, CA: Corwin Press, www.corwinpress.com. Reproduction authorized only for the local school site or nonprofit organization that has purchased this book.

Resource H

Chapter Book Template

Chapter _____

Copyright © 2006 by Karen Donohue and Nanda N. Reddy. All rights reserved. Reprinted from *180 Days to Successful Writers: Lessons to Prepare Your Students for Standardized Assessments and for Life* by Karen Donohue and Nanda N. Reddy. Thousand Oaks, CA: Corwin Press, www.corwinpress.com. Reproduction authorized only for the local school site or nonprofit organization that has purchased this book.

Resource I

PLAY RUBRIC

- General Writing (60% of grade, up to 10 points for each aspect)
  - ☐ Ideas/Content (plot)   _____ pts
  - ☐ Voice/Style (dialogue, characterization)   _____ pts
  - ☐ Fluency/Flow (including transitions between scenes)   _____ pts
  - ☐ Word Choice/Vocabulary   _____ pts
  - ☐ Organization (including "Golden rules")   _____ pts
  - ☐ Conventions/Spelling/Grammar (including "Golden rules")   _____ pts

  Total: _____pts
  (Out of 60 points)

- Technical Aspects of Playwriting (20% of grade, 5 points per aspect)
  - ☐ Appropriate use of props, implied or real, for interest   _____ pts
  - ☐ Good use of stage directions to keep actors moving   _____ pts
  - ☐ Scenes are set up fully/efficiently   _____ pts
  - ☐ Narrator does not tell the story; the play does   _____ pts

  Total: _____pts
  (Out of 20 points)

- Production (20% of grade, 4 points per item)
  - ☐ Voice and expression of actors   _____ pts
  - ☐ Transitions between acts and scenes   _____ pts
  - ☐ Familiarity with script/revisions to accommodate production   _____ pts
  - ☐ Employment of stage directions and stage   _____ pts
  - ☐ Employment of props/set   _____ pts

  Total: _____pts
  (Out of 20 points)

  FINAL TOTAL: _____

  Grade:

Comments & notes:

Copyright © 2006 by Karen Donohue and Nanda N. Reddy. All rights reserved. Reprinted from *180 Days to Successful Writers: Lessons to Prepare Your Students for Standardized Assessments and for Life* by Karen Donohue and Nanda N. Reddy. Thousand Oaks, CA: Corwin Press, www.corwinpress.com. Reproduction authorized only for the local school site or nonprofit organization that has purchased this book.

Index

**CORWIN
PRESS**

The Corwin Press logo—a raven striding across an open book—represents the union of courage and learning. Corwin Press is committed to improving education for all learners by publishing books and other professional development resources for those serving the field of PreK–12 education. By providing practical, hands-on materials, Corwin Press continues to carry out the promise of its motto: **"Helping Educators Do Their Work Better."**

Franklin Pierce College Library

00165904

DATE DUE

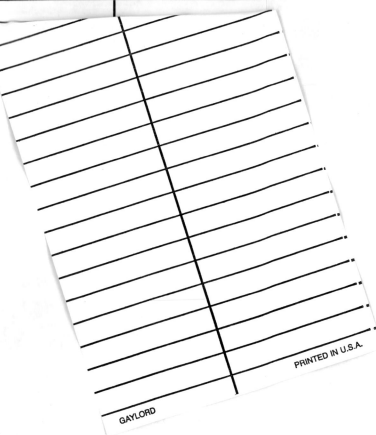

PRINTED IN U.S.A.

GAYLORD